P. J. Lydon

To

College Library

June, 1957

WATERFRONT PRIEST

Waterfront Priest

BY ALLEN RAYMOND

WITH AN INTRODUCTION BY
BUDD SCHULBERG

Henry Holt and Company · New York

In Canada, George J. McLeod, Ltd.

First Edition

Library of Congress Catalog Card Number: 54-10528

87354-0115
Printed in the United States of America

This book is dedicated to the longshoremen

of the Port of New York

FOREWORD

This story of the New York waterfront is the joint effort of two men, a Roman Catholic priest of the Jesuit Order, and a veteran newspaper reporter who is a Protestant. They had common aspirations in doing this work.

First was the hope that the book might hasten the day when social justice—rather than mob rule and excess of human greed—would govern the labor-management relations of the great harbor of New York. To that end they hope that the reading of this book will encourage and strengthen the determination of a good many brave and honest men along the waterfront in business, government, and labor to carry through to a successful conclusion the reforms now begun.

Another of their considerations was the hope that many more Christians would see the need of applying their religious principles to social situations as well as to personal and family living. In this, of course, the reporter was only an amateur Christian, whereas the priest was a professional. Yet the two men agreed that for a long time there has been a system of doing business on the waterfront which has forced everyone there to choose from among many moral evils their best course of human action.

The goal which the priest set for himself in his waterfront activities was to work with as many men as possible to see if they could, through cooperative effort, gradually transform an evil system into one more in keeping with Christian ideals. In moving toward that goal the priest was convinced that the two most important spheres of activity in most men's lives are their families and their jobs, and that unless a man is reasonably happy and secure in both, you have a man in serious trouble.

The obligation compelling him to act as he did was Christ's last command to His disciples and their successors, to teach all men "all things whatsoever I have commanded you."

The Church teaches, in season and out, the sanctity of marriage and the holiness of love between husband and wife; the sacredness of the bond that exists between parents and children—and children and parents. That same Church teaches not only that social justice should govern the relationship between labor and management, but also that their relationship should be impregnated with the charity of Christ.

In the writing of the book, the reporter's role has been merely to set down, as a partisan of its leading character, the story of the priest's arduous efforts to help the average longshoreman in the port of New York, and the port itself.

This story ends with a temporary setback for the cause of honest trade unionism. Over large sections of our country's greatest seaport, rule by known criminals is as strong as ever. But one thing is certain. The wharves of New York will someday be a far better place on which to work and earn a living, because of the efforts of all those men and women who love the great city, its people, and their God.

The Reverend John M. Corridan, S.J.
Allen Raymond

January 14, 1955

Introduction by
BUDD SCHULBERG

I welcome this book for simple and compelling reasons. Father John Corridan, the "waterfront priest," is one of the most effective human beings I have ever met. And the work to which he has dedicated himself these past nine years, the guidance of longshoremen seeking to throw off the yoke of racketeer unionism, aided and abetted by corrupt shipping executives and city politicians, is a cause vital to the health and security of the finest natural harbor in the world, our country's principal connecting point with the ports of our Western allies.

My first meeting with Father Corridan took place five years ago when I was in search of background material for a screen play I was contemplating on some phase of the New York waterfront dock scandals.

New York harbor, I was beginning to discover, was a world to itself, with its own heroes, villains, and taboos. Malcolm Johnson, a star reporter, in his challenging series for the old New York *Sun,* had described our greatest harbor as a lawless frontier, beyond the jurisdiction of police officer, jurist, or legislator. It was Johnson's bristling account that first opened my eyes to the story of crime and industrial-political corruption on the docks.

But how could an outsider begin to penetrate this jungle? Malcolm Johnson's advice was, "Start with Father Corridan. Go down to Xavier's and see Father John. He really knows the score."

The suggestion aroused my curiosity, for I had already read his provocative chapter, "Priests on the Waterfront." I remembered his description of Father Corridan as "cool as a cucumber, as patient as Job and as tough as the situation demands." And quite apart from personalities, I was interested to learn that priests in the harbor area had involved themselves in the problems of longshoremen for many years.

The truth is, despite Johnson's material, I was approaching the phenomenon of waterfront priests with a certain blindness. You might even call it prejudice. With prejudice as with burns, there are different degrees. There are the overt, running sores of prejudice, there are others just below the skin, and there are some so deeply and so long buried that the carrier has lost all conscious memory of them.

I think I may have carried the latent or "benign" type of prejudice. I examine myself on this point only because I suspect there are millions of non-Catholics like myself, people who believe themselves to be splendidly tolerant fellows who favor everyone's right to worship as he chooses. And yet there is this creeping doubt whispering in us, "What's a Catholic priest doing on the waterfront, butting into the union and political problems of longshoremen? Is this a rendering to God of the things that are Caesar's? Isn't there always the danger of religious demagoguery such as clouded the career of Father Coughlin?"

Lest any of these doubts get between you and your appreciation of the work of this waterfront priest, I invite you to come along with me on my first visit to Father Corridan at the Xavier Labor School, only a few blocks from the Hudson (or North) River waterfront, that has disturbed this labor priest so deeply for nearly a decade.

I found a tall, youthful, balding, energetic, ruddy-faced Irishman whose speech was a fascinating blend of Hell's Kitchen jargon, baseball slang, the facts and figures of a master in economics, and the undeniable humanity of Christ. His desk was cluttered with newspapers and magazines from which he had been clipping items of significance in his waterfront work. One wall was lined with filing cabinets, bulging—I soon learned—with waterfront material. There was no one of even passing interest to the waterfront story whose record could not be found in this well-organized file. "The names 'n' numbers of all the players," Father Corridan said in his breezy way, with a hearty, slightly malicious laugh I was to hear many times over the next five years.

In the course of many lunches at Billy the Oysterman's, a few blocks from St. Xavier's, Father Corridan would inevitably neglect his food as he warmed to his subject. He told me in vivid detail of the various mobs controlling different sections of the harbor, and of their multiple angles for illicit gain through control of the piers. He explained how hiring bosses with criminal records, winked at by corrupt waterfront union leaders, held the lives and earning power of dock workers in their greedy hands. He checked off the evils of the shape-up, through which longshoremen kick back part of their wages in return for the privilege of being picked for a day's work from among the hundreds of surplus workers who offer themselves for hire at each pier every morning. But I think his moral indignation was most aroused when he described the complicity of the stevedore and shipping companies who bribed and openly encouraged the underworld elements, and the compliance of the city politicians who were often in league with the dock bosses and their "respectable" protectors.

"What hurts me," Father Corridan says, "is that some of these fellers profess to be Catholics and assume they can remain in good standing just by showing up for mass every Sunday. And yet they think nothing of treating their fellow human beings like dirt every day in the week. They seem to forget that every man is precious in the eyes of our Lord and that He died for all of us, as brothers in Christ Jesus, and not just for the privileged few."

Father Corridan's words cut a way for me through the curtain of religious prejudice into the world of Catholic humanism—of Christian social ethics. There I began to sense what a powerful force for social betterment this religious tradition can be. Not that Father Corridan mentions religion in his labor classes and his strategy talks with groups of longshoremen groping their way toward some escape from the daily hell of their existence on the docks. But when he asks them what they consider the basis of economics, their answer, inevitably, is "money," "bread," "profit," or "labor supply." Father Corridan's answer is always, "Man." "Only man is capable of knowing and loving," he told me over a glass of beer one afternoon at Billy the Oysterman's. "In other words all I try to teach 'em is the dignity of man."

Father Corridan knows that the Christian strictures against man's inhumanity to man have been brought up to date in the Papal Encyclicals on the reconstruction of the social order. But, as he says with characteristic realism, "We don't want to bog 'em down with a lot of theories, religious or otherwise. The men who come in to me are men with a problem—the problem of how to live like human beings. They want practical stuff, not a lot of heavy water."

Father Corridan—or Father John as I came to know him as a friend, just as "Mike" Johnson had predicted—led me to understand that there is nothing unusual about a Catholic priest's involving himself in moral issues that find practical form in the daily lives of his parishioners. On the contrary, you will learn from him, if one takes the teachings and example of Christ to heart, one cannot do otherwise. In this regard his work, while devoted to the New York waterfront, has far broader and deeper implications.

One will close this book, I feel certain, not only with a fresh and more profound knowledge of the inner workings of political-management-union corruption in the great harbor of New York, but with a fresher sense of our moral, social, and national obligations. Whether Catholic, Protestant, or agnostic, whether Republican, Democrat, or independent, you will find something in *Waterfront Priest*—I vouch for it—that will move you and challenge you. Perhaps it may even bestir you toward a more responsible citizenship.

Budd Schulberg

New Hope, Pa.
January 13, 1955

CONTENTS

WATERFRONT PRIEST

CHAPTER 1

MURDER ON THE DOCKS

Gunmen, driven by an accomplice in a green 1948 De Soto sedan, drew up at 10:45 A.M., May 21, 1951, in front of the ground-floor offices of Local 867, International Longshoremen's Association, American Federation of Labor, at 204 River Street, Hoboken, New Jersey, near the Jersey docks of the port of New York. The gunmen left their car with motor running, walked into the doorway of the union offices, and started shooting.

There were three men in the room. One was John Nolan, 83 years old, a veteran organizer of the longshoremen's union. Another was Nunzio "Wally" Aluotto, 45, a dock worker slated that day to become hiring boss of Pier 3, Hoboken, which had been left unworked for a year or so and which was about to re-open. The third was Patrick Lisa, 28, nephew of Aluotto.

As the invading gunmen started shooting, Mr. Nolan, the octogenarian labor organizer, dropped to the floor behind his desk. He wasn't hurt. Aluotto fell with a bullet in his stomach. His young nephew, Lisa, grazed sufficiently by a flying slug so that he left a trail of blood behind him, jumped out of a rear window. He was listed by the Hoboken police as a fugitive for a good many days.

The gunmen ran out of the office. One of them tossed a .38-caliber pistol into the gutter. They jumped into their waiting car and were driven away. James Adams, an employee in the United States Bureau of Entomology, Department of Agriculture, saw the thugs emerge from the building. Mr. Adams was able to give the police a description of the automobile, its license number, and a fair description of one of the gunmen.

Nunzio "Wally" Aluotto was rushed by ambulance to St. Mary's Hospital, Hoboken. He died within 20 minutes, without regaining consciousness.

The police checked the license number of the gunmen's car. They found that it tallied with one, answering to Adams' description, owned by Michael Murphy, 28 years old, who had been the hiring boss on Pier 3, Hoboken, when the pier was closed down. The reason for the pier's inactivity had been persistent complaints by shippers that wholesale thievery on that particular dock had passed the limits of endurance, even though stealing of considerable magnitude along the docks in every section of the New York waterfront has been a common business risk for years.

The police, of course, sent out the usual interstate alarm for Murphy and his automobile. They then began rounding up a score or more of potential witnesses for questioning. Nobody was ever convicted of the murder, although several persons were indicted. There was even a trial, some two years later, of William Murphy, the leading suspect, and two of his brothers. They were acquitted.

The Aluotto case was just another of a long series of waterfront killings—murders involved in the struggle of gangsters for control of key positions along the docks, a struggle that has continued for two generations.

Many men involved in waterfront labor-union politics have been murdered. Many other dockers, involved in smuggling aliens, narcotics, cargo hijacking, loan-sharking, and bookmaking, have disappeared without a trace.

If the rule of organized thieves over New York's decaying waterfront is ever broken—and it may be some day—one man more than any other individual will have been responsible for breaking it. He is the Reverend John M. Corridan, S.J.

Father Corridan has had a lot of help during the last few years of his crusade to break the criminal rule of the New York waterfront. He recruited much of this assistance himself. Beginning by talking to frightened longshoremen—men intimidated and dispirited by oppression—Father Corridan won their confidence and enlisted their help in his fight. Many of these men formed the nucleus of a new deal on the waterfront of brief duration. The A.F. of L. longshoremen's union might not have come into existence without them. For the time being it is beaten. So is the chance for honest unionism. For eight years, since his advent at St. Francis Xavier Labor School, Father John has been a spiritual adviser to the dockers. He has also been their champion.

He found himself involved in a war, and the war goes on. It is a war against an enemy far more powerful than the dull-witted gunmen roving along the piers, an enemy formed by a corrupt alliance between dishonest elements of big business, crime-ridden labor unions, and irresponsible politicians in both New York and New Jersey. It is this evil alliance that has used gunmen to its advantage—an alliance that has made push-button murders its stock-in-trade. The alliance still exists.

In the fight now under way to break up this system, Father Corridan has made two valuable contributions. First, he saw clearly the nature of the enemy. Second, he brought to bear against this foe the one great social force which may be capable of destroying it. That force is the applied teaching of Jesus Christ, according to the tenets of the Roman Catholic Church.

Since a high percentage of the crooked politicians, dishonest labor-union officials, thieves, murderers, and extortionists in the port of New York, and 90 per cent of the longshoremen upon whom they have fed have been communicants of the Roman Catholic Church, no churchman of another faith could have wielded the power which Father Corridan found at his disposal. Against the forces of organized rascality he has pitted the strength of a tough-minded religionist and the cleverness of a canny propagandist.

It is doubtful, indeed, whether any priest other than a born New Yorker, with Corridan's own background of poverty and insecurity in boyhood, plus 15 years of rigorous Jesuit schooling, could have done the job that Father John has been doing with dedication, laughter, and, sometimes, wrath.

John Michael Corridan was born in the Harlem section of New York City, New York, on June 15, 1911. He was the eldest son of John Corridan, a New York policeman. Patrolman Corridan, who served in New York, Rockaway, Long Island, and Brooklyn, was born in Listowel, County Kerry, Ireland. His wife, the former Hannah Shanahan, who bore him five sons, was also Irish-born. Patrolman Corridan died in 1921, leaving his widow with a pension of 25 dollars a month. She soon was forced to apply for welfare benefits, which amounted to 16 dollars per month per child. Young John and his brothers spent most of their childhood on Manhattan's Upper West Side, then a German-Irish neighborhood. The boys, who attended Ascension Parochial School, worked to help support their mother. Mrs. Corridan, who took in boarders, also found part-time employment at the Old Slip Station House, making beds for the policemen stationed there.

Upon graduation from Ascension, John Corridan studied at Regis High School. Following high school he went to night school at New York University. He soon obtained a job with the National City Company, at 55 Wall Street. Within two years Corridan had risen from an office boy to a "correspondent" handling the mechanical details of sales transactions. After the crash of 1929, Corridan was fortunate in retaining his job. Early in 1931, after the first shock of the depression had sobered the entire nation, John Corridan happened to read a book by René Fullop Miller entitled *The Power and Secret of the Jesuits.* This book crystallized Corridan's thinking. It also changed his life. He shortly applied for admission to the Society of Jesus. He was accepted.

Corridan entered his novitiate at St. Andrew's-on-Hudson on August 15, 1931, thus beginning 15 years of intensive training. Two years later he completed his novitiate. There followed a juniorate of two years' duration, also at St. Andrew's. Corridan was then sent to St. Louis University, St. Louis, Missouri, to begin his philosophical studies. His philosophate lasted three years, after which he remained at St. Louis to earn a master's degree in economics. Later he was assigned to teach at Canisius College in Buffalo, New York, where he spent a year. In 1940-1941, he taught at the Crown Heights Labor School, Brooklyn, New York. At the end of 1941 he went to Woodstock College, Maryland, to begin a four-year course in theology. Corridan was ordained by Archbishop Curley, of the Archdiocese of Baltimore and Washington, on June 18, 1944, his thirty-third birthday.

The fourth year of theology was spent traveling to various parishes in southern Pennsylvania, northern Virginia, and Maryland. On September 1, 1945, Father Corridan boarded a train for Auriesville, New York, and the Shrine of Our Lady of Martyrs. At the tertianship of Our Lady of Martyrs, Father Corridan was to spend the last year of his spiritual formation before taking his vows as a full-fledged member of the Society of Jesus. St. Ignatius called similar schools, as originally founded, "Schools of the Heart." After finishing his long years of study and in preparation for his apostolic ministries, the Jesuit returns to his "School of the Heart" for a time, which is, in atmosphere, much like his novitiate. Here, Father Corridan applied himself to ten months of solitude and prayer. After 15 years of training, Father Corridan was assigned to the Xavier Labor School, 30 West 16th Street, New York. He was to work with the Reverend Philip J. Carey, S.J., director of the School.

The Xavier Labor School had been founded in 1936. Like other schools of its kind, its object was to combat communism by the explanation of Catholic social principles. More broadly, it was designed to apply Christian principles to labor-management problems. Its courses were taught by both priests and lay teachers. The men most responsible for the success of Xavier, with the exception of Father Carey, are fellow Jesuits, the Reverend John Delaney, the Reverend Ben Masse, the Reverend Joseph Fitzpatrick, and the Reverend Philip Dobson.

CHAPTER 2

A SEAPORT FOR A PARISH

The port of New York is the greatest in the world and the city created by it reflects its grandeur. Between 1946 and 1948, Father Corridan discovered the true relationship between the harbor and the city. He came to know that it was the harbor, with its tributary rivers, particularly the Hudson, that ultimately made New York the wealthiest city in the world.

He traveled the port. He walked the docks. He crossed the harbor by ferry, looking out at the freighters and liners connecting New York with every other seaport on earth. He watched the lighters, carrying their freight cars from one side of the port to another like mobile, inexpensive bridges.

Father Corridan went under the harbor waters through tunnels. He visited termini for landborne, seaborne, and airborne cargo and saw that the welfare of this harbor was linked importantly with the welfare of every man, woman, and child in the United States; linked to the inland industries and farms, relying on their share of the nation's exports and imports; linked to the security of the nation itself, as the greatest transfer point between sea and land for the country's armed men and munitions during wartime.

And everywhere Father John went, he discovered that the nation's great ocean gateway was controlled by criminals. Their names and antecedents, misdeeds and prison records, could be traced by anyone who was diligent in tracing them. Many were sheltered by disguise as labor-union officials, so that an attack on them was dismissed lightly by the ignorant as an attack on unionism.

People who travel in luxury on the great ocean liners see only a small portion of the city's harbor. It's too big to be seen, except from the air—with a good guide to point out the landmarks. Its operation is too complicated to be grasped without some study of the involved economics of international trade.

The portion of New York harbor developed for seaborne or coastwise shipping includes about 750 miles of shore line. On this gigantic waterfront there are about 1800 piers. About 200 of these handle ocean-going vessels, and these 200 handle about 400 ships at a time. About 10,000 ocean-going ships a year clear New York harbor, or one ship every 50 minutes.

More than 100 steamship lines own these ships, which sail to 155 ports in every important corner of the world. Carrying more than a million passengers a year, they handle about 35 million tons of cargo in the foreign trade alone. This cargo is valued somewhere between six billion and eight billion dollars.

Father Corridan soon discovered that the 35 million tons of foreign cargo handled in the port of New York was a carelessly guarded treasure.

Within New York harbor, cargo-handling is serviced by about 2500 tugs, barges, lighters, derricks, car floats, and scows. The railroad fleets alone move more than 750 carloads of export freight daily to 200 steamship piers. More than 3,500,000 tons of railroad freight were delivered or received at waterfront railroad stations in Manhattan alone in 1946, the year of Father Corridan's arrival at the Xavier School. This included 1,250,000 tons of fresh fruit and vegetables for the city's consumption.

The total tonnage handled within the harbor of New York, of both bulk and general cargo, domestic and foreign, during the last few years has run more than 150 million tons annually. Its annual value has ranged from 14 to 16 billion dollars.

"In order to guard a commerce like that," says Father Corridan, "you have to rely very heavily on the honesty of the people who handle it. Fortunately you can—as far as the average man goes. But what the country hasn't so far been able to guard against has been the organization of criminal gangs, in league with the political governments on both sides of the bistate harbor.

"These criminals have been winked at, or aided actively, by businessmen who have preferred to have a surplus force of cheap labor, managed by the International Longshoremen's Association, to a small well-paid force of workingmen on the docks, united in an honest labor union."

As a result the pernicious system of hiring and firing, "shape-up," and government by goon squad has remained in force. For example, examine the piers along midtown Manhattan where the big luxury liners berth. This area is under the control of the Bowers mob, who manage the loading and unloading of the *Queen Mary,* the *Queen Elizabeth,* and the *United States.* The composition of this mob is interesting reading:

1. Michael "Mickey" Bowers. Once convicted of payroll robbery and sentenced to ten years in New Jersey State Prison. Arrested three times for grand larceny, assault and robbery, and parole violation.

2. John "Keefie" Keefe. Once arrested for bank robbery, convicted of assault with intent to kill and sentenced to 12 years in

New Jersey State Prison. Arrested two other times for assault and once for illegal possession of a gun.

3. John "Apples" Applegate. Convicted of burglary and sentenced to two and a half to ten years in Sing Sing Prison. Also arrested on charges of robbery, grand larceny twice, and as a material witness for a homicide.

4. Harold Bowers, alias Frank Donald. Arrested twice for grand larceny, for robbery, for possession of a gun, and for congregating with known criminals. Sentenced to six months for criminal contempt of court as a result of the 1954 paralyzing waterfront strike.

5. John T. Ward, alias Harold Ward, alias Charles Rogers. Arrested once for carrying a concealed weapon and once on a charge of vagrancy.

The Bowers mob controls Local 824 of the longshoremen's union. John Keefe is vice-president. Harold Bowers is business agent. The president of this local was Patrick "Packy" Connolly, whom Joe Ryan, long-time president of the I.L.A., appointed an international executive vice-president. The financial secretary of the local has been John "Ike" Gannon, another close associate of Joe Ryan. This local is known as "The Pistol Local."

"Long before the State Crime Commission in 1952 and 1953 made public sworn testimony at private and public hearings that named these men, and told of their control in the I.L.A., and political influence," Father Corridan says, "they were known to longshoremen all over the waterfront."

Starting at the Battery and going up the Hudson River waterfront of Manhattan, the first piers one meets are those of the United Fruit Company's "Great White Fleet," and then the Belgian Line. Then come the Greenwich Village and Chelsea piers, where one finds the Argentine Line, the Moore-McCormack Lines, the Cuba Mail Line, the Norwegian-American Line, the Grace Line, and terminals for the United States and Panama lines.

For many years control of the I.L.A. unions and control of pier-hiring and public loading along most of these piers was exercised.

by Eddie McGrath, a notorious hoodlum; his brother-in-law, John "Cockeye" Dunn, and Andrew "Squint" Sheridan. Of these three men, two, Dunn and Sheridan, died in the electric chair in 1949 for the murder of Andy Hintz, a hiring boss.

As Father Corridan acquainted himself with the port, he learned that the East River piers were under the control of Michael "Mike" Clemente, a convicted perjurer. He found that six Brooklyn locals, known as the "Camarda" locals, because they were under the nominal control of various members of the Camarda family, were actually run by the Anastasia family. Albert Anastasia achieved national notoriety as chief executioner of Murder, Inc., during the late 1930's. His brother "Tough Tony" now rules on the Brooklyn docks. For some years the Jersey dock workers were ruled by one Charles "The Jew" Yanowsky, who had served a term in Alcatraz. The Hoboken docks were later under the reign of one Eddie Florio, a former bootlegger. Florio's chauffeur in Prohibition days, a man named Borelli, was later Hoboken's commissioner of police. In Staten Island, at the gateway to the harbor, Father Corridan found that the organizer for the I.L.A., appointed by Ryan in 1946, was a former prizefighter named Alex Di Brizzi, or Al Britton. Britton, as well as being a veteran of the prize ring, was a veteran of 15 arrests and three convictions on gambling charges and one conviction for violation of the alcohol laws.

What kind of hiring bosses did Father Corridan find dominating the piers, nominated by the I.L.A. and accepted by the stevedoring and shipping companies?

There was Danny St. John, at Pier 84, Hudson River, where the American Export and Italian liners have docks. St. John's police record, by 1953, showed 20 arrests on charges of larceny, burglary, assault, robbery, possessing dangerous weapons, and murder. It showed five convictions, four of them for petty larceny and one of them for possessing a revolver.

That a man can be arrested 20 times on the New York waterfront on serious charges, and convicted five times on minor charges, and still hold a responsible job is easily understandable. Every newspaper reporter in New York is aware that persons with political "wires" are handled gently by the lower courts. The I.L.A. influence in New York politics has always been very great. Leaders of the old I.L.A. and the bosses of some of the big stevedoring companies have usually worked together for mutual profit.

For years the hiring boss on Pier 88, Hudson River, was James "Toddy" O'Rourke. His criminal record, as of 1953, showed that he had served time both in a reformatory and in Sing Sing Prison. His numerous offenses included grand larceny, petty larceny, felonious assault, and violation of the Sullivan Law which forbids the carrying of concealed, dangerous weapons.

The New York State Crime Commission, in 1953, named more than 20 hiring foremen on the New York docks as holders of police records.

The Commission included the name of Albert Ackalitis, a member of the notorious Arsenal Mob. This group of celebrated criminals once treated Brooklyn to the Rubel payroll robbery, a 427,-000-dollar operation that is still a Brooklyn record.

Albert Ackalitis was made hiring boss at Pier 18, Hudson River, after getting out of prison. He got an excellent reference from Teddy Gleason, an officer in three I.L.A. locals. A long term in Sing Sing wasn't held against him. His criminal record, at the time of his hiring, included arrests for receiving stolen property, attempted robbery, assault and robbery, and two prison sentences served: one for attempted burglary and one for illegal possession of a machine gun.

Father Corridan, after some early studies of the harbor, soon discarded the hope that the New York City government was likely to break the grip of Joe Ryan's criminal forces on the waterfront. Ryan's political power, through the Central Trades and Labor Council and Tammany Hall, was too great. Ryan also was a friend of Big Bill McCormack, a multimillionaire known to have befriended several mayors of New York, who also was a power on the waterfront. The more Father Corridan thought of the personal and political relationships of these people who ruled the city government and the waterfront, the more he despaired of reform on a municipal level. These men obviously liked the system which he believed to be evil. They approved of it and profited by it. If he hoped to change it, he would inevitably be arrayed against them.

If any government forces were to come to the aid of the longshoremen oppressed by criminal labor leaders, Corridan believed, it would have to be at the state or national level. He began to think of the welfare of the port of New York as a bistate and national problem, rather than a local one. And he conceived of the welfare of the men on the docks and the welfare of the port as inseparable.

In 1946 he began to study the economics of the whole port area and its connection with the business interests of the American people. He sought the ammunition he would need as a propagandist for the port and the dock workers in the state and the nation.

In the next few years he gathered material for hundreds of lectures, which he made from 1950 to 1953; speaking before business gatherings, chambers of commerce, trade associations, and church groups, he addressed prominent businessmen more often than the laborers he was trying to help. But he talked to them, too. They liked what he said.

"Most people don't really understand the distinction between New York harbor and the port of New York," his talks began. "The harbor and its waterfront are merely approaches to the larger area which we call the port, and this extends back from the ocean for many miles. It is the funnel through which goods are poured into and out of the great city area.

"The port includes the termini of the 12 great railroads which come to harborside, connecting the docks with all the major industrial sections of the United States, Canada, and Mexico, and with all the farm areas, too. It takes in the great airports. The port of New York is the center of a vast network of highways, roads, tunnels, and bridges. Eight to ten thousand over-the-road trucks flow daily into and out of this great port area to supplement railroads, busses, and air lines.

"Almighty God has blessed the Northeastern, mid-Atlantic, and

Midwestern parts of the United States with all the basic materials they need for the great industrial empire we have built here. There is plenty of coal, iron ore, oil, and water power. God also has given our country great farm lands.

"But in modern civilization God has not granted our country independence of lands overseas. We are dependent on other nations for many of our raw materials, and a great deal of finished merchandise, just as lands beyond the seas are dependent upon us for much they have to have, if they are to live according to any modern standards of living.

"If we look back on early American history we can see how the harbor here in New York, with its broad, sheltered, landlocked bays, made lower Manhattan and then the shores close by it a natural place for early settlement. Then we can see how the Hudson River was a natural highway inland—a waterway—already constructed for the new arrivals from the Old World to settle the country farther from the ocean, without the need for constructing roads.

"We can see how the Erie Canal, which was an extension of the Hudson, took those old Americans still further inland, and helped, with the railroads, in the transportation of people and goods.

"New York, the port of entry, grew as the country grew.

"It is primarily because this harbor made New York the great port of entry for successive waves of immigrants that New York is the titan of U. S. commerce. Most of the human wealth of New York was funneled through Ellis Island from lands overseas.

"Because this harbor is America's greatest seaport, downtown Manhattan has become the marvel you see today. New York, above all other cities in the United States, has been built on world commerce by the American people.

"Go out and take a look at the headquarters of the great banks, the insurance companies, the financial and commodity exchanges, the import and export houses, the freight-forwarding concerns, the warehouses, and the shipbuilding and repairing facilities. Then travel over the city's outskirts, in other parts of the port.

"See the oil-storage installations, the stockyards, the produce terminals, rail terminals, air terminals, and even those miles of factories that have clustered close to the harbor.

"Then begin to figure the value of the port of New York to our state and nation.

"During World War II, about one third of all troops sent overseas by this country embarked from New York harbor, and one half of all the munitions and other material which supported them in every theater of operations was also shipped out of this harbor. What goes on in this harbor ought to be of vital interest to every American.

"What does this harbor mean to the people of New York City? Our city receives 22 per cent of its food by boat, 35 per cent by truck, and 43 per cent by rail. But most of the rail traffic finishes in barges.

"In terms of electricity, the Consolidated Edison Company has eight plants along New York's waterways that consume 25,000 tons of collier and barge-borne fuel a day, mostly coal. Electricity for New York City subways requires another 3000 tons of coal a day. It comes across the harbor in 15 barges from South Amboy and Port Redding, New Jersey.

"In terms of gasoline and oil products, harbor barges bring La Guardia Airport its weekly supply of half a million gallons of airplane fuel and bring four million gallons every 25 days to New York International Airport at Idlewild.

"Automobiles and other motor equipment use ten millions of tons of fuel gasoline every year. It comes mostly through the harbor. Yet traffic in petroleum and its by-products makes up only seven of the 900 products listed as part of the harbor's trade. They, however, amount to more than half of the harbor's entire commerce.

"What does the port of New York mean to the United States and the world? Into this area, either as commuters or as travelers, there come and go an estimated 500 million people every year. They are from every state in the Union and every country in the world. What happens in the port of New York affects all this world.

"A quarter of a million people directly earn their living from the harbor of New York. The prosperity or lack of it affects far more people than the longshoremen and the other waterfront crafts, the harbor pilots, the tugboat men, the lighter men, crane operators, dock builders, lumber handlers, weighers and samplers, checkers, cargo repairmen, and maintenance workers. It affects also the seamen and steamship personnel, shipbuilders and repairmen, the railroad workers in the marine terminals and on the 170 railroad piers, the teamsters who pick up goods at the docks, the warehousemen who store those goods, the clerks in the banks, insurance companies, in the freight-forwarding concerns, and all the personnel in the import and export houses and in the commodity exchanges.

"Another 500,000 people in New York City's 27,000 wholesale establishments, in the hotels, department stores, and service industries, are indirectly dependent for their livelihood upon the prosperity of this harbor.

"Outside the metropolitan area, millions of workers and farmers in the Northeastern, mid-Atlantic and Midwestern sections of the United States are indirectly dependent upon the prosperity of this port. Practically every industry in the country is dependent upon imports to supply at least some one essential raw material. So also the welfare of this country depends to a great degree on the smooth, regular, unimpeded flow of exports out of New York harbor.

"Exports, to some people, may seem like a very small proportion of American business. But they are vital to profit. Exports make it possible for a great many companies to spread their overhead costs across a greater volume of sales. They therefore increase the profit in the domestic as well as foreign business.

"Our American export businesses are the ones which pay the highest wages to labor. Hourly wage rates in representative American export industries exceed the national average for all manufacturing industries, in some cases by as much as 50 per cent. As for the people whom our export businesses support, in 1947 exports of 12 major industries were valued at 4,300,000,000 dollars."

If any man ever equipped himself for eloquence in the exposition of economic statistics, Father Corridan did. He did more than go digging through government reports. He went out on the piers. He watched the actual products, of which those statistics told, being trucked in and out of loading platforms, lifted by cranes and stowed in the holds of liners and freighters by the brawny and turbulent dock workers he was trying to help. Then, for a bird's-eye view of the harbor as a whole, he used to go once in a while to the top of the Empire State Building. There on a clear day, particularly in the autumn, he could see the geography of that magnificent seaport that had become his personal parish.

It revolted him personally to think of the evils infesting his harbor. He rebelled against the neglect of the physical equipment of the port as well as the oppression of the men who were working in it.

"The key to the greatness of New York's harbor today is service, and it has to be service, more now than ever," says Father Corridan, part priest, part economist. "We've got a bigger port than any other, for historic reasons, and we've built up our transoceanic sailings to an average of more than 800 monthly. Where do the ships go?

"Thirty to the Canadian Atlantic ports, 26 to the British Isles, 25 to Rotterdam and Antwerp, 25 to the Baltic, 23 to Hamburg and Bremen, 12 to the French Atlantic ports, six to Spain and Portugal, 39 to the Mediterranean.

"They go everywhere. Go over to Erie Basin in Brooklyn and see how many flags these ships fly. Look in the *Journal of Commerce* and note how many seas they plow—particularly those insignificantly small freighters which carry the bulk of the cargo.

"New York harbor has to give more and better and faster service to stop a decline that's already set in. Other harbors—lesser harbors—are reaching for the traffic which has gone through this port—and they're getting some of it.

"If service is the key to the greatness of New York harbor, then general cargo, which is packaged cargo, is also the one essential to maintenance of that greatness. By general cargo I mean 'money cargo,' in longshore language. Longshoremen are people who can express themselves pretty well when they want to. By 'money cargo' they don't mean bulk cargo like grain or coal, oil, or minerals. They mean the cargo that gives work to so many hundreds of thousands of people in the big industrial plants of the Northeast and Middle West.

" 'Money cargo?' I mean products on which a lot of work has been expended. These products need to be taken fast wherever they're going.

"Time is money in New York harbor. Every minute the ships are at the piers here, they're eating up money. They need to be loaded and unloaded quickly. They need to be kept at sea. And who are the people to keep them at sea? New York's longshoremen, when honestly organized by themselves, instead of by men with guns set over them."

As Father Corridan sees it, New York's great natural advantages as a seaport are now being sapped and weakened by a variety of causes. Bad management-labor relations are its greatest weakness. Antiquated equipment ranks second.

"Seven years ago," Father Corridan says, "a study was made of New York City's municipal piers. Thirty-nine of them were more than 40 years old. These were all built in the days when horse-drawn trucks, rather than motorized, 40-foot trailer trucks were used for vehicular hauling. Seventy-one of the docks were found to be in poor condition.

"Fewer than 20 of the city's piers could then be said to even approximate the ideal requirements of a modern pier. A modern pier ought to be 800 to 1000 feet long, with a covered area not less than 150 feet wide. It needs aprons 15 to 20 feet wide for the use of the fork-lift trucks. There has to be slip space of 320 feet between piers for the ready maneuverability of lighters, coming alongside the vessels.

"The privately owned waterfront facilities, principally in Brooklyn, were found back in 1947 to be in very little better shape than the municipal piers, if any. The New York Dock Company, which operates one of the largest privately owned marine terminals in the world, has 28 piers, used by 20 steamship lines. Few of them were built in this century. The Bush Terminal facilities, close by the New York Dock Company's facilities in Brooklyn, are considered modern by comparison, but most of its layout was built before World War I.

"Very little has been done by the governments of any municipality around the port in the last eight years to modernize the dock facilities—the Port Authority has done a good job on the New Jersey side. But a great deal more will have to be done if New York is to hold its own against outlying ports on the Atlantic seaboard with more modern equipment.

"Everybody in the shipping industry knows today that operating costs in New York harbor are excessive. And terminal and stevedoring costs for steamship lines in New York harbor amount to about 60 per cent of their total operating costs. Pier rentals are high and facilities poor. This port is slipping. In 1946 New York handled 37.9 per cent of the nation's ocean-borne general cargo. That's the 'money cargo,' in longshore terms. In 1951 this port handled only 31.7 per cent, and in 1952 it was 32.9 per cent.

"I know I have differed in my analysis of this situation from the reports of governmental agencies. I believe I'm right in my own analysis. I am absolutely convinced that to solve the port of New York's major problem of high-cost operation, as compared to competitive seaports, you've got to do one thing first. You've got to bring justice and right to the relations between management and labor on the New York docks.

"The one major cost factor here in New York harbor that can be eliminated quickly is the cost of constant wildcat strikes. These strikes have been due mostly to the men's rebellion against collusive arrangements between the New York Shipping Association and the mob-dominated International Longshoremen's Association.

"Until that collusion is broken down, those wildcat rebellions are bound to continue. I, as a priest and student, can say that with confidence. I can say it as one who has stood by the rebels, actively and openly, in full public view from the 1948 strike to the present. I say it as one who intends to stand with the men as long as my work is here."

CHAPTER

3

THE HARBOR RACKETS

For more than a generation the Greater New York waterfront has been an outlaw frontier. Law enforcement has been weakened by widespread political corruption. Standards of business ethics have been vague or nonexistent. Employers in the shipping and stevedoring industries have sought too often by commercial bribery to obtain special treatment for themselves as against their competitors. The employers' contemptuous bribery of labor-union officials to betray their followers has been customary rather than exceptional. One third of the so-called union leaders have merely been criminal racketeers in disguise.

The handling of cargo in this nation's foreign commerce has been riddled with crime and rackets of all sorts, ranging from grand to petty. Organized thievery, boosting the insurance rates on all cargo passing across the docks, has added to the cost of living of all Americans concerned with this cargo, either as producers or consumers.

There has been payroll padding, through the use of "short gangs," whereby racketeers in the labor unions and employers of the stevedoring companies have collected the pay of 23 men, the normal work-gang complement, when only 16 men were hired. Shylocks lending a five-dollar bill for six dollars in return, or 20 per cent per week, have victimized thousands of dock workers so poor and insecure in their earnings that they have put up with this usury. Organized gambling, with protected bookmakers or vendors of policy slips in the numbers racket, has been placed on a territorial basis for the benefit of known criminals by certain officers of the International Longshoremen's Association.

Control of the docks, and of the unloading and loading of ships, has given the smugglers of narcotics and of aliens their great opportunities for illegal enrichment.

From time to time honest policemen, customs officers, and United States Treasury officers have interfered as far as they could with these evil-doings. Nevertheless crime and the rackets have continued to grow, principally through the connivance of racketeers posing as labor-union leaders. These men are indisputably linked by a chain of influence to powerful people in local government.

From his little reform beachhead at the Xavier Labor School, the Reverend John M. Corridan, S.J., has observed every detail of the waterfront scene. He has publicized it, even though major powers and spokesmen in government, business, union labor, and his own church have minimized it continually. These groups always branded emphasis on the harbor's crime problem as the distortion of sensationalists.

But no defensive speeches, even by a federal official such as Harry M. Durning, then Collector of the Port, or by Edward J. Cavanagh, the former Commissioner of the Marine and Aviation Department, on the New York City government, could stave off forever the revelations of criminality made in 1952 and 1953 at the public hearings of the New York State Crime Commission. Testimony at these hearings was more than ample to corroborate all that rebellious longshoremen had been telling Father Corridan since 1946. Long before 1952 the priest had confirmed their stories by diligent collection of courtroom testimony, culled from the New York newspapers.

Father Corridan is a good librarian. He wields a tireless pair of shears. As a result, 16 filing compartments in his offices at the Xavier School have been crammed with sworn testimony about harbor crime and rackets, during trials which convicted a good many small fry.

Organized thievery has been one of the greatest plagues of the docks. The "public loading" racket, now outlawed in theory if not in fact, has been another. Since 1928 there have been more than 100 unsolved murders along the docks, attributable to the struggle for the control of these two rackets by gangsters.

How great the toll of organized thievery along the piers has been is hard to estimate. Daniel Bell, an able reporter for *Fortune* magazine who studied the waterfront rackets right after World War II, placed the total at 60 million dollars a year.

Father Corridan remembers talking with a member of the shipping association's security bureau about the amazing nature of some of this pilferage. "A few years back a detail of men stood guard over a shipment of rare French wines," the man told him. "Next morning the barrels were empty. Thieves had slipped under the pier, drilled right through the barrels, emptied them into their own barrels, and made off with their loot in spite of the guard on the pier above them."

The biggest dock theft in the last ten years was 750,000 dollars' worth of watch movements and lighters that disappeared mysteriously overnight. No one was caught. Nothing was recovered. In mid-1947, a case of diamonds, pearls, and emeralds, valued at 150,000 dollars, was sealed in front of customs and postal inspectors here. When the case was opened in London only the pearls were in it. But such thefts are rare. The huge total of pilferage is made up of many thousands of smaller larcenies, ranging from goods valued at five or ten dollars up to 5000 or 10,000 dollars.

"A cargo checker, working with a truckman, can get away with murder," says Father Corridan. "A checker and a truckman could put 40 cases of canned goods on a truck, for instance, and the receipt from the trucker might show only 20. Some time ago metal file cases valued at 6000 dollars were checked from a dock in New Jersey to the hatch of an outbound ship. Shortly after the ship sailed, the police of North Bergen, New Jersey, were checking on the garage of a suspected fence. They found several cases of these files in the basement. Nobody ever has been able to explain how the files traveled from the hatch of that ship to a garage in North Bergen.

"Of course you have cases in which the crews of ships operate in larceny on a grand scale. There was one such instance when 4000 cases of Scotch whisky were being unloaded on a New York dock. A contingent of GIs were waiting on the dock to embark for Europe. They bought more than 2000 cases of the 4000 destined to a New York consignee. On another occasion three relief ships were bound to Italy and were being loaded with macaroni, when a man walked on the pier and asked where he could buy a few truckloads. Agents of the shipping association's security bureau spotted him. They waited for him to return when he left the pier, but he never came back. The ships arrived in Italy a month apart. The first showed a shortage of 13,792 cases of macaroni; the second, 14,789; and the third, 20,824.

"Nobody could figure out how that macaroni could have walked off the docks. But there have been other thievery cases just as unexplainable. One day four tons of coffee seemed to have walked off another pier mysteriously. That coffee was no good unless it was mixed with a special bean. Seven days later the necessary amount of the special bean disappeared too."

This thievery was easy because of the domination of the port watchmen's union by officers of Joe Ryan's International Longshoremen's Association and their muscle men. Because of this rule, the watchmen on the piers were so intimidated that they refused to report a great deal of stealing of which they had knowledge.

Organized robbery has also been easy because there has been an alliance between cargo checkers, the hiring or dock bosses, and the truckmen who serve the piers. This alliance in criminal enterprise has been maintained despite the fact that the hiring bosses have supposedly been representatives of management. Actually they have all been members of the I.L.A., and many of them have been imposed on the management by Ryan's union, over management protest.

The ship companies normally do not report many thefts as thefts. They say merely, "The goods are missing." Frequently they do not know the goods are missing or stolen until reports come back to them from consignees who may be halfway around the world.

Sometimes these thefts have been accomplished by means of false invoices handed to truckmen, showing receipt of goods for shipment that actually were speedily diverted to nearby warehouses, or "drops," to be disposed of by the receiver, or fence.

The invoices given truckmen might either be signed by a false name or show a larger amount of merchandise than actually was delivered. Such a theft would not be discovered until after the ship supposedly bearing the cargo to a foreign port had reached its destination. At such a time consignees would naturally complain that the expected goods either had failed to arrive or were short in amount. Then there would be an investigation of the docks by employees of the insurance company concerned. Investigators would simply run into the fact that no person bearing the name signed to the invoice ever had been employed on the pier. Or they might meet a blunt denial that the amount shipped out had been any less than was marked on the invoice. Very likely they would hear a shrugged remark that "there's always plenty of stealing around here, but nobody knows just how it's done."

One factor in the thievery along the docks is certain. The 2000 members of the port watchmen's union, ruled in fact, though not in name, by their "adviser," John J. "Ike" Gannon, a vice-president of the Atlantic Coast District Council of the I.L.A., have been so terrorized by beatings and threats through the years that they have been pretty useless to protect harbor cargo. Three of the port watchmen, two of them with broken noses suffered for temporary adherence to duties for which they were hired, testified to this before the New York State Crime Commission, on January 21, 1953.

One of the broken-nosed watchmen, Michael Cronin, testified that when he was new to his job on Pier 34, Hudson River, and was trying to do his job, he was beaten up by a widely known waterfront thug, one "Buster" Monahan. Cronin immediately filed assault charges with the police. He withdrew them after the defendant obtained two adjournments in Magistrates' Court. The beaten-up watchman expressed the consensus of the waterfront in his testimony to the Crime Commission.

"The waterfront clique has a good connection with the courts," he said. "I was new on the waterfront at the time. If I'd known then what I know now, I wouldn't even bother bringing the man to court."

If the beaten-up watchman was unfair in his appraisal of the magistrate who handled his complaint against Monahan, he merely reflected the low esteem in which the magistrate's courts generally have been held along the waterfront ever since the Seabury Investigation of the 1930's revealed the influence of criminals and ward heelers within them. Ill repute dies hard even when the reasons for it may possibly have passed.

Another pier guard, Charles Gulizia, testified that a longshoreman he caught stealing a case of gloves on an American Export Line Pier 84 in 1947 was suspended from his job for four days but was not arrested. He said his union's boss, "Ike" Gannon, reprimanded him for turning in the thief to the pier superintendent. He said Gannon told him, "That isn't the way to do things," and asked how he would like it if he, himself, were suspended for a few days.

Still another pier watchman, Thomas Launders, testified that after he had thwarted the theft of two cases of meat from the

Moore-McCormack Lines' Pier 32 in 1946, the pier hiring boss came to him with a dollar bill and said he was taking up a collection for flowers. When the watchman asked who the flowers were for, he was told they were for him because he was going to be thrown into the river.

With men of criminal records controlling the loading and unloading of trucks, and the hiring of all cargo-handlers and watchmen, New York City's police have had an uphill fight at all times to keep down the daily toll of robberies. The best they could do was arrest an occasional group of small operators, caught stealing such things as 50,000 dollars' worth of lumber, destined for export; 500,000 dollars' worth of cotton and rayon textiles by one gang operating for about 18 months; truck lots of whisky and even steel rails.

The thieving crews have even developed specialties, one gang taking freight cars of general merchandise, and another such commodities as frozen meats, butter, and other refrigerated foodstuffs.

It has been common knowledge for years that a large part of this country's supply of illegal narcotics flows through New York harbor, supposedly directed by "Lucky" Luciano or some of his colleagues in the syndicate. Control of the docks by mobs like Murder, Inc., has made drug smuggling easy for the syndicate.

Abe "Kid" Reles, a gunman of Murder, Inc., who turned informant, testified as follows before his mysterious death at Coney Island's Half-Moon Hotel, while under police custody. "In Brooklyn," said Reles, "we [Murder, Inc.] all are together with the mob on the docks—and it takes in from two to five blocks in from the water, too. . . . Albert A. [Anastasia], who is our boss, is the head guy on the docks. He is the law."

All the agents whom the U. S. Treasury and U. S. Customs departments have placed in New York harbor are only a token force. As of 1952 the U. S. Customs had only 135 pier guards, working eight-hour tours of duty five days a week, on a beat extending from New York to Poughkeepsie, New York. It had 500 inspectors and only about 35 members of its intelligence unit, or detectives. Of these detectives, only two have been assigned to narcotics control.

How close is the connection of I.L.A. officers with this dope-smuggling racket? For years since the Murder, Inc., scandals, a large section of the Brooklyn docks has been under the control of "Tough Tony" Anastasia, and his brother, Jerry, if not their more renowned brother, Albert. Tough Tony's power was never so great as it is today. His brother Jerry was formerly business agent of I.L.A. Local 338-1. Are they in the dope racket? It has never been charged against them. Albert Anastasia and Luciano have been close friends.

But the link between this country's dope smugglers and Joe Ryan's I.L.A., with all its political influence, can be pinned down in two places at least. As of June 15, 1952, Saro Mogavero, a convicted extortionist, ex-vice-president of Local 856, I.L.A., was the operator of a truck-loading concession on Pier 25, East River. On his criminal record were arrests for burglary, jostling, assault, and homicide. Once he was convicted of homicide, only to have the jury's verdict reversed.

In 1954 Mogavero was convicted of harboring Salvatore "Tom Mix" Santoro and John "Big John" Ormento, when they were fugitives facing a narcotics charge in 1951. When the pair were caught, they pleaded guilty to smuggling opium from Mexico. This opium smuggling was only a side-line with Santoro, who was a big-time heroin merchant in Harlem.

Santoro's friend, Mogavero, owes his truck-loading concession and union office to Mike Clemente, undisputed waterfront racket ruler of the Lower East Side docks, and business agent of Local 856, I.L.A.

Another I.L.A. figure, who by 1952 was known to be involved in the dope racket, was Philip "Phil" Katz Albanese. He has been rated high on the U. S. Narcotics Bureau's list of major violators of the narcotics laws, and has long been regarded as kingpin of the dope organization on the Lower East Side. Albanese served nine months in prison in 1945 on two drug charges, and was convicted of income-tax fraud in 1954. He was originally a protégé of Joseph "Socks" Lanza, the jailbird who preceded Clemente as East Side racket boss.

This man, Albanese, known to be involved in the dope racket, has operated a truck-loading concession, on piers of the Pennsylvania Railroad, 27, 28, and 29, Hudson River. These piers are run by no other than William J. McCormack, the "Mr. Big" of the waterfront, previously mentioned patron of Joe Ryan.

A devout churchman, doubtless Mr. McCormack would frown on dope peddling, particularly in view of recent revelations of juvenile narcotics victims.

The professional Shylock, or loan shark, charging usurious rates of interest for loans to the needy, has never been a popular type during human history.

It has been one of the peculiar infamies of Joe Ryan's I.L.A. that it did more than parcel out control of loan-shark privileges to racketeers on many a pier, knowing that the casual longshoreman was a first-class prospect for loan sharks.

With union backing, the Shylock's toll was made a part of the price which many longshoremen have had to pay if they hoped to be picked by the hiring boss. The hiring boss and the Shylock united to exploit the jobless men who came to the docks to earn their living. Getting a loan at the usurious rate of 20 per cent a week from the loan shark was one way in which the job applicant could be sure to catch a favorable nod from the hiring boss when he entered the morning shape-up. Without that loan, the job went to another man—presumably more desperate for employment.

Collection of loan and interest for the Shylock was certain. All he had to do was to pick up that brass check from the longshoreman which alone would entitle the longshoreman to his wages. It would be the loan shark and not the longshoreman who would appear to collect the man's wages. The Shylock would collect the pay before the longshoreman got it, and pay him the balance after deducting the interest. The profits of the racket are sure.

A single loan shark on the Brooklyn waterfront, "Blackie"

Ruggiero, one of Tough Tony Anastasia's associates, was found to have 29 of these brass pay discs in his pocket when he was arrested in January, 1952. He was charged with violation of the gambling laws and convicted. In Ruggiero's pocket was a collection of policy slips. Playing the numbers was also forced on jobless longshoremen as another manner of kickback. It was just a different facet of the same method of exploitation.

How large the toll of the racketeers from shylocking along the piers has been would be hard to say. Some law-enforcement officers prosecuting those Shylocks who have been caught have given out fancy figures to the press for publicity purposes. Figures like 30 million or 40 million dollars a year have been mentioned.

Chief Justice Irving Ben Cooper once declared, "I am filled with amazement at the loose practices of those who pay the longshoremen where one man can turn in a batch of pay discs and get the pay of several men. The companies are under a duty to plug up this loophole which makes it possible for loan sharks to take advantage of these poor men who borrow only to make ends meet."

Some idea of the Shylock's profits might be gleaned from a single news story. In 1948 Mrs. Mildred C. Leahy, of Rye, New York, sued her husband, Edmund J. Leahy, for a separation. She asked 500 dollars weekly alimony.

Leahy was a loan shark, she alleged, and also had a share in a used-car business. He was worth more than 200,000 dollars, although used to lavish spending. She estimated his income at a great deal more than the 30,000 to 36,000 dollars a year he had been giving her.

Mrs. Leahy said that her husband collected loans from hard-pressed longshoremen by collecting their pay discs, and that although he himself was nominally employed on the docks, he did no actual manual toil there. During their marriage, she said, he had kept no bank account, but had given her between 2500 and 3000 dollars a month for household expenses. At times he had also showered her with expensive gifts, such as 15,000 dollars in jewelry, a 4000-dollar mink coat and a 600-dollar beaver coat.

During three winters, she said, he had sent her and their children to Florida, at an average cost of 3000 dollars per trip.

Aside from the gifts he made to her, she charged, the man whom she alleged was a loan shark had his own little luxuries, including a diamond-studded watch costing 3500 dollars, clothing and underwear made to order, and plenty of seats for all the baseball games and fights.

"He thinks nothing," she said, in papers filed in the Supreme Court, "of buying 14 ringside seats for the fights at 20 to 50 dollars apiece."

Their breakup came, she said, when she discovered that he had developed a fondness for another woman.

Leahy denied all his wife's charges. He alleged in his reply that although his wife and children lived smartly in that house in Rye, New York, his income was not more than 5000 dollars annually. Saying that both he and his blonde wife came originally from the Hell's Kitchen portion of West Side Manhattan, the defendant said his wife had "reverted to type" and was nothing more than a "gold digger" who recently had been going out with other men.

Allowing for a bit of inaccuracy in both the wife's and husband's versions of their dispute, this little vignette of New York life gives a rough idea of what a minor Shylock's profits and manner of living, on the way up from Hell's Kitchen, via dockside-loan enterprises might be. The angry wife's charge that Leahy was a loan shark was never proven.

The Shylock's occupation, however, in waterfront neighborhoods has not been one on which life-insurance companies would wittingly gamble. Many practitioners have wound up tied in sacks and strangled to death in lonely fields; shot dead and left in gutters or stolen automobiles; or simply ice-picked through the heart by acquaintances not yet identified.

The distinction between alien smuggling and the harboring of aliens who have entered the United States illegally may be a shadowy one, but one thing has been sure along the docks of New York for many years. I.L.A. racketeers and hiring bosses, willing to connive with the stevedoring companies and split 10,000 dollars a day in profits of hiring "short gangs," have always found a way to get illicit newcomers from Italy jobs on the docks and I.L.A. memberships. This has been particularly true in Hoboken, New Jersey, controlled by Eddie Florio, an Italian, and along the Brooklyn waterfront where members of the Anastasia family have ruled the I.L.A.

The United States Immigration Service has very few men with which to deal with the illegal entry of aliens in New York harbor. Once in a great while the service stages a raid to bag a few illegal immigrants with the help of large numbers of New York or New Jersey police or plain-clothesmen.

Standard procedure is for the raiders to descend on the docks just before a morning shape-up of longshoremen, and to round up a few-score job seekers. Raids such as this cannot be staged too often. It would interfere unduly with the harbor's business. Sporadic raids, however, featuring large numbers of national and city law-enforcement officers cooperating in rounding up the unwanted aliens serve at least to give a city's police force and the Immigration Service favorable publicity in the press for a day or two. These raids are utterly inadequate, of course, to cope with the basic problems of illegal immigration.

Taking a few sample raids at random from the files of Father Corridan, one may note that on June 12, 1951, 185 policemen and federal agents arrested 85 longshoremen on four piers in Hoboken as illegal ship-jumpers. These men had somehow obtained union buttons showing that they were members in good standing of the I.L.A.

Twelve hundred longshoremen were questioned before the 85 were hustled off to Ellis Island. According to Isidore Dworkin, the assistant district attorney of Hudson County, one of the illegal immigrants had only been in the United States four days but had gotten work on three of them. Meanwhile native Americans were left in the shape-up standing jobless.

Such a news event naturally aroused a patriotic howl of anguish from Mr. Ryan, as I.L.A. president. He demanded that Ed Florio, his I.L.A. organizer in Hoboken, launch an immediate investigation to see how those aliens happened to get I.L.A. buttons. Presumably the investigation was launched, but nothing ever was heard of it. The importation of aliens on the docks by those I.L.A. bosses, who combine the role of *padrone* with that of union official, continued without interruption. It would be surprising if it does not so continue to this very day.

Raids on the Brooklyn docks brought similar discoveries that alien ship-jumpers were working on them, equipped with I.L.A. membership books and buttons. After a series of such theatricals, some newspapers no longer took the raids too seriously. The New York *World-Telegram,* in a facetious editorial, noted that more than 400 such illicit immigrants had been rounded up in one series of raids.

"Most of them," it observed accurately, "were caught working as longshoremen on the waterfront, sporting union buttons and apparently in good standing with Joseph P. Ryan's International Longshoremen's Ass'n. Officers of that union say they are conducting an inquiry into how the buttons got into the hands of the illegal entrants. In this connection we can suggest one source of information. They might question Albert Anastasia, whose brothers, the Kefauver inquiry brought out, had no difficulty jumping ship and landing responsible jobs with the union."

But illegal entry in New York harbor has been no laughing matter to U. S. army and navy officers, charged over the last 15 years with guarding against sabotage in the nation's mightiest seaport. One of those ship-jumpers, picked up working on the docks at Hoboken in 1951, with I.L.A. protection, was a wartime saboteur.

He was identified as Guistino Arrivo, one of Mussolini's agents in World War II, who had been convicted in 1943 of having helped sabotage the steamship *Ircania.* Convicted of this crime in Tallahassee, Florida, he had served 18 months in a federal prison and then been deported. Yet here he was back again in the United States, at work on its vulnerable waterfront.

Far from the greatest waterfront racket in point of plunder, or financial gain, the "public-loading" racket was started during World War I, as a kind of petty extortion by a few strong-arm boys of the dockside areas. In time loading became legitimized by co-operation of the I.L.A. and New York City government. The powers wielded by public loaders and hiring bosses are the keys to most of the crime in the harbor. Any alliance between a hiring boss and a public loader can tie up a pier.

All the hiring bosses and loaders have been in alliance, through membership in Ryan's International Longshoremen's Association, even though both of them are employers of labor or representatives of management in the shipping and stevedoring industries rather than actual laborers. An accountant for the New York State Crime Commission set the annual sum extorted by public loaders from the shippers of merchandise along the New York City docks alone at about eight million dollars a year. This extortion and the public-loading system, as known in New York, have not been known in any other port.

Originally, public loaders were casual laborers, completely unorganized, who hung around the docks. They would volunteer to help teamsters load or unload their wagons. Back in the horse-drawn-vehicle days, these loaders were very simple men. They had strong backs and arms and were ready to work for anyone for modest sums. If teamsters were able to load or unload their own wagons, they certainly did so, for many years until the racketeers took over the loading function.

Of all the harbor rackets, this one of the public loaders has probably caused the most outcry, even though not the most costly to the port. The squawks of anguish came first from the merchant truckmen, the initial victims. They were being shaken down for exorbitant fees to keep their trucks moving. They were being denied the rights to bargain for a price of their helpers and to choose what help they wanted.

The truckmen gradually gave up a struggle against thuggery. They simply passed the exorbitant loading charges along to the importers. These, in turn, passed the charges along to the ultimate consumers.

The Committee on Transportation of the Commerce and Industry Association of New York, Inc., put up the best fight it could, in 1933, to make the steamship and railroad companies take over the responsibility of loading and unloading shipments on the piers. Nothing came of it. Steamship and railroad companies declined absolutely. The Commerce and Industry Association tried to get the city to amend its pier leases so that the racket might be ended.

By 1942 extortion and capricious overcharge by public loaders, who actually did no work but controlled dockside concessions, was at such a height that truckmen, importers, and others appealed to Joe Ryan to bring some system into the business. Ryan convened a series of meetings between truckers, shipping officials, importers, and loaders. A standard loading fee was established over many kinds of merchandise. An impartial arbiter was selected to adjudicate all disputes. But that failed to end abuses of the system. It remained for the public hearings of the New York State Crime Commission to bring out such damaging evidence against the public loaders in 1953 that the whole racket was outlawed by the laws adopted in New York and New Jersey setting up a bistate harbor authority.

The Crime Commission hearings showed that the loaders kept very few records, and that while their incomes were demonstrably high, their income taxes were low. They paid no unemployment compensation taxes or workmen's compensation taxes, and no deductions for old-age insurance for their employees. Most of them paid no rent for the piers on which they had established squatter sovereignty. Many of them had no equipment for loading heavy cargo, but borrowed it from shipping and stevedoring company employees. Their only stock-in-trade was a strong-arm terror or their ability to call on their I.L.A. allies, the hiring bosses, for "quickie" strikes to bring about settlement of disputed charges on their own terms.

Such were the main rackets which Father Corridan found had been flourishing for many years before he came to Xavier. Someone asked him one day whether they hadn't slowed up harbor production and cost the shipping industry dearly.

"Up to 1946, they didn't," the priest replied. "The only additional cost to the shipping companies may have been the cost from thievery, and the insurance companies paid most of them. Thievery, anyway, has amounted to less than 1 per cent of the value of cargo handled in the harbor. All the costs of the rackets came from the hides of the longshoremen and the pocketbooks of the general public.

"After 1946, however, because of the rackets, a great many longshoremen have been in a perpetual state of rebellion. Their wildcat strikes have certainly slowed down production, noticeably, and have increased the cost of production to the shipping industry. Only an end to the rackets, now, will restore production to its proper level and cut down costs that are ruining the port."

CHAPTER 4

THE PATTERN OF POWER

For almost a generation, before the arrival of Father Corridan at the Xavier School, the one man along New York's waterfront who typified untouchable power to veteran West Side longshoremen was William J. McCormack. "Big Bill" was a multimillionaire industrialist, born of lowly origin within their own neighborhood. Their eyes had followed his rise.

The one man who symbolized to those old-timers a somewhat smaller power was their union president, Joseph P. Ryan, or "Joe." He also had been brought up in their neighborhood and they had watched him climb.

These old-timers knew that McCormack and Ryan had worked together as political and business allies on both sides of the harbor, in New Jersey and New York. They knew that of the two men, McCormack had always been the stronger, the tougher, and the smarter. "Big Bill" was the leader, and Joe Ryan the follower.

For most of these years McCormack was seldom in the public eye. His climb to great riches drew very few newspaper headlines. Ryan, the follower, was often in the news as a labor-union leader and politician. Although McCormack admits today to 64 years of age and might be even five or six years older than that, the newspaper reading public heard very little of him until the great scandals uncovered officially by the New York State Crime Commission in the early 1950's began to reveal themselves. Then suddenly he became known as the harbor's "Mr. Big," or, by his own words, "The Little Man's Port Authority."

According to a brief biography of McCormack, for which he paid a press agent in 1952, New York harbor's "Mr. Big" was born in New York in 1890. He was the son of one Andrew McCormack who migrated to New York from County Monaghan, Ireland, after the Irish potato famine of 1849. His mother was Julia Moran, a second-generation Irish-American, whom Andrew McCormack married here after his arrival.

The elder McCormack was a wagon driver. He never emerged from poverty. After 39 years of work, six days a week, ten to 12 hours a day, he was hospitalized for a while. His employer let him go and paid him only seven dollars for one half of his final week's pay, since he only had worked three days.

Then and there, young Bill, the youngest of four children, two boys and two girls, vowed he never would let such a thing happen to himself. When he grew up he was going to be one of the bosses, and independently wealthy. He had gone to work when he was ten years old, delivering meat before and after school and on Sunday mornings for two dollars a week. At 13 he quit school to become a wagon boy. A juvenile Hercules, he became a wagon driver at 15. At 16 he owned his own one-horse truck. By that time his family had moved to Jersey City. He and his older brother, Harry, went to work as teamsters in the perishable vegetable market in Jersey City, known as the "Peach Yard."

In those days fights and physical violence were a normal part of a teamster's life along the waterfront. The two McCormack brothers soon became known on the Jersey City piers as two of the hardiest brawlers in the neighborhood. They were always ready to use their fists to reinforce their words in any argument. They also had business acumen. When Bill McCormack was 20 he owned three teams of horses. When he was 23 he bought out a trucking company which had 15 wagons and 30 horses.

In those years he became a close friend of Frank Hague, who for many years was mayor of Jersey City, undisputed boss of Hudson County politics, and one of the most influential Democratic Party politicians in the eastern part of the United States. He also became a stanch friend of Dan Casey, who for many years was Mayor Hague's chief of police. Before they were 30, both McCormack brothers were stout pillars in Frank Hague's political machine, and their trucking business grew prosperous.

By the time World War I had rolled around, their trucking concern was large enough to handle most of the meat shipped to the AEF. In 1920, right after World War I, McCormack joined with several other truckers in forming the U. S. Trucking Corporation, installing himself as executive vice-president in charge of labor relations. The then-Governor Alfred E. Smith had just been defeated for governor by Nathan L. Miller, Republican. McCormack, and his friends, made Al Smith the president, or front man, for their company. Thereby they showed an acute perception of the value of political prestige to any concern which wants to grow rich along the New York waterfront.

When Smith was re-elected governor in 1922, he made McCormack, his former business associate, chairman of the New York State Boxing Commission's License Committee. This committee had absolute authority over licenses to everyone, fighters, managers, handlers, referees, judges, and promoters, in professional boxing.

By 1927, when a great building boom was under way in New York, McCormack sold out his interest in the U. S. Trucking Corporation. He went into the sand and gravel business. He was a great friend of the late Sam Rosoff, builder of many New York subways—an occupation which also requires political connections of a very high order. He also became a great friend of an Italo-American newspaper publisher and politician who was in the sand and gravel business, Generoso Pope. Soon after entering the business, McCormack began supplying ready-mixed concrete to builders of all kinds.

In 1930, through contacts, partly political, which he had formed while in the trucking business, he obtained the contract to handle all the stevedoring business of the Pennsylvania Railroad, largest shippers into the metropolitan area. This contract brought him back into the handling of a large part of the city's perishable food products, along the piers of the Hudson River, where he had worked as a lowly wagon driver's helper when a boy of 13. In 1932 he organized the Jersey Contracting Company which took over the handling of all the Pennsylvania Railroad's work on the Jersey side of the harbor. Entry into the oil-distribution business followed swiftly. Today a chain of McCormack-owned filling stations is the largest independent chain in New York. Bill McCormack's business enterprises in New York today include the following:

The Transit-Mix Concrete Company; Penn Stevedoring Company; Jersey Contracting Company; William J. McCormack Sand Company, which dredges sand from the bottom of Long Island Sound, and the Morania Oil Tanker Company, which is named for Julia Frances Moran, his mother. He also is president of the Lincoln Fields Race Track in Chicago, but is said to serve this institution without salary. All told, his enterprises are said to gross some 20 million dollars a year, and McCormack personally is reputed to have rolled up a fortune of many millions.

Joe Ryan, the protégé and friend of Bill McCormack, although neither so tough nor so smart as the man above him, was tough enough to manage most of the men on the docks, because of the gunmen under him or political pals.

Ryan, the child of Irish immigrants, was born in Babylon, Long Island, May 11, 1884. Both his parents died before he was nine years old. A stepmother brought him to Manhattan, where he lived through his early years in Chelsea.

Chelsea and Greenwich Village are close enough together on the Lower West Side so that they merge into each other almost imperceptibly. Ryan and McCormack are known to have been acquaintances in boyhood. Their friendship only ripened as Ryan became a labor-union leader, after World War I.

Ryan went through several of the primary grades in the Xavier Parochial School. He left school when only 12. For a time he swept floors, was a stock boy and clerk in several stores, and then became a conductor on a cross-town trolley car. He was 28 years old before he got his first job on the docks. Like McCormack, Joe Ryan was then a big and powerful man, known to be handy with his fists.

He worked on the docks for less than a year. Then while he was working the hold of one of the ships, at 15 dollars for a 60-hour week, a load of lead ingots was dropped on his foot, so that for a short time he was sent to a hospital. He had bought a membership in the I.L.A. in 1916 for only two and a half dollars. That was the going rate for a union book. In later years he was wont to jocularly refer to this purchase as the finest investment he ever made.

A friendly official of the old I.L.A., knowing Ryan to be penniless and liking him, as countless acquaintances have liked him since, got him the post of financial secretary for the Chelsea local of the I.L.A. No. 791. This was then a part-time job. Soon afterward he was advanced to full-time work as an organizer at 30 dollars a week. It was the most money Ryan had made in all his life. He then discovered his natural talent. He was good at a certain type of sentimental and humorous oratory, and he was grand as a politician—meaning a go-between, or fixer. He made himself solid as a faithful henchman of the Democratic Party organization of Manhattan known as Tammany Hall.

By 1927 Ryan became president of the I.L.A. by favor of local leaders who controlled its inner politics. He was never popular with the rank and file. By 1943 the local leaders made him president for life, at a salary of 20,000 dollars a year, plus 7,200 dollars for expenses. This money was only a small part of the financial rewards of his office, as the public hearings of the New York State Crime Commission were to reveal in 1953.

Ryan, like McCormack, was always a good churchman. In New York politics that is an asset. He has for years been a trustee of the Shrine Church of the Sea, where his good friend, the Right Reverend Monsignor John J. O'Donnell, is pastor. Monsignor O'Donnell, as honorary member of Ryan's I.L.A. and as chaplain of the port, has been stanch in Ryan's defense at all times. Ryan with a wife and two daughters is also known as a good family man. He also has been capable of outbursts of generosity toward poorer acquaintances during his own times of affluence.

A big, burly barrel of a man, fat in his later years but with plenty of brawn, Ryan in affluence went in for Cadillacs and suits and shirts of the finest tailoring. He developed a penchant for dining and wining long and heartily at such restaurants as Toots Shor's in midtown Manhattan, and Cavanagh's on West 23rd Street. Cavanagh's has been a hangout for influential Tammany politicians as well as a haunt for discerning gourmets for more than a generation. Ryan also became a member of the Elks, the New York Athletic Club, and the Winged Foot Golf Club in Westchester County.

Beyond all else he became the so-called "standard-bearer" of the Joseph P. Ryan Association. This was a political club with two paramount and intertwined objectives: to advance the fortunes of Tammany Hall and Joseph P. Ryan.

The Joseph P. Ryan Association, with the aid of the Central Trades and Labor Council, waxed fat in political power. It gave an annual dinner and dance for many years, either at the Hotel Commodore or the Waldorf-Astoria. This dinner-dance was a great deal more than a festive occasion. It served to dramatize, once a year, the great power and influence which Ryan and his closest associates wielded in New York City's government; their affiliations with businessmen of undoubted means and some respectability; and their influence over thugs and murderers. A sprinkling of murderous hoodlums was always at these Ryan dinners in close proximity to judges of the courts, district attorneys, heads of city and borough governments, and ranking bureaucrats in the city's many governmental departments. For many years the chairman of the committee of arrangements for this festive occasion was Ryan's great and good friend, Big Bill McCormack.

Although these dinners were given always in Ryan's honor, the real insiders of New York politics knew since the middle 1930's certainly, that Big Bill McCormack, the rising industrialist, was a bigger man than the guest of honor. Chairman of the committee on arrangements was a very good title for him. Back in 1931 there were two chairmen of the dinner, Mayor Jimmy Walker of New York and Mayor Frank Hague of Jersey City.

In 1937 the late Mayor F. H. La Guardia and his police commissioner, Edward P. Mulrooney were listed as guests at Table 26. The late "Cockeye" Dunn, murderer, was a member of the committee on arrangements. Philip Mangano, another murderer now gone to his reward but then a flourishing member of the Anastasia-Adonis mob, sat at Table 80.

In 1938 Mayor La Guardia stayed away. But Mayor O'Dwyer was at the dinner in 1950, sitting at Ryan's own table. Mayor Vincent Impellitteri was a regular attendant at the dinners for years. In 1948 the listed diners included Police Commissioner Wallander, United States Attorney McGohey, District Attorney Miles McDonald of Brooklyn, District Attorney Frank Hogan of Manhattan, District Attorney Foley of the Bronx, and District Attorney Sullivan of Queens. Charles Yanowsky, the Alcatraz graduate who was then running the Jersey City waterfront, sat at Table 115.

The dinner of 1951, on the very eve of the State Crime Commission's investigations, was as good as any. Its committeemen and guests, drawn from political and business life and the underworld, suffice to show the pattern of power which has governed the New York harbor for two generations. Once again, McCormack headed the arrangements committee. Harry M. Durning, Collector of the Port, was a vice-chairman. Members of the committee included Harold Beardell, president of J. T. Clark & Son, a stevedoring concern, who testified openly before the New York Crime Commission of his money payments to union officials. Frank Nolan, president of the Jarka Stevedoring Company, since then convicted of commercial bribery; Eddie Florio, Ryan's old bootlegger henchman from Hoboken, later in prison on a perjury rap; William J. Tracey, a big tugboat magnate; and Hugh E. Sheridan, impartial chairman of the trucking industry.

The dinner-dance committee was equally eminent. Its chairman was John J. Casale, a boss trucker. Vice-chairmen? The five borough presidents of Manhattan, including Robert J. Wagner, now mayor.

Others on this committee were Mike Clemente, the perjurer now serving five to ten years, Inspector McQuade of the New York Police Department, and John Mangiamelli, an I.L.A. leader who later pleaded guilty of stealing union funds. Also "Connie"' Noonan, who refused to answer questions at the Crime Commission hearings on the ground his answers might tend to incriminate him.

The chairman of the entertainment committee was Colonel Ivan Annenberg, circulation manager of the New York *Daily News*. The vice-chairman was the Honorable Albert Goldman, United States Postmaster. Members of their committee included Harold Bowers, business agent for the I.L.A. "Pistol Local"; and Anthony V. Camarda, head of one of the Anastasia locals in Brooklyn who was later jailed for stealing union funds.

The two chairmen of the reception committee were the Honorable Hugo E. Rogers, a former leader of Tammany Hall, and the Honorable Charles W. Culkin, a great Tammany power. Two of the members of their committee were Willie Cox, a pier loader who once served a term in Elmira for biting off an opponent's ear during a brawl on a New York excursion steamer, and Inspector Herbert Golden of the New York Police Department.

Guests at this dinner included Chief Magistrate John Murtagh, John A. Coleman, former governor of the New York Stock Exchange, Carmine De Sapio, current boss of Tammany, and "Joe the Gent," I.L.A. leader in Newark.

The dinner of 1952 was the last of the dinners. In 1953 Father Corridan was speaking on waterfront problems at a dinner of hotel executives in the Hotel Commodore. He was introduced as the man who had knocked the Joe Ryan dinner out of the city's social life.

"As a result of this," the toastmaster said, "the grand ballroom of the Commodore is now available next Saturday night."

Reporters for years got chuckles from these dinners, because of the odd mixture of businessmen, politicians, and widely known thugs to be found there. In recent years reporters were not welcome. But as recently as 1950 Governor Thomas E. Dewey of New York was sufficiently cognizant of the political power represented on these occasions so that he sent his polite regrets to Ryan at being "unable to attend."

The governor's letter follows:

> *Dear Joe:*
>
> I would surely be delighted to come to the annual affair of the Joseph P. Ryan Association on Saturday, May 20th if possible. As it happens, Mrs. Dewey and I have accepted an invitation to the marriage of Lowell Thomas's only son that week-end and we just can't possibly make it.
>
> It is mighty nice of you to ask me and I wish you would give my regards to all the fine people at the dinner.
>
> On behalf of the people of the entire state, I congratulate you and thank you for what you have done to keep the Communists from getting control of the New York waterfront. Be assured that the entire machinery of the Government of New York State is behind you and your organization in this determination.
>
> With warm regards,
>
> SINCERELY YOURS,
>
> *Thomas E. Dewey*

This letter was written by a New York politician who had

ridden to power on his reputation as a racket-buster when in the district attorney's office, even though the waterfront rackets flourished during his term in municipal office as they still were flourishing when he wrote the letter as governor. It was carefully written, sending regards only to the "fine people" at the dinner and ignoring the others.

To many the Ryan dinner was a symbol of either Ryan's or McCormack's power. But to Father Corridan it epitomized the moral corruption which, leechlike, was sucking away the life blood of the harbor. It sickened him, Father Corridan says, to "see that same corrupt influence extended in recent years to some of the harbor's Catholic communion breakfasts.

"It was in early 1950," Father Corridan remembers, "that a Chelsea longshoreman, 'Happy' Donahue, came to me and asked for advice on how to run a longshore communion breakfast. I suggested three simple rules to protect the integrity of the occasion.

"First, the committee running the breakfast should be composed of strict rank-and-file longshoremen. Their chairman should be a man well over 60 known to have no political ambitions, a man respected by the longshoremen as a 'God-fearing' man.

"Second, the mass preceding the breakfast should be rotated among the waterfront churches, to help every pastor to build up his church, spiritually and materially.

"Third, at the breakfast itself, no union or company official should be seated on the dais.

"There is no differentiation at the altar rail," Father Corridan told Donahue, "and there should be no differentiation at the communion breakfast. Let them keep that for their political dinners."

On May 7, 1950, the first longshore communion breakfast was run, with honor given to much the same cast of characters as appeared at the Ryan dinners. What grieved Father Corridan, he says, was not the fact that many of those listed on the program as "Our Guests," were later revealed in the State Crime Commission hearings to be poor advertisements for virtue.

"It was the fact," Father Corridan says, "that independent of any Crime Commission revelations, the longshoremen knew the unjust dealings of those men on a daily basis for years. When one longshoreman said to me, 'Father, some of the biggest bums we have in the harbor, both in the union and in management, were honored at the breakfast this morning,' I shared in his bitter frustration. I recalled Pius XI's admonition:

" 'For there are some who, while exteriorly faithful to the practice of their religion, yet in the field of labor and industry, in the professions, trade, and business, permit a deplorable cleavage in their conscience and live a life too little in conformity with the clear principles of justice and Christian charity.

" 'Such lives are a scandal to the weak, and to the malicious a pretext to discredit the church.' "

Later in the early fall of 1950 Father Corridan was invited by a pastor in Newark to be the principal speaker at the first longshore communion breakfast in Port Newark. "I had to decline," says Father Corridan, "because I knew that the cochairmen of the breakfast, Pat Ferrone and Joe the Gent, business agents of the Newark I.L.A. locals, had just shaken down some fur importers for 70,000 dollars. A year or so later Joe the Gent had died in such circumstances that he had to be refused Christian burial."

The communion breakfast, however, that violated all the norms of religious decency, Father Corridan says, was the twenty-eighth communion breakfast of the United States Customs Service. It was held on March 24, 1952. A short time before, the New York State Board of Inquiry had published its report on the corrupt conditions which caused the 1951 wildcat strike.

Another Jesuit, Father Laurence J. McGinley, president of Fordham University, Father Corridan remembers, was asked to waive his rule of not speaking at communion breakfasts. Father McGinley consented to give a spiritual talk on the assurance there would be no political atmosphere in the occasion.

"That breakfast reeked with the cheapest kind of politics, as anyone could gather from reading the New York *Times* on the following day," Father Corridan says.

According to this *Times* report, Harry M. Durning, Collector of the Port and a speaker at the breakfast, "denied allegations that the New York waterfront is a racket-ridden community."

"Referring to newspaper and magazine articles that pictured the New York waterfront as a haven for criminals and racketeers, Mr. Durning said they were part of a widespread campaign to drive business away from New York to other seaports. He characterized the whole idea as an effort to knock down the port for selfish reasons."

The New York *Times* account went on to say that Edward F. Cavanagh, Jr., Commissioner of the city's Marine and Aviation Department, was another government official who spoke in similar tenor at the breakfast.

"The Commissioner took sharp issue with 'individuals who, with little or no knowledge of the facts and, for purposes of their own, find the New York waterfront a cesspool of iniquity,' " the *Times* narrative ran. " 'I have no illusions about the political aspects of the situation,' Mr. Cavanagh said. 'Of course, with millions of dollars going to our allies there are legislators who are anxious to see their states get the business.'

"Mr. Cavanagh admitted that certain types of crime have existed along the waterfront, but suggested that further facts be obtained before any conclusion was reached."

At the time of that breakfast, attacks on Big Bill McCormack, as "Mr. Big" of the waterfront, were beginning to be spread through magazines and newspapers. Mr. McCormack was on the dais. Mr. Durning asked him to stand up and take a bow. McCormack obliged. Then the Collector of the Port continued:

"Bill is a very able man, a religious man, a family man, and a patriotic American who has worked on the port for 40 years. New York City and the country at large are under obligation to him, not only for what he did during the war years, but what he did during the administrations of Mayor La Guardia, Mayor O'Dwyer, and Mayor Impellitteri."

Mr. Durning had praise, too, for Joseph P. Ryan, as president of the International Longshoremen's Association. Durning said he had known Ryan as he had known McCormack for about 30 years. Ryan, he continued, was also a very good friend of his, although he did not always see eye to eye with him. He predicted that there would be some improvements worked out in regard to problems involving longshoremen. Then he asked two United States district attorneys, Myles J. Lane of Manhattan and Frank J. Parker of Brooklyn, who also were seated on the dais, to stand up. Both men did.

If there were any corruption on the waterfront, Mr. Durning said, "these two outstanding public-spirited citizens would start proceedings."

"If religion is on the decline as a moral influence in the lives of many people, breakfasts such as these, as much as the corrupt conditions on the waterfront, are a cause," Father Corridan says.

CHAPTER 5

WHAT CORRIDAN LEARNED FROM CAREY

Back in 1941, five years before Corridan's arrival at Xavier Labor School, Father Philip J. Carey had tried to help a group of dock workers. As Father Carey tells the story, four men came into his office in August of that year. They were coopers, or more particularly, fruit-cargo repairmen employed at the produce piers on the Hudson River. At that time most of the fruits and vegetables for sale in New York came into the city over the Erie and Pennsylvania railroads. After the freight cars were lightered to Manhattan docks and unloaded, the coopers were put to work to repair damaged cases so that a buyer could not tell whether the crates had been packed in California or New York.

This made a great deal of difference to the Railroad Perishable

Inspection Agency, a self-insurance organization sponsored by the railroads to keep down losses on damaged cargo. The monetary difference at that time went from two and a half dollars down to 80 cents as between an undamaged and a damaged crate.

The four men informed Father Carey that they had been working for two concerns. One was the Aetna Cooperage & Stevedoring Company, which was under contract to the Erie Railroad. Aetna was run by the late Harry McCormack, brother of Big Bill McCormack. When they were not working for Aetna, the men said, they worked for the Penn Stevedoring Company. That was one of "Mr. Big's" own concerns.

The four men maintained that they and their fellows had worked a great many hours of overtime for many months without being paid proper overtime rates. "We used to belong to Local 202 of the Teamsters," said Charlie Iburg (one of the four), "when Harry McCormack was the wheel, and we worked on the Erie piers. We were hired by the railroad. There were some pretty funny strikes in those days. I remember one quickie when the Erie was caught with a whole freight train of peaches that couldn't be unloaded over in Jersey. The strike lasted one night, and then the contract for handling cargo repair work was handed over to McCormack's Aetna Company from the Railroad Perishable Inspection Agency, which had handled the work before. Then Harry McCormack became our boss. Immediately there was a terrific difference in our working conditions. We stopped getting time-and-a-half for overtime, which we got when we worked directly for the railroad.

"We asked McCormack about it. He said, 'Look, you used to have a contract with the Erie, but you don't have any contract with me.' We went down to 202 to see what they could do about it. They wouldn't do anything. McCormack was running the union. He paid us a flat seven dollars per day regardless of the hours worked. We worked quite regularly between ten and twelve hours a day, with occasional longer stints caused by high tides."

That was way back in the early 1930's. In 1938 the Fair Labor Standards Act was passed. These coopers did not realize that they might get help under its provisions until 1941. This gives you a rough idea of how much waterfront labor understood labor legislation from that section of the New York press which the men were accustomed to read. But in 1941, at any rate, some of the men filed a case for reimbursement of their overtime pay with the Wages and Hours Board.

They were advised for their own security to join a union that would protect them. At first they sought affiliation with the Brotherhood of Railroad and Steamship Clerks. They were turned down because that union had just come off second best in a jurisdictional contest with the Railway Expressmen from Cincinnati. Its leaders were in no mood to take on a fight with the powerful teamsters' union in New York.

George Donahue, leader of the Wholesale and Retail Department Store Workers, C.I.O., offered them an affiliation with his union. They were hesitant at joining the C.I.O. at that time. Harry Bridges, West Coast longshoremen's leader, was trying to break into New York harbor.

Bridges, to them, was a Communist. These men wouldn't join any union he ran. They saw no hope in Joe Ryan's International Longshoremen's Association, since men were working car floats with Ryan's tacit consent at less than the union rate of one dollar and five cents an hour. They also knew that Ryan's I.L.A. was permitting its members to work under conditions below contract standards on many a pier. They wanted no part of Joe Ryan's union.

Finally they decided to organize a union of their own. Meetings were held at first in City Hall Park. They couldn't afford to hire a hall. The first meeting was held on August 30, 1941. The very next day the men were informed that a meeting had just been held in Hoboken in the office of the Commission of Public Safety, at which Secretary MacDonald of the Employing Truckmen's Association, W. J. McCormack, Bob Burker, an officer of Aetna Cooperage & Stevedoring Company and others were present.

Iburg told Father Carey that his new union members were warned that it wouldn't be healthy for any of them if they persisted in their plan for an independent union. By whom?

By men who they believed, rightly or wrongly, represented their employers, as well as Teamsters' Local 202, which had failed to represent them for years. They believed then, as the New York State Crime Commission hearings were to show publicly 12 years later, that Local 202 was a crooked labor union, which would fail absolutely to represent their interests.

On August 26, 1941, these men formed their own union in defiance of warnings, with Bernard H. Fitzpatrick, a lawyer, drafting their constitution. They called this new union the Independent Coopers and Cargo Repairmen of New York. All the men were working on the produce piers, in spite of threats. It was a busy season on the Erie Railroad for fruit transportation. The very night they acquired their new constitution, plug-uglies who, the coopers said, represented Local 202, showed up on the piers. There was some disorder, but not much, since their work was needed.

The men filed proceedings before the National Labor Relations Board, seeking recognition as an independent union to bargain on wages and working conditions for their own group. Almost concurrently, they instituted suit in the Federal Court to recover back pay from Harry McCormack's company. The men were less interested in recovering the money than in writing the future conditions under which they would work on the docks. The theory was that as a condition of settling the back-pay action (which carried a double pay and attorneys' fee penalty) the employer could be forced to extend recognition to their union or to arbitrate the matter.

The next move was up to Harry McCormack. It came fast. The members of the new union were informed that the Aetna Cooperage & Stevedoring Company had just signed a closed-shop contract with Local 202. They were told that if they would pay up their back dues and become members in good standing within 202, all would be well. They could go on with their work at the usual rates, which did not include any payment for overtime.

The men refused and were locked out. They applied to the National Labor Relations Board for an immediate election to show which union the coopers really wanted, their own or Local 202 as run by "Joe" Papa. This man, Papa, was to be shown up publicly 12 years later as so flagrant an offender against unionism's code of ethics that he was removed from office by Dave Beck, president of the teamster's international union.

The countermove by "Joe" Papa, through his lawyer, one Ed Kaplan, according to Father Carey, was so wide of the truth as to be funny. Papa charged before the N.L.R.B that the new independent coopers' union was "employer-dominated." Here were these men, locked out because they would not yield to their employer, after he had signed a closed-shop contract with a racketeering union. Such an allegation was on the face of it monstrous. Yet the local officers of the National Labor Relations Board, says Father Carey, dragged their heels in investigating and dismissing the unfair practice charge. Meanwhile, the N.L.R.B. would not permit an election since the charge was pending.

This case of the aggrieved coopers, as it stuck in the craw of Father Carey for many a long year, might now be relegated to the limbo of forgotten causes, or the wrongs of small groups of humble workmen without any influence, except for one thing. Father Carey could never forget it.

He passed the story along to Father Corridan. It contained within it the pattern of oppression, against which the longshoremen of New York were to rebel again and again through the coming years. This was the pattern which Corridan set out to smash just as quickly as he documented thoroughly its wider ramifications, and became an adviser to the men being hurt.

Let Father Carey take up the story. "The investigator assigned to this case by the Wages and Hours Agency," he says, "was a man of remarkable integrity. He got all the proof he needed that the men were right in their claims. Then the investigator, himself, was warned to lay off the case. He told me about it. Someone who said he was Commissioner of Public Safety in Hoboken telephoned him one day at the height of his investigation and asked him if he didn't know that Mayor Hague of Jersey City, undisputed Democratic boss of New Jersey at that time, was personally interested in the case.

"The investigator replied that this made no difference to him. He intended to do his duty as he saw it. The voice replied, 'Well, good-by, sucker, you'll be hearing more about this.'

"The next morning the investigator was called into the office of the Regional Director of the Wages and Hours Agency, an appointee from New Jersey. He was asked to bring all his files on the case, and was then relieved of it. The investigation was handed over to another inspector and died a natural death in his desk drawer. Meanwhile, some of the men still working on the piers were forced to sign statements that they had received their overtime, under threat of being fired if they didn't.

"Those men who had come to me, after going first to their parish priest, were on my mind through many waking moments. I sought the counsel of some men whom I knew. Ed Flynn, Secretary of Labor in New Jersey, referred me to Peter McGuinness, a Brooklyn politician. He told me Joe Ryan was the man to see."

McGuinness, self-styled "Mayor of Greenpoint, the garden spot of the universe," was the registrar of records in Kings County at that time, and a man of broad political knowledge. McGuinness knew the inside of the inside. Joe Ryan, he told Father Carey, would be "just the man to tell you the right thing to do to settle the problem."

McGuinness went further than that. He called Joe Ryan himself. Joe wasn't in. McGuinness left a message. McGuinness told Father Carey to go back to the rectory at St. Francis Xavier and wait for Ryan's phone call. Father Carey waited most of that day. He phoned Ryan at 5 P.M. Mr. Ryan's secretary told Father Carey that Ryan had received Registrar McGuinness' message and knew all about the case. That was all the answer that Father Carey could get, at any time, from Joe Ryan.

Father Carey is a gentle soul and a shrewd one. He has one of the kindest smiles about the eyes that any man could wish to see. But he really hasn't the direct-actionist impulses of his assistant, Father Corridan. They are a good team, particularly as Corridan has just a faint touch of the gladiator about him. Carey can understand all these labor problems, too, and give wise counsel. But the Waterfront Priest is of the same strain as John L. Sullivan, once world heavyweight champion. This helps him a great deal around the docks.

"All the time," as Father Carey recalls it, the men who had come to him for help were out of work on the street. "I walked around with them, sitting on park benches, as they were looking for employment. I was able to fix up a couple of marriages and straighten out a few families. I even locked one of the boys in my room one night to keep him from killing a Local 202 delegate who kept hounding him from one job to another. This man was worried about his boy, who was a marine on Guadalcanal and was badly wounded.

"The men's law suit dragged on in the Federal Court. The men didn't have any money to pay their lawyer. Finally their case was arbitrated before the State Mediation Board. The independent union took the initiative. Twenty-six men testified openly before the arbitrator, despite the danger that they would be blackballed on the produce piers. Mr. Jacob Goodstein represented the McCormack interests. 'Joe' Papa and Ed Kaplan, his lawyer, represented Local 202.

"Fitzpatrick was summing up the case around noontime one day when the secretary of the Mediation Board broke in and asked if Mr. Fitzpatrick and I would step outside." When they went with him, the secretary informed them that the case before the arbitrator, Louis Yagoda, had given the board great anxiety.

"On the merits of the case and the evidence, he said, the decision would have to go for the men. But for certain reasons he was not at liberty to state, the board did not want to be put in a position where it would have to give any such decision. Mr. Yagoda, as arbitrator, would step down after lunch. This secretary of the board thought Mr. Fitzpatrick and I would be well advised to work out a compromise deal with Local 202 of the Teamsters' Union."

Father Carey was enraged.

"I didn't think the sell-out all along the line would reach in here," he told the board secretary. "Sir, this is a fix." It was a charge made in righteous anger which he could never prove. But the fact that the men could lose a case they deserved to win was peculiar. Doubtless, board members immediately concerned acted properly under their official instructions.

The board secretary tried to mollify the priest. He assured him that mediation rather than arbitration would bring full justice to the plaintiff coopers. Neither Fitzpatrick nor Father Carey was satisfied. They stormed over to the offices of the Reverend John Boland, chairman of the State Labor Relations Board. He was sympathetic but informed them that the case was outside his jurisdiction. He could do nothing about this case, he said, though he found it shocking.

Father Carey went to Arthur Meyers, then head of the Mediation Board, and asked for some assurance that the men would obtain, through a face-saving device in mediation, that decision to which they were entitled by right and justice. He was blunt in condemning the failure of arbitration as a "fix." He remembers being told that Mr. Meyers never would work under any compulsion or threat, and being asked what he intended to do about it.

The good priest knew at once, of course, that there was not anything he could do about it. He felt right down to the bottom of his shoes that the case had ended in vile injustice for the men concerned. Rightly or wrongly he was absolutely convinced that their cause was lost in something more than bureaucratic red tape.

It was lost, he felt, because the employer in the case, allied with a crooked labor union under "Joe" Papa, was able to reach into the governmental agencies charged with protecting the men and to rob them of their money and rights because of political influence. That is exactly the way the men felt about it also.

Thereafter, as an anticlimax, Father Carey was present when a deal was worked out with "Joe" Papa, as boss of Local 202, whereby the men who had fought for their rights would at least suffer no harm for their efforts.

" 'Joe' Papa shook hands with me on his promises," he says,

"and broke them within a month. Most of the men drifted away from the docks. They were afraid to go back."

Such is the story which Father Carey, as director of the Xavier School, told Father Corridan, when the younger man arrived at Xavier in 1946, all brimming with energy.

"How would you like to try your hand at the longshoremen's situation?" Father Carey asked his junior.

"I'll be glad to," said Corridan.

CHAPTER 6

THE GATHERING OF KNOWLEDGE

When Father Corridan volunteered to take over that part of the Xavier School which dealt with the counseling of longshoremen, he was not completely devoid of knowledge of waterfront problems. Father Corridan had first encountered waterfront problems in 1941 when assigned to the Crown Heights Labor School in Brooklyn. He met two men there who gave him the basic knowledge which he later developed by personal work with the dock workers.

These men were Monsignor Edward E. Swanstrom, of the Diocesan Commission for Catholic Charities in Brooklyn, and George Donahue, a member of the Association of Catholic Trade Unionists.

Monsignor Swanstrom, who had written the book, *The Waterfront Labor Problem* (published in 1938 by the Fordham University Press), had become interested in waterfront labor problems because of his meetings with the families of many longshoremen, in his efforts to alleviate the lot of the poor. George Donahue's viewpoint was that of a professional labor-union leader. Donahue had been a dock worker in his early years, and had participated in the rough business of bucking gangster control of his local in the I.L.A.

Monsignor Swanstrom's contribution to knowledge of labor conditions in New York harbor, given as author and scholar, was very great, because prior to the book he wrote in 1938 there was very little written material on longshoring in any port of the United States. A sociologist named Charles R. Barnes had written a book called *The Longshoreman,* in 1915. As Father Corridan studied the two books he could see that the basic ills that plagued dockside labor in the 1940's were merely aggravations of the casual labor system in effect around the docks before World War I.

Under this system the great shipping companies, with the stevedoring concerns, had successfully maintained for more than two generations a dockside force of casual laborers, two to three times as large as needed in their industry. These were kept in a state of complete insecurity, always close to the boundary line of hunger. The employers had maintained this force of available workers with the connivance of a labor union that professed to represent these workers' interests but never did. Maintenance of this surplus labor force, frequently desperate for any work at any rate of pay, was easy as long as the International Longshoremen's Association would do just one thing. That was to keep the union books open to anyone who wanted to work on the docks, who was willing to pay union dues.

Within the system, as it developed through the years, the hiring boss became one of two key figures by which the mass of casual laborers were exploited. He became the arbiter who could determine on any given day, two to three times a day, whether the men and their families would eat or go hungry. He could determine this by reason of the historic method of hiring, called the shape-up, or the shape.

Here is the way the hiring was done. At any pier in New York harbor which awaited a ship for unloading, or contained a ship to be loaded, aspirants for the work have lined up in a semicircle outside the shed, in any weather, at the shrill blast of a hiring boss' whistle. Within this semicircle, men accustomed to work on the decks of the vessels in port assembled at the left. Those aspiring to work down in the holds have gathered just to the right of them. To the right of these were men seeking work on the docks. Then came drivers of "fork trucks," upon which cargo is moved around the piers. On the extreme right of the semicircle was the extra or surplus force of job-seekers, ready to take the place of anyone in moving ship's cargo.

Some of the longshoremen's work is highly skilled. Some requires little mental ability and a great deal of brawn. Skilled or unskilled, all the men who have assembled in these dockside semicircles had to be I.L.A. members in order to get work, theoretically. Actually that was not the case.

There was no system of enforceable seniority for men who had worked within the union for years. Some of the job aspirants have been required to pay in the regular, formal way for their union books. Others—and a great many others—simply came to the docks with a card from a political leader to the hiring boss to give them work. Others had preference in the gaining of work because they had gone into debt to loan sharks with whom the hiring bosses made business arrangements. Others arranged to pay kickbacks on their pay in various ways to nearby saloon keepers, who worked out similar business arrangements with hiring bosses.

Theoretically, the hiring bosses on New York piers have been the representatives of the shipping or stevedoring companies. Actually, these hiring bosses have been members of the I.L.A., that is, the same union as the men they hired. They often have been forced on the stevedoring or shipping companies who have not wanted to employ them. Some of the stevedoring companies, however, have knowingly employed ex-convicts as hiring bosses—particularly ex-convicts known to be quick with gun, knife, or fist. These employers have held that longshoremen are a tough lot, at best, and need to be kept in fear by hoodlums, if they are to give adequate production. Other employers have acquiesced in this hiring of gangsters, as selected by the I.L.A., because they have known they could get special treatment either by Joe Ryan or his principal lieutenants. Ryan & Co., as bosses of the union, were willing to let favored employers work union members in smaller gangs than those which strict adherence to union contract would have required.

Such have been the conditions of employment faced by New York harbor's longshore workers, as they stepped up to shape-ups daily, at the sound of a whistle. From 1915 to 1938, when Father Swanstrom wrote his book, the number of shapes were reduced to three a day. One was at 7:55 A.M., and another at 12:55 P.M., and there was a third at 6:55 P.M. if work needs to be done through the nighttime, as it usually must when a ship is in port.

Looking back today on his first reading of Monsignor Swanstrom's book, Father Corridan is struck by how closely the findings of the Brooklyn priest's original research in 1938 paralleled those of the New York State Crime Commission in 1953. According to Father Corridan, Monsignor Swanstrom's analysis of the reasons why thousands of brawny workingmen, living in tenements close to the piers, have been willing to accept their status as victims of the corruption above them, is as valid today as on the day it was written. "The dock worker is a most unusual type of man," Msgr. Swanstrom wrote. "He accepts many of the conditions he finds along the waterfront as part of the industry. He looks with suspicion upon anyone coming in from outside. He knows the strength of the union machine and those who control his destinies, and he is not willing to jeopardize the little he has already by any disclosure of prevalent abuses. He knows that it is all too easy to have him excluded from all available work opportunities.

"Because of the competition for work it is easy to understand why he is willing to accept a little less than he is supposed to be receiving, if the difference will assure him of more regular work from those who can supply that work. He is not likely to complain when he knows that complaints will probably mean the loss of all, or nearly all employment."

The information that Father Corridan obtained from George Donahue, the professional labor leader, back in 1941, was of a different nature, but it shed added light on the problem.

"I first met Donahue when I was at the Crown Labor School," Father Corridan recalls. "I had known of him previously by reading *The Labor Leader,* a publication of the Association of Catholic Trade Unionists. Donahue is a graduate of Manhattan College. But in the depression years he was working as a checker of cargo on the docks. In 1936 he was instrumental in getting the International Longshoremen's Association to organize checkers hired by his employers. They were enrolled in the Coastwise Checkers' Local, 1,346. It wasn't long after the organization of the checkers that he became alarmed by the presence of nonmember thugs at his union's meetings.

"Donahue complained of this to 'Teddy' Gleason, who had been made an officer of the local. When he made his complaint, Gleason shrugged and made the following comment: 'I'm not going to throw them out. Do you think I want to get killed?' "

In March, 1937, a jurisdictional strike of the checkers' local was called by Gleason and two of his associates, Daggert and John "Cockeye" Dunn. When Dunn's reign of terror on one sector of the waterfront was in full flower, Donahue as a Catholic trade unionist made the mistake of criticizing the jurisdictional strike which Dunn and his pals were leading. His criticism was made to Gleason.

That afternoon Donahue was visited on the pier by Daggert and three ex-convicts constituting his union strong-arm squad, "Barney" Baker, and two others. After Daggert informed him, "I'll blow your head off and throw you in the river if you don't mind your own business," the strong-arm boys beat him up and left him lying on the pier.

Donahue had courage. That very evening he went into a meeting of the local and denounced the criminal forces working within the leadership of the I.L.A., as he had come to know them. He appealed to fellow members to back him up if he were fired from his job because of the fight he proposed to make on these criminals. The members at the meeting voted to back him.

Donahue went out and lodged a complaint with the police against the only two thugs among his assailants whom he knew by name—Daggert and Baker. Daggert disappeared from the waterfront for a while, but Baker was picked up by the police. He was then a parolee. "Barney" was sent back to prison for violation of parole. Two weeks after the assault, Donahue told Father Corridan, he was fired from his job of checker on the docks because of alleged "inefficiency," even though he was a college graduate. He appealed to "Teddy" Gleason, the union organizer. Gleason, he said, refused to back him up on the ground that he had "caused the arrest of a union brother."

"I believe it was George Donahue," Father Corridan says today, "who first called my attention to the post-Prohibition migration of mobsters from the old bootlegger gangs into the loading rackets along the waterfront. With the end of Prohibition, all the criminals who had made this vast outlaw trade their business had to find other employment. A great many of them were strong-arm boys with a shrewd nose for easy pickings on the fringes of legitimate business.

"The smartest of them, of course, worked their way into businesses that could serve as a respectable front for their criminal activities. The old gangsters of the Prohibition era certainly were familiar with the New York docks and with the trucking business. They knew politics, also, since political influence had always been used to protect them in the days when Prohibition made drinking illegal, and New York's population demanded illegal liquor.

"Donahue pointed out how the boss loaders at the piers, organized as I.L.A. members, though they were really employers, had achieved by sheer squatter sovereignty the right to load all incoming cargo on trucks at the piers, and how lucrative the racket was.

"Long before I came to the Xavier School I had learned how veteran gangsters killed each other for control of this commerce. I remember that among others killed in rivalry over pier-loading concessions in 1936 were Joe Butler and George Keeler along Lower West Side docks; and Johnny Costello on those same docks in 1937. In 1939 and 1940 Dave Beadle and Richard "The Bandit" Gregory were killed along uptown West Side piers. The "Pistol Local" of the I.L.A., managed by the Bowers boys, now rules the uptown piers.

"Donahue already had seen the pattern of mob control in the I.L.A., back in 1940. He was convinced that phony labor leaders, who really were criminal racketeers, had seized control of the docks for many purposes outside the law, under the protective coloration of labor unionism. You have to remember that during the growth of organized labor in the 1930's very few people recognized how racketeering had become a force in it. A large part of the American people who had followed President Roosevelt and the Democratic Party in its New Deal reforms, and been conscious of benefits from them, looked askance at any attack on labor leaders, as such. Naturally leaders of labor unions generally, who were keenly aware of how bitter had been the fight to organize unions, tended to discount attacks on other leaders of unions.

"Donahue believed—as I came to believe—that the shipping and stevedoring companies went along with this labor union setup on the docks because it enabled them to get maximum production out of the dock workers without the installation of those conditions of regular labor and safety for the workers which establishment of honest unionism would have entailed.

"Violent deaths over control of the dock rackets were not confined to the West Side. They occurred along the Brooklyn waterfront and over in New Jersey, at Jersey City and Hoboken. I remember when a Brooklyn longshoreman named Peter Panto tried to lead a rank-and-file revolt against the control of six Brooklyn locals of the I.L.A., which stemmed from Murder, Inc. Panto's lime-encrusted body was dug up near Lyndhurst, New Jersey.

"That was back in January, 1941, when I was at the Crown Labor School. Bill O'Dwyer, who later became Mayor of New York before he departed for Mexico, was then district attorney in Brooklyn. At one time he expressed some confidence that he would 'break' the Panto case and bring the murderers to justice. He never did. As district attorney, he took over the investigation of the waterfront in Brooklyn which had begun very promisingly under John Harlan Amen. The investigation died.

"At the Crown Labor School I learned other things about the waterfront rackets, both from Monsignor Swanstrom and from Father Thomas Darby of the New York diocese, a chaplain for the Association of Catholic Trade Unionists. They told me of Father Swanstrom's unsuccessful efforts to get Joe Ryan, as president of the I.L.A., to do something about cleaning up his union. During the 1939 I.L.A. convention, they told me, Father Swanstrom tried to pass out circulars, advertising his book, to the union delegates at the Hotel Commodore. Ryan ordered the sergeant-at-arms at the convention to take his circulars away from him, and asked the management of the Hotel Commodore to put the priest out of the building."

It was back in Brooklyn that Father Corridan first began to study the interplay of politics and the shipping industry. He learned that more than half of the piers on the New York City side of the port were municipally owned. He found that the Seabury Investigation had turned up cases of improper leasing of some of these docks to boss stevedores and shipping companies. He learned how important a part federal subsidies played in the development of the American merchant marine, so that close personal association between representatives of the shipping industry and the officials of the federal government played its part in the obtaining of subsidies. He learned, too, how generally recognized it was that the Central Trades and Labor Council, within which Joe Ryan was no minor power, was an important adjunct of Tammany Hall.

He began to see clearly that pattern of mutual interests, that web of personal alliances, that existed all around the perimeter of the harbor. Because of it the shrewd, hard, and practical businessmen, politicians, and so-called labor leaders rose to wealth and eminence within the greater community. Because of it, also, the brawny dock workers were kept in such subjection that they stayed poor and insecure, despite advances in living standards by organized workingmen, no smarter than they, who worked in other trades.

Once at the Xavier School, after Father Carey had assigned him to work specifically for the dock workers, Father Corridan went to work to lay his hands on all information that might be available to him, concerning their lot and the industry employing them. He learned early that longshoring is probably the most dangerous work that any man in American industry may do. He learned, too, that neither the labor-union leaders nor the shipping and stevedoring companies took any substantial interest in cutting down the rate of costly accidents on the piers of New York until after World War II.

No adequate report of injuries along the docks exists to this day. The most indicative governmental study of injuries and their causes in the longshoring industry that Father Corridan has been able to find is one dated 1944. It is the work of two statisticians for the U. S. Bureau of Labor Statistics. For the industry record of the bureau in that year, Frank S. McElroy and George R. McCormack reported in part as follows:

"More than 138 longshoremen experienced disabling work injuries in the course of every million employee-hours of longshore work performed during the year 1942. No other industry for which injury-frequency information is available had a record even approaching this unfavorable figure. The highest injury-frequency rate recorded for any other industry in 1942 occurred in the highly hazardous operations of logging, where there were 89.6 disabling injuries for every million employee-hours worked. In the iron and steel industry, the rate was 10.4 and in the construction industry it was 36.7."

The report, according to the U. S. statisticians, probably covered about one fourth of the longshoremen in the country, so that the probable volume of disabling injuries to longshoremen, in the nation's ports as a whole, would run to about 22,000 a year. "In 1942," the report said, "the chances for an individual longshoreman were approximately 1 in 560 that he would be killed or completely disabled for life; 1 in 48 that he would experience a permanent physical impairment; and 1 in 4 that he would lose time because of temporary injury."

The fact that workers in the holds suffer twice the number of injuries sustained by other longshoreman explains a traditional practice among longshoremen. The work is reserved, if possible, for the foreign-born, or recent arrivals on the waterfront. Most of the old-timers are too smart to go down into those holds if they can get any work on ship decks or docks.

Father Corridan quickly learned, too, that the irregularity of employment for dock workers characteristic of New York was not characteristic of a great many other big seaports, where the unrestricted shape method of hiring had long since been abandoned. Various schemes to regularize employment of longshoremen and to bring about better relations between labor and management had been developed over the last 40 years elsewhere. The port of Hamburg, Germany, had pioneered in a "decasualization" program as far back as 1906. Liverpool followed in 1912. American seaports that had managed to work out systems of more regular employment for longshoremen than New York included Seattle, Washington, in 1921; Los Angeles, in 1922; Portland, Oregon, in 1923, and San Francisco, in 1934.

Why had New York failed to follow suit? The hiring system along the New York docks had been the subject of severest criticism, down through the years, beginning with a report of a committee appointed by Mayor John Purroy Mitchel in 1916. That report declared that: "Conditions of hiring [meaning the shape] are degrading in the extreme. They do not ensure selection of the most efficient workers. They are open to the danger of graft, and are in themselves a continued source of dissatisfaction."

The more Father Corridan studied the New York waterfront, the more he realized that this description of employment conditions, written before World War I, remained equally true after World War II. He realized also that every time the hiring system, which was one of the more basic evils of the port, was publicly attacked, it was jointly defended by the New York Shipping Association representing the employers and the I.L.A., which was supposed to represent the interests of the employees. They spoke with one voice.

Why was that? To be sure, the hourly wage rate for longshoremen had risen through the years. It was 95 cents an hour, on an average, in October, 1934, and had been 85 cents when Joe Ryan became president of I.L.A. in 1927. Rebellious longshoremen were damning Ryan as "Woolworth Joe," or "Five-and-Ten Joe," when Father Corridan arrived on the scene. Between 1934 and 1942 Ryan had negotiated five contracts with the employers, four of which brought the men a nickel-an-hour raise in average wage rate, and one of which brought ten cents an hour.

This raise in wage rates lagged behind increases received by other unions and far behind the rising cost of living, once wartime inflation set in. During all those years Ryan's negotiating committee never had advised the men to strike for a better deal than the shipping people were willing to give them. And even after negotiating a contract, he and his union leaders had permitted favored stevedoring companies to break it with impunity —notably the Jarka Stevedoring Corporation, largest in the United States.

The more Father Corridan studied the waterfront problem, and the more he talked to dock workers trickling into the Xavier School for advice and instruction, the more he became convinced that the I.L.A. was a "captive union." It was not completely a company union, but it was almost that. It was dominated by the employers more than by the men on its roster and was in no real sense of the word a labor union at all.

CHAPTER 7

TIMES ARRIVE THAT FAVOR REVOLT

In many ways the timing of Father Corridan's arrival at the Xavier School was fortunate for the longshoremen whom he came to serve. World War II was ended. The war in Korea had not yet begun. Veterans of army and navy service, who were born and reared near the New York docks and who had worked on the piers before they entered the service, were coming back to them, to pick up their old jobs and earn their livings.

In 1945, with V-J Day a recent memory, rebels against the rule of the I.L.A. staged the first of a series of so-called wildcat strikes by which they were to win better terms from the New York Shipping Association than their president, Joe Ryan, had consented to make for them. One section of the 1945 wildcat strike, on the

Brooklyn docks, had been Communist-led, but the bulk of the strikers were anti-Communist. By a walkout well-nigh spontaneous they won a raise of 25 cents an hour, the biggest increase in hourly pay of any new contract in all I.L.A. history. They also won a right to vacation pay for that small minority of them who succeeded in getting 1350 hours of work per year.

To understand the temper of those younger men in the old I.L.A., to whom Father Corridan became a spiritual adviser in their rebellion against oppression, it is necessary to note that the great majority of them were native-born Americans, schooled in the public and parochial schools of New York City and northern New Jersey. Many had worn their country's uniform in combat. They were not so easily to be pushed around—even by gunmen with records of murder—as were their fathers, who often were recent immigrants in a strange, new country, without even elementary schooling.

Father Corridan began his work at a very propitious moment in the history of New York harbor. Very few longshoremen, indeed, were attending the Xavier School when he got there. But a few of them were. More came quickly after they learned that a priest was there who was working hard for them, and that the school building had so many entrances and exits that their comings and goings need not be observed.

The first longshoreman whom he met in the school, Father Corridan says, is one whom he will long remember—a deeply religious, middle-aged man, now dead, named "Christy" Doran. Doran was a family man, with wife and three children. Before he died he had found steady employment with the Turner & Blanchard Stevedoring firm as a hiring boss on Pier 42, Hudson River. But Doran, though hiring boss for Turner & Blanchard, still was a member of the I.L.A. He was interested, when Father Corridan met him, in efforts of younger rebels along the piers close to his own in Greenwich Village and Chelsea, to break the controls exerted within their union by known racketeers, particularly by the Dunn-McGrath mob.

Another early arrival at the school was a veteran longshoreman who now is teaching there at its evening classes, Arthur Brown, or "Brownie," a veritable sea lawyer, with a memory of waterfront history and personalities as accurately arranged and commodious as a well-ordered filing cabinet. "Christy" and "Brownie," according to Father Corridan, taught him much about harbor-front actualities, as he was feeling his way during his first year at the school.

A little later a navy veteran Johnny Dwyer came to Xavier. In 1954 Dwyer was to become port chairman of the new A.F. of L. longshoremen's union contesting the power of the old I.L.A. throughout the port. Along with Dwyer came Joey Cuervo, Jackie Mullins, and Eddie Barry. All these men were veterans of the United States armed forces during World War II. They did not like what they found along the docks when they came back home. Already they were forming a rebel nucleus in the Chelsea and the Greenwich Village neighborhoods of the city which was shortly to win control of a key pier by insurrection. All these men contributed to Father Corridan's knowledge after he gained their confidence. But it was "Christy" Doran, he says, who first traced back to him a few historic grievances of the men all around the harbor which led to the wildcat strike of 1945.

One of the greatest of these was the so-called "ammo case." This was a grievance over nonpayment of wages for the traveling time which longshoremen had to spend on their way to and from work far down the bay on the Jersey shore, loading ammunition aboard ships bound overseas for the U. S. armed forces. For more than a quarter of a century prior to World War II, the terms of the longshoremen's contract covering the handling of ammunition and explosives specifically covered both the day's rate of wages and a rate to be paid for travel time. Practically all of this ammunition loading was from piers at Leonardo, New Jersey, an isolated point close to Sandy Hook, where the Jersey highlands act as a buffer against damage to any community in case of explosion. Longshoremen working on munitions received money for traveling time during the years when the United States was shipping a great deal of ammunition to Great Britain for the war against Hitler.

Suddenly, early in 1942, after the United States government entered the war via Pearl Harbor, the men discovered that their pay envelopes were short. The men were angry. They appealed to the business agents of their local unions who promised them support in their claims, but nothing happened. They brought their appeals to such local meetings as were held in the I.L.A., but meetings were rare in many a local, so they brought their complaint up to the district council of New York. This council agreed that the men were right, but did nothing to get them their money. They took the matter up with the I.L.A. executive board for the Atlantic coast and were again told they were rightly aggrieved, but they got no money. The men then brought their grievance to the national I.L.A. convention in 1943. There the matter was pigeonholed by the steering committee of the convention and never was brought out on the floor for discussion by delegates.

"Instead of helping them press their claim on a clearly violated contract, the men's own leaders had agreed secretly with somebody to forget the whole thing," says Father Corridan.

Early in 1946, some of the men affected began to sign up with lawyers who agreed to take their case on a contingency basis. Here, strangely enough, the men's move for back pay was openly opposed by Joe Ryan, their own president. Once this was made known, only about 1200 men were willing to sign their names as plaintiffs, although about 10,000 men were eligible to receive the back pay if the validity of their claims was upheld. Why did not the rest of the eligible longshoremen join in the suits?

Some West Side rebels told Father Corridan that it was fear of Ryan and their own union leaders. About 1200 men, however, instituted suits in the courts of New York and New Jersey, and those suits are unsettled to this very day.

"I always hark back to this case," says Father Corridan, "as a definite proof that the old I.L.A. leaders, under the presidency of Joe Ryan, did not in fact represent the interests of the union members. In the first place they entered into an agreement whereby they deprived their own members of contractual rights. Then they frustrated efforts of the members to obtain those rights under union procedure. Then they tried to stop the members from taking their cases to the courts, and forced them into unnecessary legal expenses.

"I believe that the history of this case, rankling as it did through the years, will be found to be one of the basic causes for the downfall of Joe Ryan from his leadership of the old I.L.A. The men who sought to be repaid were from all parts of the harbor. They were men from the old West Side docks of downtown Manhattan, from Brooklyn, and from across the harbor in New Jersey. They all learned a lesson that kept them united on a harbor-wide basis through many years."

Almost an exact parallel to the "ammo case," in Father Corridan's opinion, was the so-called "overtime-on-overtime case." In this case, longshoremen who believed they were deprived of pay due them under contract went into the courts to get it over the opposition of their own union leaders, and won. They still didn't get the money. The case was complicated by a great differential between day rates of pay and night rates, traditional within the industry. But one thing was simple about it. Rightly or wrongly—and the courts said "rightly"—the more intelligent dock workers around the port have believed that 26,000 of them lost about ten million dollars in wages due them. The men believed they lost the money because of collusion between Ryan and the N.Y.S.A., and the political influence of the shipping industry in Washington.

In all the contracts for longshoring in New York harbor up to 1945, the men's basic pay scale for night work was 150 per cent of the pay for day work. Ever since 1872, back in the days before there was any longshoremen's union, the pay for night work has run a great deal higher than the pay for day work. It had to be to get the men to work at night. The night work was dangerous.

Longshoremen have held—and the courts have agreed with them—that this higher rate for night work was not true overtime pay. The men have believed, therefore, that if they worked more hours than their contract called for, during dangerous nights, they should be paid true overtime, above that night-rate differential.

This theory of the men's was tested out in the courts in 1941. Local 841 of the I.L.A. then filed suit in the Federal District Court of Milwaukee against the National Terminal Company, charging that it was breaking the Wages and Hours Act through failure to pay due overtime on the night-rate differential. The men won their suit on May 15, 1943, in that court. The company appealed the decision, but the men were upheld again by the Seventh Circuit Court of Appeals on January 28, 1944.

Seven times the courts have ruled that the night differential paid historically to longshoremen is not true overtime. The U. S. Supreme Court finally upheld the claims of longshoremen for overtime pay above that differential. Did the men get their money? They did not. The shipping industry stalled. Union leaders stalled. Then in 1949 the United States Congress passed a law which removed men in the stevedoring trades from the overtime provisions of the Wages and Hours Act and made this new law retroactive. Thereby the Congress outlawed all claims which the longshoremen had against either the shipping and stevedoring companies or the federal government. As a matter of fact, 90 per cent of the money the men claimed was due them would have had to be paid by the federal government, because of its cost-plus contracts with the shipping and stevedoring companies during World War II.

The fact that Ryan, as union leader, backed the New York Shipping Association, rather than the claims of his men, was admitted openly by Ryan himself in 1952. "I would like to remind those operators who accuse the I.L.A. of failing actively to enforce the contract obligations, that in the overtime-on-overtime struggle, the operators were fully supported by the I.L.A.," he said.

They were, indeed. But the more Father Corridan studied the realities of the longshore industry, through 1946 and 1947, before he stepped out into the public view as a spokesman for the longshoremen, the more evidence he amassed that Ryan, in general, was on the side of the shipping industry instead of the men whom he was morally obligated to lead.

Father Corridan could never find any justification, for instance, for the failure of the I.L.A. to enforce its contractual relations equally throughout the harbor against all employers. Why, for instance, he asked himself, did Joe Ryan permit for a long time the payment of an hourly rate of a dollar-fifty to a dollar-sixty an hour to members of Local 976, Marine Freight and Warehousemen, on piers controlled by his good friend and patron William J. McCormack? The prevailing wage for similar work in the harbor elsewhere was ten cents an hour higher and the men in addition were entitled to a pension under the Railway Labor Act.

"Christy" Doran first told Father Corridan of the fight begun by a few veterans of World War II to wrest control of I.L.A. Local 895 on the Lower West Side from the Dunn-McGrath mob. This mob exercised its power through a pair of brothers named Thompson. One of these brothers, Sonny, was the local union delegate, but this was not his only line of business. He was the proprietor of Sonny's West Shore Bar and Grill, which faced the Hudson docks on West Street in lower Manhattan. Sonny's bar was a hangout for the loan sharks and numbers game racketeers who preyed on the men, and for gangs of pilferers who preyed on the cargo coming through Piers 45 and 46, North River. Sonny's brother, Eddie Thompson, was hiring boss on Pier 45, with absolute control over the destinies of the men who worked that pier.

In 1945, when the young rebels headed by Johnny Dwyer first started their campaign to regularize work on Pier 45, their union local, 895, had not held an election in 20 years. While a few of the more skillful longshoremen were fairly certain of regular work, many more could only catch the eye of the hiring boss by playing ball with the racketeers in Sonny's Bar and Grill. Men of no skill whatever were able to get jobs as casual laborers on an occasional day-to-day basis and were a danger to older hands, particularly when working below decks.

Dwyer and a few of his friends began to pester the I.L.A. leaders close to Ryan for a real election in the local. They were so persistent that orders went down for the Thompson boys to give them their way. The rebels were to have their election, and a lot of good it was going to do them. Polls were established in the basement of St. Veronica's Church on the waterfront. When the regular longshoremen of the neighborhood showed up for the vote they found the place swamped by several hundred men they never had seen before. They soon found the intruders had been brought in from Brooklyn, all equipped with shiny new union buttons and with dues books in order. Some 300 of these strangers voting the straight Thompson ticket kept the old mob in power. The voting was accompanied by fist fights outside the church, which won the rebels nothing.

The winter of 1945-6 was like Valley Forge to the men who backed the rebel ticket. They and their families lived mostly on home relief or unemployment insurance between odd jobs away from the waterfront. Major leaders of the revolt were blacklisted all over the harbor. The Greenwich Village mob was now their sworn enemy, and back of Dunn and McGrath stood the I.L.A. hierarchy. The local's mob-backed officers were apparently to be in power for another five years.

But Dwyer and his men were too tough to surrender. They turned to the Association of Catholic Trade Unionists for help and received free legal counsel in the person of Ed Scully. A "Longshore Conference" of the A.C.T.U. was called for January 18, 1946, in St. Veronica's Parish Hall on Christopher Street, with "Bibbles" Barrieo, a leading rebel, in the chair. Among the speakers were the Reverend Edward Bergin, assistant A.C.T.U. chaplain, and Mr. Scully as counsel to the Catholic Labor Defense League. A resolution was adopted asking the help of Mayor O'Dwyer in getting back the jobs of the neighborhood longshoremen under blacklist of the mob.

"Joe Ryan made desperate efforts to discredit that meeting," says Father Corridan. "So did others in the I.L.A.'s roster of officials. The pastor of St. Veronica's, the Reverend Martin Conboy, was abused and threatened for permitting the meeting in his church, and the Chancery Office was informed that the meeting was backed by Communists. That last move only hardened the temper of the rebels by making them madder than they were before. They were all good Catholics, and they've always gotten mad when Ryan & Co. have tried to pin the Red label on them."

On March 14, 1946, Mr. Scully instituted suit in the New York Supreme Court to have the rigged election in I.L.A. Local 895 declared void. "One hundred men," says Father Corridan, "put their waterfront livelihoods on the block by signing the petition to the court. They all went without work."

For some time they would have been without work on Pier 45, anyway, because the United States Navy, which had kept it running through the war, abandoned the use of it. The pier had acquired a bad record for pilferage, and some time elapsed before the Alcoa Steamship Company and the John W. McGrath Stevedoring Company occupied it. Sonny Thompson and his allies tried to provide the McGrath Company with longshoremen, but neighborhood sentiment by this time was riding high with the rebels. They picketed their pier and kept it closed.

To break the strike, an officer of the stevedoring company turned straight to Dwyer, as outstanding leader of the rebel forces, and offered him the job of hiring boss. "I was scared to death," Dwyer remembers. "I knew the mobs, and I knew what a hiring boss has to do. He's got a tough job at best. You have work for maybe a couple of hundred men, and there's 300 or 400 or maybe 500 standing in every shape-up, just staring at you, begging for a day's work and ready to call you every name in the book if you turn 'em down. Their eyes go right through you. That job's a terrible responsibility."

Terrible or not, Johnny Dwyer took the job. Within a short time Supreme Court Justice Henry Clay Greenberg appointed Professor Milton Handler of Columbia University to supervise a new election in the local. By agreement reached in court, the Local 895 officials who had been chosen in the phony election of 1945 all resigned. The new election was held on November 26, 1946, and was the first really secret, legitimate ballot ever cast for that local's officers. The rebels won three out of seven positions in a very close contest, but one of these posts was secretary-treasurer. Their strength was sufficient to make certain that Dwyer would continue as hiring boss. Sonny Thompson, former union delegate, actually failed to run for office. He just lost interest. He beat a strategic retreat to Miami, where he is reputed to have taken up an easy and profitable life at the race track.

When Johnny Dwyer first blew the hiring boss's whistle on Pier 45, back in August, 1946, he ushered in a complete New Deal for the longshoremen living in the neighborhood of the pier, the men who had been accustomed to look to it for their regular living. There was no way to end the shape-up as long as it remained the official system of hiring in the harbor, backed by the shipping interests and the I.L.A. leaders. But Dwyer brought to it a keen sense of fair play and sound judgment. Regular gangs were formed from men who were known as reliable workers who had families to support. The work was rotated in an effort to give at least some work to as many of the old-timers as possible, who under the old regime had often seen themselves pushed aside in favor of outsiders from other trades. Principles of seniority began to be observed. The pier became known as a good one to work on.

This new regime had a great significance for Father Corridan. By early 1947 he had won his way into the confidence of the rebel leaders. He became their counselor to some degree. He set down John Dwyer's local in his books as the nucleus for an honest trade unionism which he hoped might be spread in time throughout the harbor. Already there was a nearby local in the Chelsea neighborhod, Local 791, which was democratically conducted. The priest could count on Local 791, too, as free from the mobsters' rule. Ironically enough, this was the very local that Joe Ryan had joined when he first worked on the docks, and he still held a card in it. But by 1946 the members of Local 791 were so anti-Ryan that they had a special rule limiting him to five minutes, if he wished to address them, even though he was international president of the whole I.L.A.

These two locals together, if they wished to buck any bad contract the I.L.A. leadership and the N.Y.S.A. might wish to put over in the future, had enough power so that with the aid of just one more local, No. 1258, in which they had influence, they could stop work on every pier along the North River from Fulton Street on the south to 23rd Street on the north. If supported by Local 808 in Brooklyn, they could tie up the whole harbor.

For a year, working conditions on Pier 45 were so greatly improved that the men did not expect them to last. They were right.

"The remnants of the Dunn-McGrath mob still held key jobs on Pier 45," said Father Corridan. "Organized stealing became so heavy that in the summer of 1948 the Alcoa Steamship Company was compelled to move to a dock in Brooklyn. Pier 45 joined Piers 42 and 46 as 'hot' piers. The city stood to lose 400,000 dollars a year in rentals as long as those piers remained idle. More important still, a whole neighborhood was put on a starvation diet as 700 men were now out of work.

"Action, however, was not taken by the city until after Malcolm Johnson's Pulitzer-Prize-winning series of articles in the *Sun* called 'Crime on the Water Front.' These articles made the docks a political hot potato. In late November Mayor O'Dwyer ordered an investigation by the Marine and Aviation Department of the three hot piers. Edward F. Cavanagh, Jr., then Deputy Commissioner of the Marine and Aviation Department and Samuel London, a confidential inspector of the department, conducted the investigation. Their report was not made public, but 'Mike' Johnson and I were able to find out a good deal that was in it. This knowledge helped me advise the rebels when the time was ripe for Pier 45 to reopen as a clean pier."

Portions of the report were made public three years later in the New York *Journal-American.* The portions said that labor conditions were bad on Pier 42, Pier 45, and Pier 46 where union factions were fighting each other. It said that although most of the longshoremen were honest and willing to work, a handful of bad ones controlled Pier 45. "If dissident elements were thrown out of the union everything would be satisfactory," the report said.

"In other words," says Father Corridan, "if the rebels, who were trying to clean up the place, could only be thrown off the dock, and the old mobsters, responsible for the thievery, left in control, everything would be lovely. Personally, I found that report pretty misleading."

Several of the rebels, led by Johnny Dwyer, consulted Father Corridan on future strategy, early in January, 1949. A short time before, they had attended a special membership meeting at St. Veronica's. At this meeting one of Ryan's lieutenants, "Teddy" Gleason, took the floor in defense of the I.L.A. president, then under fire from the men.

"Johnny Dwyer stood for what Gleason was saying for a bare three minutes," says Father Corridan. "Then he jumped to his feet and denounced him openly as a stooge not only for Ryan but for Big Bill McCormack, whom he named as waterfront czar."

"I'm walking out and everybody who agrees with me can follow me out," Dwyer shouted.

Every longshoreman in the hall followed him. Although Alcoa had moved to Brooklyn, Dwyer was still in the employ of the J. W. McGrath stevedoring concern, as an assistant pier superintendent. The very next day he lost his job through I.L.A. pressure.

"But he'd won something bigger," says Father Corridan, "he had won the overwhelming support of the membership of his local."

The rebels came to Father Corridan at this time because the Grace Line was about to move into Pier 45 on a contingent basis, namely, that the line was free to move out at any time, after giving the city 30 days' notice that conditions were unsatisfactory. The rebels were afraid that the same elements of the Dunn-McGrath mob through I.L.A. pressure would return to their key positions and, after lying low for a while, would get itchy fingers all over again. If they did, the company would move out and the men would be out of work again. In their desperation the rebels had been thinking of pulling a strike at the first shape to get rid of the trouble-makers.

Father Corridan advised against such a move. He counseled them to do as they had done before and set up a public meeting through their A.C.T.U. Longshore Conference, as "The Committee of Longshoremen of St. Veronica's Parish." He explained that this was a mayoralty year and the waterfront had been a sensitive issue in Malcolm Johnson's series. He advised them to invite everyone from the mayor down who had a stake in their problems to attend the meeting, and predicted they would get good newspaper coverage and action, if they did that.

The meeting was set for Thursday, January 27, at St. Veronica's Hall. The Sunday preceding the meeting, Father Edward Head, a curate at St. Veronica's, made an extended announcement at all the masses. After each mass the men distributed leaflets advertising the meeting and inviting all to attend. On the day of the meeting Malcolm Johnson ran a page-one story in the *Sun* with a two-column lead, "Idle Dockers to Tell Story."

"On the night of the meeting Joe Ryan showed up outside St. Veronica's Hall but did not enter," Father Corridan recalls. "Father Head opened the meeting by introducing John Dwyer as permanent chairman. Dwyer immediately read the telegrams of regrets for their absence from all the invited city officials including Mayor O'Dwyer, and commented acidly: 'I'm glad my name doesn't begin with an O. I guess we working stiffs aren't as important as all those dinners. I wonder if they care how hungry we and our families get.'

"After Dwyer spoke, Chris Doran, Pete Loughran, and Jackie Mullins, as spokesmen for Piers 42, 45, and 46 respectively, stressed the recent increase in pier rentals as the principal reason for the steamship companies staying out of the area. George Donahue, A.C.T.U. president and a former member of the I.L.A., referring to Johnson's exposures of racketeering on the docks said, 'We know there are evils on the waterfront, but you people are not responsible for them.'

"To sum up the sense of the meeting a prepared motion was put on the floor to the effect that if the committee did not hear from City Hall by Sunday evening, the men would go to see O'Dwyer personally on Monday morning in three buses paid for by the parish, or, if the mayor was unavailable, they would begin to picket City Hall.

"The overflow crowd roared their unanimous consent. Father John P. Monaghan, Pastor of St. Margaret Mary's in Staten Island and an old favorite at St. Veronica's, closed the meeting with the pointed remark: 'When the Church and the community cease to be interested in the men that labor, both the Church and the community die.' "

Malcolm Johnson not only carried the account of this meeting on the first page of the *Sun,* but at Father Corridan's suggestion put in a couple of phone calls to City Hall and to steamship officials as to what would happen next. Johnson particularly wanted to know if notorious waterfront hoodlums like "Bullhead" Kennedy, just to name one, were going to get key jobs on Piers 42 or 45 when they reopened.

That clinched it. The St. Veronica's Parish Committee of Longshoremen was called down to City Hall on Sunday afternoon. The pier was opened shortly afterward. It was opened with Johnny Dwyer's rebels in charge. Father Corridan was happy.

CHAPTER 8

FATHER CORRIDAN'S PROBLEM

Little men frequently have good ideas. Larger men often are possessed by only one. Between the years 1946 and 1948, as Father Corridan studied the complex problems of New York's waterfront, a single idea took hold of him. How could he best, as a priest of the Jesuit order, assigned by the Xavier School to work with longshoremen, give the dock workers a chance to live better lives?

As a teacher in the school, he was supposed to be an educator. He was also a citizen. But above all else he was a priest and man of action, subject only to his conscience and the discipline which his calling imposed on him. It was late in 1948 before he decided to pitch himself actively and publicly into the fight which the rebels in a few longshore locals were making against the men who tyrannized over them.

Father Corridan decided to step into a war that was grimy and ugly, a war that was being fought with guns, threats, briberies, and slander. When he made his decision to step out publicly, on the side of rank-and-file dock workers who were often being maligned as Communists, he made it with absolute faith that he would be fighting for the ultimate welfare of the whole community, for his church, and for the Kingdom of God.

It was a long step to take, and a gentler, more philosophical man would not have taken it. It was risky, in some ways, but not as risky as the dangers encountered by rebellious longshoremen. These men faced the gangsters' guns. Father Corridan was warned of the dangers that would confront him personally, even before he took that step of siding publicly with the rebels. He was warned partly by his own common sense and his native knowledge of Manhattan's West Side. He knew that the very fact that he was a priest gave him some protection from gunmen.

He knew also that he would be opposed in what he was doing by some men, both priests and laymen, within that church which he aimed to serve. He knew that some of these men would rank far higher than he. He knew that some would seek to discredit him, and would strike at him if possible through that very Jesuit order and the larger church which were dear to him.

Added to the warnings of his own intelligence, Father Corridan says, was a spoken warning given to him by a great friend of his father's whom he highly regarded. This was the late Chief Inspector John O'Brien of the New York Police Department. Chief Inspector O'Brien knew young Corridan well enough to call him "John" instead of "Father" when addressing him. Many longshoremen today call him "Father John" instead of plain "Father."

"When I was first getting into this work among the longshoremen," Father Corridan remembers, "Inspector O'Brien warned me —God rest his soul! 'John,' he said, 'don't you ever leave Xavier to meet anyone in the labor picture or in the government part or in the business part of the waterfront, because I can tell you now there are certain elements among all three of them who would do anything they could to destroy you.'

"I followed the inspector's advice for a good two to three years, after we first talked over waterfront problems and he gave me that advice. By that time I felt I was strong enough in the public eye so that I would not be in such jeopardy as O'Brien had foreseen."

Father Corridan says he thought out nine principles for his own conduct to guide him as he went into battle. The first one was to stick to Xavier and keep out of the public eye till the time was ripe for public appearance. He even speaks of his first efforts, working with the longshore rebels against the rule of mobsters in I.L.A. leadership, as working "with the underground."

His second determination, once he knew he would step into the public eye as a speaker and expert on waterfront problems, was never to put an overemphasis on organized crime in his writing and speeches.

"I knew," he says, "by studying the newspapers how headlines are apt to stress the more sensational side of any speech, by anybody, to attract the readers' attention. I knew there would be danger of distortion of what I said in short news stories put into the newspapers as fast as they have to be, even by reporters who try to give good accurate news accounts. Most reporters try to do this, but not all.

"I knew that the complicity of the business interests involved in New York's shipping, and the complicity of the political leaders in letting evil waterfront conditions continue, would be harder to show than the crime element in the picture. It was more complex, and it would frequently be too dull for the average reader for whom newspapers of great mass circulation are written.

"I knew, too, how a great many longshoremen felt, about overemphasis concerning crime on the waterfront. They were helpless to do anything about it. But they have always felt that some of the disrepute and dirt spilled over on themselves and their families. Therefore I determined to emphasize economic and political factors in all the talks I intended to give, and keep the crime phase of the waterfront controls in proper perspective."

Thirdly, Father Corridan says, he determined early in the game to keep personalities out of his remarks, insofar as he could, even though he was bound to attack some practices of some men.

"What I've been attacking in the harbor has been a system that has grown gradually, which has involved many men, through many years, in business, in politics, and in labor," he says. "Of course I have had, at times, to attack Joe Ryan, and I certainly have criticized Bill McCormack, or 'Mr. Big,' and many others at times. But I always remember these men, too, are children of Almighty God, as well as members of my own church. These men, and many others, I have said, partly by acts of commission and partly by acquiescence in evil, have had a share in the responsibility for the evils which have gripped the port.

"But I always remember that the men I'm forced to criticize—because longshoremen rely on me to call a spade a spade, and wouldn't rely on me if I didn't—are themselves in part the products of a deeply rooted system of corruption. The system has grown up historically, for many reasons, in the harbor. The ultimate responsibility to end that system rests on thousands of people, who have been made the prisoners of it.

"In the fourth place, I resolved early, when I took up my work at Xavier, to remain uncommitted to anyone but my church and my work. I decided I would never accept any honorary positions or official posts of any group whatever. I determined to be perfectly free to be consulted by all people involved in the waterfront struggles, and capable of telling anyone the truth as I saw it, if I felt myself privileged as a priest to tell it. No priest can tell all he knows, since much comes to him in confidence either within the confessional or under circumstances very close to it.

"Point five: In dealing with law-enforcement agencies, such as the police or district attorneys, I have had to be careful not to be an informer, and have concentrated in talks with men of these agencies on waterfront labor-management relations as the underlying cause of crime. I have made an exception, of course, in a few matters of physical violence and murder.

"Now for a sixth point. I have been on the side of the men. You can take that for granted. But I have tried to work with representatives of both unions and management, to make both sides see the other's point of view more clearly and to understand it better. I've tried as best I could to work toward that ultimate goal of industrial peace with justice which the harbor needs—which everybody needs.

"I was determined to work very patiently and leave much to time and to others, to work for limited objectives, and to try to work in such a way that longshoremen would not jeopardize themselves unnecessarily. The men, in their rebellion, have had to face dangers. Battlefield dangers. Dangers from gunmen. But I have always cautioned them.

"For a man in my position, as a Jesuit priest, there was one very important rule which I understood thoroughly and have always tried to follow. That rule was to keep my superiors informed of all I was doing or saying, not only for the permissions that were necessary for me to obtain but for the welfare of the church.

"I knew that for the welfare of the church I must always be sure that my superiors would be in a position to give correct answers to anyone who might come to them, criticizing my activities. I have also held that I had no right, as a Jesuit, to engage in any activities which my superiors within the order believed to be wrongful or harmful, since part of the training of a Jesuit is in obedience to properly constituted authorities within the church.

"Finally, I knew that opposition would come to me from certain elements in the business world, and very possibly in the political world, rather than directly from the mobsters who ran large segments of the waterfront itself. I resolved simply to consider all attacks at first as due to ignorance rather than malice; to try to answer questions of anyone concerned with the waterfront problems; to be patient but to defend those positions taken within my knowledge and conscience at all times against anyone.

"This last, both Father Carey and I have had to do. We both have been threatened, though very rarely, by Catholic businessmen who knew better. We have been told that funds would be withheld from our order because of our activities in strengthening the hand of Catholic and other workingmen, working in trade unions. Naturally it has made no difference in our course of action."

It was just before the big wildcat strike of 1948 that Father Corridan decided that the time had come to leave his "underground" and to stand in the open as a champion of the men. His files by this time were loaded with information on the shipping industry. Longshoremen who trusted him were on many a pier. He wanted his first appearance in public discussion of harbor problems to get right down to the religious fundamentals.

The first audience before which he would speak would naturally be composed of laymen of his own church. His voice must ring with all the fervor of which he was capable, in terms which these laymen would understand because they, too, were members of his own communion. Knights of Columbus were among the first to hear him. In a speech before these laymen called "Christ Looks at the Waterfront," Father Corridan set the tone for future addresses within his own natural constituency.

"It's funny how everybody ducks the main problem of the waterfront," he said. "They plan to fix up the piers, and though the piers really need fixing, the men are in greater need than the piers.

"A bill is passed to fingerprint watchmen to protect cargo, as if cargo were more precious than men. Some stab is being made to protect the profits of cargo-handling by cleaning up the loading racket, but you can't find anybody planning to give all the men a decent annual wage. The 'boys,' however, are fencing nicely . . . knowing that time and politics and steamship profits are on their side.

"The police pick up a few loan sharks, but nobody thinks of setting up a loan service for the longshoremen operated on a nonprofit basis. You would think the union would, but the union isn't interested in the men any more than the shippers of goods or the steamship companies.

"You want to know what's wrong with the waterfront? It's love of a lousy buck, whether it's one or a thousand or ten thousand . . . God or no God. A man is going to get them in any way he can. In many ways you can't blame the mob . . . even if the mob is Catholic. They see supposedly Catholic-educated men chase a buck as if Christ didn't exist, and hide behind their professional Catholicity.

"All this is not a technical definition of the shape. All it tells you is that it's a system calculated to produce the most bucks for all the interested parties except the men.

"The men can keep begging for work, and their wives and children can eke out an existence in the midst of heartache. Some think that a few bucks in the collection or an ad in a church journal is more important to Christ than the souls that He died to save . . . as if Christ died to save them in want and insecurity. What a shock they are in for, an eternal and everlasting shock.

"You often wonder about the men who fought against injustice until a job or the hope of a job was slipped under their nose. For a few bucks they sell out and drink heavily once in a while to forget the silent contempt in which they are held . . . little dreaming of the profound contempt in which Christ holds them.

"Too often men have risen from the ranks in the name of justice and turned out worse than those they supplanted. The workingmen's wrongs cry out to heaven for vengeance, but none so much as those inflicted by workingmen who sell out their fellows.

"I suppose some people would smirk at the thought of Christ in the shape. It is about as absurd as the fact that He carried carpenter's tools in His hands and earned His bread and butter by the sweat of His brow. As absurd as the fact that Christ redeemed all men irrespective of their race, color, or station in life.

"It can only be absurd to those of whom Christ said, 'Having eyes, they see not; and having ears, they hear not.' . . . Because they don't want to see or hear.

"Christ also said, 'If you do it to the least of mine, you do it to me.' So Christ is in the shape . . . as sure as every man there in the state of grace is His brother and the others are called to be.

"Christ has bread and butter and meat bills and rent to meet. He stands in the shape knowing that all won't get work and maybe He won't. What does Christ think of the efficiency argument for the shape?

"Christ works on a certain pier. He knows that He is expected to be deaf, dumb, and blind, if He wants to work. Some people think that the Crucifixion only took place on Calvary.

"Christ works on a pier and His back aches because there are a fair number of the 'boys' on the pier. They don't work but have their rackets at which so many wink. What does Christ think of the man who picks up a longshoreman's brass check and takes 20 per cent interest at the end of the week?

"Christ goes to a union meeting. Sees how a meeting is run. Sees how few go. Sees how many don't speak. Sees a certain restraint. At some meetings He sees a few with $150-dollar suits and diamond rings on their fingers . . . drawing a couple of salaries and expense accounts . . . handing out the stuff from 14th and Eighth" (The offices of the I.L.A. are at West 14th Street and Eighth Avenue in Manhattan.)

"Christ goes for a walk in the evening in the waterfront area. He loses count of the number of bars but has great difficulty in finding a supermarket or playgrounds.

"Christ walks into a tenement and talks with the wife of a longshoreman. Her heart is heavy . . . and this is the Christ who in anger drove the money-changers from the temple.

"Christ steps into a school and looks over the kids. Sees how they are dressed. Wonders *how* they eat. 'See that you do not despise one of these little ones; for I tell you, their angels in heaven always behold the face of my Father in heaven.'

"Christ steps into a confessional and hears the confessions of children. He hears things that He shouldn't hear and gives His judgment of the *efficient* shape and all that goes with it: 'Whoever causes one of these little ones who believe in Me to sin, it were better for him to have a great millstone hung around his neck, and to be drowned in the depths of the sea.'

"For those longshoremen who are straight and are good family men, God be praised. For those who slip every once in a while and lose hope, God have mercy. To those responsible, God grant the grace to see things on the waterfront as Christ sees them, for the time is growing short when God will show no mercy."

That is the way Father Corridan talks to Catholic laymen—longshoremen, politicians, and others.

Father Corridan's decision to minimize, in his own public appearances, the problem of crime on the docks was made in the deep conviction that this was not as great a social evil as the corrupt relationship between the rulers of the harbor. He knew also that the problem of crime, in human society, has many aspects, and that the rehabilitation of men who have broken laws and been imprisoned is one of them.

"It's true," Father Corridan says, "that perhaps as high as 25 per cent of the men on the waterfront have police records of some sort or another, but most of them are minor ones. We have to look this problem of the employment of ex-criminals squarely in the face if we are to deal with it in any spirit of justice. Society has not been any too successful in its attempts to rehabilitate men and women who have fallen afoul of the law and gone to jails or prisons. There is plenty of evidence to show that mass imprisonment tends to harden first-time offenders and that punishment, rather than rehabilitation, has been a basic principle of too great a part of the nation's penal system.

"Men who have served their time, as punishment for their offenses, have fulfilled their debt to society. They have to have employment somewhere if they are not to turn to criminal pursuits once more as a source of livelihood. One practical way in which to help the rehabilitation of the ex-criminal is to assure him steady employment at a fair rate of pay. One of the few places where a man from a New York prison has been able to go, here in New York City, to earn a fair hourly rate of pay, if not to get steady employment, has been the New York waterfront. It hasn't been the best place in the world in which these men could rehabilitate themselves. But it would be absolutely unjust to bar men with prison records from handling cargo.

"Ex-criminals have proved dangerous on the waterfront only when disguised as union officials or placed in a supervisory post to terrorize over the rest of the men or discipline them."

The problem of dealing with crime on the waterfront, Father

Corridan says, is one of making law enforcement possible. It has not been possible for any agency dealing with crime to do much about it, for many a long year, in his opinion.

"You take the Police Department," says Father Corridan. "Policemen have no power of subpoena. The power of detectives is pretty limited. Unless a policeman is actually on the scene of a crime when it occurs, the department has to gather evidence about it from people who know the facts. These people have to be willing to testify in a courtroom. It has been completely impossible, in many cases of crime on the waterfront, to find any witnesses willing to testify. The men who work around the docks are notoriously tight-mouthed. They have had very good reason to be.

"The district attorneys in the harbor cities have certainly been unable to cope with waterfront crime. Of course, they have the power of subpoena and the power to launch investigations. But each district attorney has jurisdiction over only one small segment of a bistate port. Each district attorney is the product of the political machine that elects him. The machine itself is steeped in corruption. Then, too, a great deal of lawbreaking in the harbor involves the breaking of federal rather than local laws.

"The United States attorneys around the harbor are subject to most of the limitations that hamper district attorneys. They are also accountable to their superiors in Washington, who can order them to give priorities to some activities and to steer clear of others. We have a whole lot of specialized agencies of law enforcement also. We have the FBI, the Coast Guard, the Narcotics Bureau, Customs agents, and others. Very few places in the world, if any, have more law-enforcement agencies set up within them to protect life and property than New York harbor.

"Yet of 100 known murders around the docks in the last 25 years, only two cases have been solved—the murders of Andy Hintz and Barney Dietz. Both of them, incidentally, were solved by the same man, Lieutenant Joseph P. Sullivan, of Manhattan. Why has law enforcement been impossible?

"You can never enforce the laws against crime around the New York docks as long as union officials who are really criminals are allied by business interest with the shipping companies, and by political interest with whatever municipal administration has control of police and courts."

It was to smash this triple alliance of business, politics, and union racketeering that Father Corridan set out late in 1948. In the long run, he believed, it would have to be broken if law enforcement on the docks was to be made possible and the dock workers were to live under any other regime than fear. The priest had friends among the leading longshore rebels. He sized up the odds against them. They would never be able to win, he felt, unless the powers of government in state and nation were brought in to help them. The cards were stacked against them too heavily in the harbor cities.

At first the priest winced at the full extent of governmental intervention, which he was sure would be needed. Some of his closest friends advised him he was taking the wrong tack. The decision as to his own course of action, however, had to be made by Father Corridan alone.

In an early memorandum which he wrote to Father Carey, shortly after he arrived at Xavier, for their own discussion, Father Corridan had defined the function of a labor school as he saw it: "Labor schools are not pulpits, writers' bureaus, or research institutes. Their purpose is to infiltrate Christ's interest into economic self-interest; not in any 'pie in the sky' way, but in a hard-boiled way, that at times jockeys through successive choices between two or more evils."

There spoke a priest who was groping his way forward. He knew that the "infiltration of Christ's interest" into the "economic self-interest" of New York's commercial society was a major objective in his becoming teacher of labor-management relations at the Xavier School. How to accomplish it?

When he got into actual combat, on behalf of Christ's interest as he saw it, Father Corridan took to the pulpit, wherever he could find a pulpit open to him, from which to expound his ideas on his assignment, the moral problem of the waterfront. He became a one-man research institute. Thereby he contradicted in action his original statement to Father Carey. He became a first-class publicist, a tipster to news men, magazine writers, book writers, motion-picture scenario writers, and radio script writers. He became a pamphleteer on the docks themselves.

Through it all he prayed. He and Father Carey, in lighter vein, have clung to a favorite old prayer by a man named Sir Jacob Astley, who uttered it out of a full heart to his God, just before going into the Battle of Newbury. The prayer runs as follows:

"Lord, I shall be very busie this day. I may forget Thee, but doe not Thou forget me."

CHAPTER

9

THE WILDCAT STRIKE OF 1948

On Tuesday morning, November 9, 1948, at 7:55 A.M., *Local* 791 of the I.L.A. struck against a contract which had just been negotiated by Joe Ryan. The strike spread swiftly, first throughout the harbor and then up and down the Atlantic coast from Portland, Maine, to Hampton Roads, Virginia. It lasted 18 days.

In the life of Father Corridan, this strike stands out for several reasons. It was the first wildcat strike in which he publicly supported the men and became a figure in the news. It was at this time that he earned for himself the soubriquet of "The Waterfront Priest."

Before the strike was started, Father Corridan had cautioned his closest associates in the rebel locals against it. He was trying to work out with them a policy of continual limited gains, or fringe benefits, such as welfare appropriations, seniority rights, and vacation pay to supplement the modest hourly wage increases which were continually being tossed to them. These wage increases, they all knew, were lower than more aggressive unions were winning. Perhaps, with fringe benefits to supplement them, the men could keep on with their work without utter rebellion, without loss of pay envelopes or undue hardships on their families.

Looking back on the 1948 strike, Father Corridan says it is important to see the pattern of negotiations clearly, as conducted between the I.L.A. and N.Y.S.A., to understand it. These negotiations began on July 12 to draw up a new contract for one that was to expire on August 21.

As usual, the union's wage-scale committee was an unwieldy 125-delegate body, representing longshoremen in all the Atlantic coast ports, from Portland to Hampton Roads, and six allied crafts: the checkers, clerks, cargo repairmen, general maintenance workers, miscellaneous workers, and marine carpenters. As always, most of the delegates were self-appointed, in violation of the I.L.A. constitution, which called for their election by their locals. Most local leaders simply named themselves. Thereby they received an extra 25 dollars a day for all the time they served.

When they were gathering to start their negotiations, Father Corridan got a laugh at the comment of a policeman who saw the committeemen meet.

"Most of these mugs," the West Side policeman told the priest, "I seen for years. The only rank-and-filers are from the West Side locals."

The conference committee of the N.Y.S.A. was made up of 15 representatives of the membership. The N.Y.S.A. membership consisted of 66 steamship lines and steamship agents, 58 contracting stevedores, one cargo-repair contractor, 15 contractors for checkers and clerks, two contracting maintenance agencies, and 19 contracting marine carpenters.

When the union and shipping representatives first met, they exchanged formal proposals and counterproposals. The I.L.A.

asked for an increase of 50 cents an hour in the straight-time rate ($1.75 to $2.25). In addition the union asked for the establishment of a union welfare fund. The employers did not specify definitely what increase they would be willing to grant, but conceded they would grant one. Before granting any monetary increase, the employers said, they wanted a complete settlement of the much-discussed "overtime-on-overtime" problem.

This problem was not resolved by August 17, so President Harry S. Truman invoked the national-emergency section of the Taft-Hartley Law to give negotiations more time. He appointed a three-man board of inquiry, consisting of Saul Wallen, chairman, Joseph L. Miller, and Julius Kass. The next day these three men reported back to the President that a longshoremen's strike along the Atlantic coast was imminent, as of midnight, August 21, 1948. On that day Judge Harold R. Medina, in the United States District Court for the Southern District of New York, issued a temporary restraining order against a strike or a lockout. With the consent of both parties, on August 24, he replaced the restraining order with an injunction, to remain in force until midnight, November 9. In early October the I.L.A. and N.Y.S.A. agreed to place themselves under Section 7(b)(1) of the Wages and Hours Act as a temporary solution to the "overtime-on-overtime" problem. This was an escape clause, written for the benefit of industries employing casual labor, exempting them from most of the restrictions of the act.

With the roadblock on overtime-on-overtime removed by the union's surrender, negotiations returned to a familiar longshore pattern, known along the docks as "chop-chop." Under this pattern the I.L.A. always started out by asking for "pie in the sky," and wound up by accepting far less than would have been accepted by a bona-fide union without a strike.

By October 21 no agreement was reached, and under the terms of the Taft-Hartley Law the employers submitted a "final offer," to be voted on by the I.L.A. membership under a secret ballot to be conducted by the National Labor Relations Board.

The board of inquiry then reported to President Truman the

New York Shipping Association's final offer and Ryan's reaction to it. Ryan felt, the members of the board said, that further consideration by the employers of the retroactive date of the wage increase and the I.L.A. demand for a welfare fund could give the wage-scale committee an agreement which they would recommend to the membership. The board definitely believed that intensive negotiations with the aid of the conciliation service could bring an agreement before midnight, November 9, the expiration date of the injunction.

Meantime, Father Corridan was concerned about two phases of the negotiations. The first involved Arthur "Brownie" Brown of Local 791, the Chelsea local.

" 'Brownie,' " says Father Corridan, "had been approached by the waterfront section of the Communist Party to sit in on their planning, not only for the current contract and possible strike, but also on the overtime-on-overtime question. 'Brownie' consulted me. We agreed that from an intelligent viewpoint it could prove extremely helpful if Brownie were to sit in on the party's deliberations. The party, after all, had captured temporarily the Brooklyn part of the 1945 wildcat strike.

"I counseled 'Brownie' to get clearance from Joe Ryan so that he might not run the risk of being branded a 'Commie' at some later date. 'Brownie' got Ryan's O.K., he told me, in the presence of the business agents of 791, John J. 'Gene' Sampson and Jay O'Connor.

"Three interesting points developed out of 'Brownie's' sitting in on the party's waterfront deliberations. In the first place, the party didn't have a legitimate longshoreman sitting in on their strategy meetings other than 'Brownie.'

" 'Brownie' didn't receive one cent for expenses from the secret Ryan anti-Communist fund although he had to give up work on many days in order to attend the Communist Party's waterfront meetings. When his party contacts asked him to go to Washington with them to meet John L. Lewis, 'Brownie' asked Ryan to cover his expenses. Ryan refused and immediately accused 'Brownie' of being a 'Commie.' 'Brownie' is no more a 'Commie' than I am.

"By his efforts as an undercover man, we knew that the Communist Party had no influence whatever on the 1948 strike. The 1945 strike marked the high-water mark of Communist efforts to get a beachhead on the New York waterfront."

Father Corridan gave four talks just before the strike to Holy Name and Knights of Columbus groups in waterfront sections in Brooklyn and Jersey City. "Most of the longshoremen seemed to feel," he says, "that the length of time consumed in solving the overtime-on-overtime problem by Joe Ryan and the New York Shipping Association was just an act put on for the benefit of Congress, where consideration was being given to retroactive legislation on the matter, and a smoke screen to conceal an approaching sellout. The men were right, as Congress finally voted the retroactive law that wiped out their pay claims."

Father Corridan says he didn't allay the men's suspicions when he pointed out early in the negotiations that Section 7 (b) (1) of the Wages and Hours Act was at least a temporary solution to the N.Y.S.A.'s and the I.L.A.'s overtime-on-overtime problem. When Ryan and the shipping association, in early October, adopted this obvious solution to the problem, the men's suspicions of a "sell-out" were confirmed.

Frank Huttick, a longshoreman friend of "Brownie" and Father Corridan, was a 1948 wage-scale delegate from Local 791. He dropped into Father Corridan's office during the negotiations. He asked Father Corridan what the actual cost of a welfare fund would be. The conference committee of the shipping association was then refusing to consider the demand on the grounds that the cost would be prohibitive, he said. Huttick told Father Corridan that no effective rebuttal to this claim of the shipping association was being made by the I.L.A. Father Corridan, "Brownie," and Huttick sat down that night with Edward Chave, a teacher in the Xavier School who was well versed in the benefits, costs, and mechanics of welfare funds.

Together they went over a welfare plan that had been initiated the year before by the teamsters' union, Local 807. Longshoremen had some familiarity with the plan from their daily contact with the drivers of that local who picked up and dropped off cargo at the docks.

The plan called for the following benefits for the workers: (1) 1000-dollar life insurance; (2) 1000-dollar accidental death and dismemberment insurance on an off-the-job as well as on-the-job basis; (3) 25 dollars weekly off-the-job accident and sickness benefits. Benefits were made payable from the first day of an accident off the job and from the eighth day in case of sickness.

The foursome then discussed protection involving family coverage. "Eddie Chave pointed out that the longshoremen could choose either Blue Cross hospitalization benefits, with family coverage for a wife and for all unmarried children under 18 years of age, or purchase hospitalization from an insurance company for about the same cost," Father Corridan remembers.

"We decided that coverage by an insurance company might be preferable to the Blue Cross scheme, as a family could be covered for 31 days instead of 21 as under the Blue Cross. Maternity could also be covered, whereas we felt that it was not adequately covered under the Blue Cross. 'Brownie,' I remember, was asked by Ed Chave if maternity was a problem on the docks.

" 'Definitely! Maternity on the docks is a headache,' said 'Brownie.' "

For a few more meetings they wrestled with the complicated cost problem, as posed by conditions peculiar to longshore industry. The principal problem was that no figures were published at that time either on the number of legitimate longshoremen in New York as compared with the part-time workers or "connected men," or on the number of hours which either category worked.

Father Corridan was able to get from the National Labor Relations Board the approximate figures. Only 14,000 men out of 46,000, the board said, were able to get 1350 or more hours of work a year in New York harbor. This was the vacation eligibility minimum of the preceding two-year contract.

Father Corridan estimated that no more than 18,000 of the 46,000 men who were legitimate longshoremen were able to get at least 800 hours of work a year on the docks. On that basis, and with the other 28,000 men contributing, according to the total number of their hours worked, Ed Chave estimated that the cost of insurance coverage should be somewhere between three and four cents per man-hour worked. All during these meetings, Father Corridan acted as the interpreter between Mr. Chave, the scholastic teacher, and "Brownie" and Huttick, reducing cold insurance calculations into longshoremen's terms. The priest, like his longshore friends, was reared on the West Side.

The fact that only 14,000 longshoremen out of an annual total of 46,000 men receiving pay as longshoremen were able to get vacation paychecks of 70 dollars (minus deductions) pointed up another sore spot in the 1948 picture to Father Corridan.

"Four cents per man-hour worked had been paid into the vacation pay fund for the industry," he says. "Assuming that at least 40 million man-hours were worked (the best figure we could find), 1,600,000 dollars must have been paid into the vacation pay fund, out of which less than one million dollars was paid out to the men who had 1350 or more hours. The longshoremen wanted to know what happened to the remaining 600,000 dollars and the surpluses of the preceding years.

"They looked upon the money as being their money and wondered why the men who only worked 800 hours in a year weren't paid a week's vacation, since 18,000 men, multiplied by 70 dollars per man, was less than 1,300,000 dollars. But the men never were told what happened to their money. They just suspected."

These were some of the factors that caused Father Corridan to sense that the danger of a wildcat strike in 1948 was real. It was certain if the N.Y.S.A. and the I.L.A. did not heed the demands of the men for a welfare fund and more equitable vacation pay. The economic costs were negligible, the priest believed, in comparison to the psychological benefits to be gained by the companies. The men would consider they had been dealt with squarely if their demands were met, and carry a grievance if they were not. Yet all indications seemed to point to the negotiators' ignoring the wishes of the rank and file.

"I tried to give the men's viewpoint to the regional Federal Conciliation Service, but I couldn't because a conciliator appointed to the case was a former Catholic who was particularly bitter against priests," Father Corridan says.

He turned then to Bernard Fitzpatrick, a staff member of the Commerce and Industry Association of New York, who was a teacher in the Xavier School. "Bernie," says Father Corridan, "considered the danger of a strike serious enough to warrant a trip to Washington."

As Fitzpatrick and Father Corridan saw it, on Wednesday, November 3, the day after the re-election of President Truman, the rejection of the employers' final offer by the men on the coming Friday, November 5, in a secret N.L.R.B. ballot, was a foregone conclusion. That would leave too little time for the successful conclusion of contract negotiations before the antistrike injunction expired on November 9. A "no" vote was taken for granted, since the I.L.A. had recommended a "no" vote to its membership. When the injunction expired, the I.L.A. would be forced either to call the first harbor-wide strike in its history or risk watching its members hit the bricks in their second major wildcat strike since the war because of the union's complete surrender to the employers.

Neither Fitzpatrick nor Father Corridan could say surely at that time whether the Communist Party might not pop up at some few piers in the harbor to give the men the leadership they would need for a wildcat strike, just as had happened in 1945.

Furthermore, the national-emergency section of the Taft-Hartley Law was defective in meeting such a situation, Father Corridan believed. All the President could do upon being apprised of the crisis would be to give a complete account of it to Congress. Congress was not in session. Yet both Father Corridan and Mr. Fitzpatrick believed the situation was still manageable. A strike might yet be averted.

"Fitzpatrick telephoned John Steelman, President Truman's labor adviser, at the White House, and arranged for an appointment for the two of us for noon of November 4," says Father

Corridan. "Early that morning we met at the Pennsylvania Station. We left for Washington on the seven-thirty train. We had breakfast on the train and, of all things, talked about the coopers' case. Bernie had been the men's lawyer in that case. From there we went into the whole waterfront problem and how to resolve the conspiracy of the triple alliance—business, politics, and Ryan's union.

"The only way to end it, we both agreed, was how to build a decent union. But how to do it? As an optimist, I thought I could see the beginnings of one right in Chelsea and the Village, right in my own back yard.

"We arrived in Washington at 11:30 A.M. and left immediately for the White House in a cab. It was a beautiful fall day, with something extra added. You could feel the electrifying atmosphere of President's Truman unexpected but popular re-election and the four-year reprieve granted to the Democratic Party and its officeholders. In the White House itself you could sense that same 'out of the valley of death' elation. We didn't have too long to wait before we were ushered into Mr. Steelman's office.

"Mr. Steelman was particularly gracious. His affable manner was proportionate to his ample frame and expanded somewhat when he told us he was leaving on the morrow to join the President at Key West, Florida, to bask in sunshine and the joys of Democratic victory. He listened intently to what we had to say on the New York situation.

"When we concluded, he jocularly remarked, 'Gentlemen, you are not going to leave that hot potato in my lap.' He reached for the phone. As he did so, the phone rang. It was his secretary, informing him that Joe Ryan was calling from New York. Mr. Steelman instructed her to tell Ryan that he was not in and to get Cyrus Ching of the Federal Conciliation Service on the phone at once. Mr. Steelman arranged for a 2:30 P.M. appointment at the Conciliation Service offices between Bernie and me and Mr. Ching.

"After a leisurely lunch we walked over to the Conciliation offices. The offices were in one of the old government office buildings with their large marble halls, spacious offices, and high ceilings to mitigate Washington's summer heat. Peter Seitz, counsel for the Conciliation Service, sat in on the conference. After greeting us, Mr. Ching slumped back into his large swivel chair.

"I judged Mr. Ching to be some 70 years of age. His large frame, stretched out over some six feet and five inches, radiated quiet strength. A former vice-president of the United States Rubber Company, Mr. Ching first created the impression that he was something of a New England cracker-barrel philosopher. He puffed away on his meerschaum pipe and spoke in general of his labor-management philosophy.

"It wasn't long, however, before Mr. Ching got down to brass tacks and listened to our account of the present situation on the New York waterfront and the likely developments. He wanted to know if I had apprised the regional office of the Conciliation Service in New York of the facts and opinions that I was giving him. I told him that I had gone over the situation with some of the local conciliators, but not the man directly in charge of the case. Naturally I couldn't tell him why.

"He asked what I would propose as a solution. I pointed out that I was more competent to speak on the nature of the problem than to propose specific solutions. That problem belonged to the I.L.A., the N.Y.S.A., and the government.

"I told him, however, that it seemed likely that a package deal—including money, welfare fund, and vacation pay—was the likely key for the immediate problem. Then I went further. I had been thinking of this problem for years. I knew that Bernie agreed with me, and I was sure I was right. I spoke as eloquently as I could.

"Any temporary solution of the present crisis through a successfully negotiated contract would prove to be just a temporary palliative of an evil condition." I told him. "There was a great need for a thorough study of the whole labor-management setup in the harbor if the fundamental causes of the instability in the harbor were to be corrected.

"The aspects of national safety as well as the free flow of international commerce in a bistate harbor argued that the federal government, which subsidizes American shipping as an auxiliary arm of national defense, was the only competent body to undertake such a difficult assignment.

"Ironically, I told Mr. Ching that if war ever broke out between the Soviet Union and the United States, security could be more easily gotten in Harry Bridges' piers on the West Coast than on Ryan's docks in New York. Bridges' centralized hiring would make the checking of saboteurs far easier than Ryan's sprawling shapes. I reminded him that government security agents had told me they thanked God the Soviet Union was our ally in World War II.

"On that note, Bernie and I bowed ourselves out. Mr. Ching seemed impressed. Of course I couldn't tell how much. But I had spoken the burning truth as I saw it. We returned to New York to await, on the following day, November 5, the outcome of the first secret ballot ever conducted by the government on the New York waterfront. The men rejected the N.Y.S.A.'s final offer by an overwhelming 10-to-1 margin. That was what Ryan asked them to do.

"Immediately after the results were announced, I called up Father Ben Masse, S.J., labor editor of *America,* to ask him if *America* would care to have an article on the longshoremen's strike. I was now convinced the strike would break out on the following Tuesday or Wednesday. Father Masse agreed to take my article. We made the arrangements whereby I would hold out the copy until just before the magazine went to press at noon on Tuesday. We also reached an agreement whereby I was to get 10,000 reprints of the article before the magazine itself was run off.

"I was convinced that the strike would come. I was sure of it. And I was determined to come out openly—on the side of the wildcat strikers.

"Upon the resumption of negotiations, the N.Y.S.A. modified its final offer only to the extent of reducing the contract's duration from two years to one year and offering to move back the retroactivity of the ten-cent wage increase to September 15. In the early hours of Tuesday morning, November 9, the I.L.A. wage-scale committee, that had recommended a "no" vote to the membership on the N.Y.S.A.'s first final offer, gave its approval to virtually the same agreement which it had rejected. Only the three rebel West Side Locals 791, 895, and 1258 objected.

"At the 7:55 A.M. shape, later that morning, Local 791 men at the Cunard piers, 54 and 56, North River, reported sick for work. They did not want to be in technical violation of the injunction which did not expire until midnight.

"The wildcat strike was on before a vote was taken. The men were afraid of a Ryan count both in and out of New York.

"Right after eight o'clock, when I got the word that the strike was on, I jumped to the typewriter to hammer out in one-finger fashion this prenote to my article in *America:*

" 'Since Father Corridan, assistant director of the Xavier Labor School in Manhattan, submitted this article, his worst fears have been realized. As we go to press, the port of New York has been paralyzed by a widespread rank-and-file walkout of longshoremen.'

"I had no sooner finished the prenote than the phone rang. Father Masse was at the other end of the wire. My nickname in the order has been 'Pete,' for some reason I've never been able to fathom.

" 'Sorry, Pete,' he said, 'but we can't take your article.'

"I laughingly said, 'How come, Ben?'

" 'Why,' he said, 'I just read in the New York *Times* that an agreement was reached early this morning.'

" 'Ben,' I said, 'that's what the *Times* may think, but it's not what the men think; they are already slipping off the piers.'

"Father Masse asked, 'Will it go all the way?'

"I said, 'Definitely.'

" 'Well, then, Pete,' said Father Masse, 'get that article up here *quam primum.*'

"May Golden, our secretary, had come in. She typed out a clean copy and I was off by the Seventh Avenue Subway to the *America's* editorial offices at 325 West 108th Street, one block away from where I was raised as a kid. I'd scored a news beat on the *Times*.

"Early Wednesday morning, 'Brownie' and I picked up the bulk of the 10,000 reprints at J. P. O'Brien's printing house on the Lower East Side. Some of our friends came into the school and were off to scatter 'Longshoremen's Case' by Father John M. Corridan, S.J., all over the harbor."

From that moment on, all around the New York waterfront the rank-and-file longshoremen knew they had found a friend. They had found a defender and a champion.

"The 'overtime-on-overtime' issue is not at the root of the present difficulties," Father Corridan wrote in his article for *America.* "Neither is the root of the present impasse to be found in lack of respect of a contract, which a federal judge charged against the rank and file of the union a short time ago. The longshoremen respect a legal contract.

"Racketeering and graft are not at the base of the troubled conditions along the docks. Racketeering and pilfering are merely manifestations of a condition spawned by the JOINT CRIMINAL NEGLECT OF THE SHIPPING ASSOCIATION AND THE UNION LEADERSHIP."

There was the straight-from-the-shoulder punch that Father Corridan delivered, from the heart of his own beliefs and the beliefs of many longshoremen. Early in his career at Xavier, one of the longshoremen had said to Father Corridan, "Take Joe Ryan and J. V. Lyon off our back. They always work together."

J. V. Lyon was the executive secretary and spokesman for the New York Shipping Association. When Father Corridan charged that the men's troubles and the wildcat walkout in the harbor were due to the "joint criminal neglect" of the men's welfare by the shipping association and union leaders, he won an audience. And when he was willing to stand up to a federal judge, and say the longshoremen would respect a legal contract, even though they might defy one they believed to be illegally ratified, he won friends on the waterfront.

"Nor is Communist agitation the root of the present delicate situation," Father Corridan continued. "It was not in the past, and it will not be in the future if the present longshore mess is cleaned up. Communism thrives best where conditions are unhealthy, and they are plenty unhealthy along the docks."

Then Father Corridan spelled out in language so plain that anyone could understand it just what was the trouble on the waterfront that brought about the wildcat strikes—with their damage to everyone in the port—and the racketeering and the pilferage and other evils. Longshoremen knew he was right.

"The heart of the matter is the system of hiring along the waterfront," Father Corridan wrote. "Men are hired as if they were beasts of burden, part of the slave market of a pagan era. A longshoreman tends to work on only one pier. He is known on that pier. If he is not hired on that pier he won't ordinarily find work on any other where others have priority.

"The longshoreman's work difficulty flows out of each company's policy of striving to build up a large labor reserve to meet the peak period of activity on its own piers. Peak periods are, too often, few and far between. There are always more men looking for work than there are jobs, and this holds good on every pier. The union leadership has made little effort to curtail the number of cards. So long as a man is willing to pay the initiation fee and keep up regular payment of dues, he can join. . . .

"The 'shape-up' cries against every standard of decency and justice, particularly when you consider the hundreds of millions of dollars spent on docks, shipping, and harbor improvements. . . . It is a waterlogged relic of the days of the clipper ships when the first anyone knew of a ship's arrival was the cry of the shore watch.

"Other great ports of the world have long since adopted the hiring hall as a solution to the problem. Anyone familiar with casual labor knows that there must be a closed shop, and hiring must be done through central bodies. You just have to have some regulation if men are not scramble over one another for jobs like dogs for a bone. The present legal difficulties to the hiring hall should be removed by the new Congress. Whatever physical justification there may have been for the demoralizing 'shape' has long since disappeared with the coming of air mail and ship-to-shore communications.

"The *Queen Mary* is a fast ship. The morning she leaves Southampton for the four-day run to New York, her manifest is flown by air mail to the Cunard Lines in New York and is in their hands within 30 hours. All loft space and disposition of cargo are plotted out and checkers' books are laid out for them while the giant ship still steams through the Atlantic. Off Sandy Hook, radio and telephone communications, weather and tide will tell you when she will be tied up at one of the midtown piers. Yet, though the material matters are all prepared for, the men are still hired in slave fashion from the pierhead at 7:55 or 12:55 or 6:55 the day the ship is berthed."

An understandable indignation breathed through the priest's words. There was fire in them, as well as reason. "Is it unreasonable to suggest that a little of the care shown the cargo be used for the men who handle it?" he asked. Then once again he coupled the shipping association with the union leadership. "If the shipping association and the union leadership can't throw off their apathy, intellectual indolence, and moral blindness," he asserted, "the government of the United States should set up a competent commission of inquiry to investigate and to solve this cancerous condition in a free society."

Then Father Corridan paid his respects to those newspaper editors who were complaining that any interruption of service on the waterfront would jeopardize movements of goods bound to Europe to aid in the recovery of war-devastated lands.

"It is ironical," he said, "that so many should be concerned over the movement of European Recovery goods, and so few should give any thought or action to the men who move those goods at the cost of so much fear, sweat, and blood."

In conclusion, Father Corridan stated the social implications of the case for the men on the docks with an eloquence that begged all Christians to join to end waterfront evils.

"From the irregularity and danger of the work there flow many evil consequences," he said. "How is the mother of a longshoreman's family to plan her budget if she is totally uncertain as to whether her man will have three days or one day or no work at all in any given week? And the longshoreman himself? He's prepared for work with his lunch under his arm. He is not called at the 7:55 shape. There is nothing for him to do but to idle about with the rest of the men until the 12:55 shape, in the hope that this day will not be wasted.

"If this goes on day after day it is easy to understand the corrosion of a man's character. If you should blame him, then you should blast the system which produces him. Living from hand to mouth can do something to a man's ideas of fairness. One's ideas of justice fade when injustice is rampant. . . .

"If a longshoreman can't keep straight and can't make good at a 'racket,' drink comes easy. He succumbs to the loan sharks and the installment hawks. To get himself out of their clutches he needs to make a 'killing.' He'll despise the chance of a fairly steady income for the chance to clear himself at once. Does one blame his wife if after years of this she becomes improvident? And what of the children? Do you think that living on the fringe of society in the backwash of the city will bring out the best in them?

"The docks are thought of as a refuge for society's misfits and failures. Don't let the rough working clothes and the surroundings fool you. Ninety per cent of the men are as fine a group as you'll find in any walk of life—real, big-hearted family men, some of them condemned at the age of 15, because of home needs, to a lifetime at hard labor.

"Tragedy comes often to the docks, and the men have no way of meeting expenses except out of their own depleted pockets and passing the hat. Do these men need a welfare fund?

"More than 3,000,000 workers are covered by health and welfare funds under collective bargaining. Yet longshoremen need a health and welfare fund even more than miners, or the workers in the clothing and textile, steel, auto, and electric industries. Will they get one? A decent one? Not as long as there are two to three times as many men as there are jobs. Not as long as the industry doesn't put its own house in order through the hiring hall and the closed shop. Not as long as the government doesn't set up a commission of inquiry to help, and if need be goad the industry into living up to its responsibilities.

"The cause of the men of the docks, the hard-muscled, honorable men whose work means so much to our daily living, is a challenging call to all Christians. For these men are our brothers, redeemed in the precious blood of Christ, and one cannot rest secure if His dignity in them continues to be violated and outraged."

With these words Father Corridan opened his public campaign in the port of New York for an honest labor union with a closed shop and for government intervention, if necessary, to set up the conditions whereby the men could obtain such a union. At the very outset of his campaign he declared the shipping association to be equally culpable with the union leadership in the International Longshoremen's Association. Throughout his campaign he kept reiterating the culpability of the employers for the continuance of conditions in the harbor he found so degrading as to outrage believers in Christ who knew the facts.

His attitude was a far cry from that of those voices from the upper reaches of New York daily journalism who portrayed the shipping industry as being victimized by an inept union and the men as probably being under Communist influence.

As the strike spread and the entire harbor became affected, the first week's news was naturally of the discomforts of passengers aboard the luxury liners who were forced to carry a good deal of their baggage ashore, when it had passed through Customs inspection on the piers, and to leave some trunks on shipboard.

Then came news of the diversion of ships to other ports. The *Mauretania* put in at Halifax. On November 13 the railroads placed an embargo on all freight for export bound for the port of New York. By November 15 more than 200 ships, awaiting loading or unloading, lay idle at the piers. The *Times* asked editorially of the shippers' association and the longshoremen's union, "Are these costly interruptions necessary?"

On November 16 sailings of the *Queen Elizabeth* and the

America were canceled. Postmaster Albert Goldman complained on November 19 that 150,000 sacks of mail were now being delayed.

The best that Mayor William O'Dwyer could do to end the strike was to offer his labor-relations adviser, Theodore W. Kheel, to help Mr. Ching of the Federal Conciliation Service. Mr. Ching sent one of his deputies, William N. Margolis, to New York on November 17. After a week of conferences, Mr. Ching himself arrived on November 24. He brought the shippers' association and the longshoremen's wage committee together in a final meeting to make an agreement which had been in the making for about a week.

Under the agreement, instead of a rise of ten cents in the hourly wage rate, with 15 cents for overtime, the longshoremen received a rise of 13 cents in the hourly rate and 19½ cents in the overtime. They received doubled vacation benefits and the establishment of a welfare fund, although not quite as liberal a one as had been worked out at the Xavier School in the conference of longshoremen with Father Corridan and Eddie Chave.

All told, it was a victory for the rebels. They may have "gotten off on the wrong foot" in starting their wildcat strike, as the New York *Herald Tribune* had informed its readers, editorially. But the wildcat strike, or rebellion against their own leaders, as waged between contracts, became in 1945 and 1948 the one demonstrable way by which the men might win higher wages and better working conditions than the Ryan leadership would fight for. It was a tactic which won the approval of Father Corridan as the only effective weapon available to the men at the time.

CHAPTER 10

THE GREAT HUE AND CRY

In early November, 1948, only a few days before the bitter wildcat strike began, an event occurred which played directly into the hands of Father Corridan. Malcolm Johnson of the *Sun* began writing the first of his articles on the waterfront.

As they began to appear, letters flowed into his newspaper office. Among others was one from Father Corridan. Edward Bartnett, city editor, turned it over to Johnson with the remark, "You'd better go around and see this man; he seems to know what he's talking about."

Corridan and Johnson met. Thereafter Father Corridan became an assiduous tipster for the star reporter. Together they set off a great hue and cry against the waterfront racketeers.

Johnson was the first man in New York to call attention in journalism to the dominance of criminals in the leadership of Joe Ryan's union. He named them. He gave their criminal records. Johnson, too, was the first man with any wide audience to call attention to the key controls of the waterfront by the public loaders and the hiring bosses of the shape.

Johnson showed how some of these mobsters were allied to the national crime syndicates, the leaders of which were operating in the race tracks, in gambling, narcotics, and the smuggling trades, after some education in Prohibition era bootlegging.

It was Johnson who first collected into one continuous and thorough exposé the stories of such hoodlum-unionists as the Socks Lanza gang, Johnny Applegate, Richard "The Bandit" Gregory, Emil "Big Moe" Nizich, David "The Beetle" Beadle, Johnny Dunn, Charley "the Jew" Yanowsky, and Eddie McGrath.

Johnson's most complete and perfect picture of the close alliance between vicious criminals in the waterfront rackets and the powers of politics was in his story of John M. "Cockeye" Dunn, who ultimately went to the electric chair with one of his pals, Andy Sheridan, for the murder of Andy Hintz, a hiring boss for Pier 51, at the foot of Jane Street, North River.

Both Dunn and Sheridan were notorious killers long before they were convicted. But they were no more notorious along the docks than others of their time. The only reason they would stand out in the history of New York harbor today is this one fact: It was through the story of Dunn's crimes, his ultimate downfall, and the help which men high in government tried to give him that Johnson first traced for general public knowledge the pattern of the alliance between hoodlum unionism and government.

John M. "Cockeye" Dunn was born in the borough of Queens, New York, August 24, 1910. His father was a merchant seaman, lost at sea when the boy was four years old. His mother later became a charwoman at Madison Square Garden. Little is known of her second husband except that he was comparatively poor and was killed in a railroad accident when Dunn still was a boy.

By the time Dunn was 15 he was roaming the streets with a

neighborhood gang of boys with little parental surveillance, and was found robbing a hardware store. For this juvenile offense he was sent to a Roman Catholic protectory, which failed to reform him, for at 19 he was once again in trouble with the law—this time for robbing a grocery store of 625 dollars. He was sent to a reformatory, where he spent two years, emerging in 1931. In 1932 he was convicted of robbing a card game at the point of a gun and sent to Sing Sing for two to four years. For some unfathomable reason he was paroled within a year.

Once out of Sing Sing he teamed up with another hoodlum, just as vicious as he, named Eddie McGrath, who later became his brother-in-law. In 1935 both he and McGrath were arrested on a charge of homicide but were discharged for lack of evidence.

Just one year later Dunn became a labor-union organizer by a simple process: picking the waterfront as his scene of operations. At this period of the 1930's, new labor unions, encouraged by the Wagner Act, were springing up around New York by the dozens. Joe Ryan's I.L.A. was an easy parent union from which an enterprising, would-be labor leader could get a charter to form a new local union. Dunn, with a small group of pals, got a charter from the I.L.A. for Local 1,346-1 to represent terminal checkers and platform men in collective-bargaining negotiations with trucking companies.

Then Dunn got a charter from the A.F.L. for another union, the Motor and Bus Terminal Checkers, Platform and Office Workers, Local 21,510, while one of his close hoodlum friends, Andy Sheridan, got one for the same group of workers, numbered 21,512, in Hoboken. This gave them control of a fairly large labor force along both sides of the Hudson River.

Dunn set up his union offices at Eighth Avenue and West 14th Street in Manhattan, where Ryan had his offices. Dunn and Sheridan first signed contracts for their labor force with the Motor Carrier Association of New York, comprising about 500 trucking companies, by guaranteeing to provide them plentiful labor at 55 cents an hour. Within nine years they jacked up the price to a dollar-thirty-five per hour.

In that same office building which housed Joe Ryan and Dunn, the murderer, was the headquarters of a waterfront concern known as Varick Enterprises. This concern for more than a decade was a respectable mask for many a criminal operation along the docks. It was started on the New Jersey side of the harbor back in the Prohibition era when an accountant found that some of the trucking companies were keeping two sets of books to conceal their activities in the moving of illicit alcohol. The accountant notified a labor leader. He gave him the wonderful idea that, when the trucking companies transporting bootleg liquor kept two sets of books to hide their crime, there was plenty of opportunity for blackmail.

By 1937 Varick Enterprises, Inc., had moved to the Manhattan side of the river. As Prohibition was ended it found a profitable field for company activities in being the collection agency for boss loaders along the docks. Eddie McGrath, Dunn's hoodlum brother-in-law, was with Varick Enterprises. Varick Enterprises once had the task of making collections for the boss loaders, with every truckman along the North River from 14th Street, South, paying tribute of varying sums, usually in cash. The collections were enforced by goons armed with guns or blackjacks. Truckmen paid under threat of violence to have their trucks unloaded.

Dunn and McGrath waxed fat and prosperous. By 1938 Dunn was living in a very pretty home in Kew Gardens, Queens, for which he had made a down payment of 5000 dollars. On January 17, 1942, with three of his gang, Dunn was convicted of coercion. The three pals were Eddie Thompson, then a hiring boss on Pier 45; J. J. "Peck" Hughes, a checker on that pier; and George Donovan, a simple gunman. They were sent to prison.

In a campaign to control the hiring on Pier 51, North River, by a boss named E. J. Kelly, who resisted him, Dunn had beaten up Kelly in a saloon at West and 10th streets. He then called a strike of his checkers to get his own man hired in Kelly's place. He won his point, but only after two British freighters which were loading at the piers were delayed through two convoys. The United States was then at war.

It was after this conviction that the hoodlum's influence in the business and political world began to make itself felt. Persons prominent in both worlds interceded to get him free. Within a few days of his conviction, letters from officials of leading trucking companies went to the New York City Parole Board saying Dunn was an upright, honorable citizen with whom it was a pleasure to do business. On January 30, 1942, A. Clayton Powell, Negro city councilman from Harlem, wrote a letter to the Board, saying Dunn had done much for Negro longshoremen.

On February 26 United States Representative George Holden Tinkham, Democratic representative from the 10th Congressional District of Massachusetts wrote a similar letter. Dunn was then in the city's penitentiary as Convict No. 7291.

On February 1, 1943, Lieutenant Colonel Charles E. Martin and Majors John J. Lane and John Bridge of the U. S. Transportation Corps, concerned with the movement of shipping, wrote long letters to New York City Parole Commissioner Samuel Battle, saying Dunn's services along the docks were urgently needed for the promotion of the war effort. Another letter to Commissioner Battle, also portraying Dunn as a very valuable man for the war effort, was sent by Colonel Frederick C. Horner, chief of the Highway Division of the Army Transportation Corps. Just who engineered these efforts at intervention on Dunn's behalf has always remained a mystery. They were balked temporarily because Commissioner Battle consulted Mayor Fiorello H. La Guardia on the matter. Mayor La Guardia was outraged. He wrote to Henry L. Stimson, then Secretary of War, and Stimson personally withdrew the Army's requests for Dunn's release from prison.

The penitentiary, however, could not hold the influential criminal long. On September 16, 1944, after serving two years, the parole was granted. "Cockeye" Dunn went back immediately to his criminal activities on the docks. Within a few days of his parole, Cornelius J. Noonan, president of Local 21,510 of the Motor and Bus Terminal Checkers, Platform and Office Workers, I.L.A., advised the parole commission that Dunn had been reinstated as vice-president and business agent of that union at 60 dollars per week, with 25 dollars expenses. For the duration of his parole the parole board forced Dunn to resign his union office. He resumed it after his parole expired.

Dunn's actual income from criminal activities, of course, ran into many thousands of dollars a year. When his fellow hoodlum, "Peck" Hughes, was made hiring boss at Pier 51, at his request, the pilferage in the single commodity of rice alone ran up to 8000 dollars in a single month. Hughes was fired.

As far as Dunn was concerned, his criminal career as a union official ran unchecked until January 8, 1947. At seven o'clock that morning, Andy Hintz, who had been the hiring boss on Pier 51 for the previous seven months, was shot dead as he stepped into the hallway of his Greenwich Village home, 61 Grove Street. Hintz was just getting started for work. Six bullets were pumped into him by three men he met in his tenement hallway, but he was tough enough to live until January 29. Before he died, he broke the usual waterfront code of silence. He told his wife, "Johnny Dunn shot me." After an inquiry detectives arrested not only Dunn but Andy Sheridan, the killer who had pioneered with him in organizing West Side checkers and platform workers back in 1936, and a former prizefighter named Danny Gentile. Ultimately all three were convicted of murder in the first degree.

It was brought out at the trial that Dunn and his pals had shot Hintz because he had been reckless enough to resist their efforts to replace him on the dock with one "Ding Dong" Bell, another plug-ugly of the Dunn-McGrath mob.

"Tell Dunn to go to hell," Hintz had said publicly.

That challenge was his death warrant.

Testimony at the trial of Dunn, Sheridan, and Gentile indicated that Dunn, the killer, was far from a small-time mobster. Just before the murder of Hintz, it was brought out, Dunn was spending some time in Hollywood, Florida, in a hotel with Meyer Lansky, and was telephoning friends in New York from Lansky's room. Lansky was for years a member of the same gang as Buggsy Siegel, the gangster murdered in California in the summer of 1947. A check on the telephone calls from Lansky's room in Florida, during the time when Dunn was with him, showed calls to Joe Adonis, racketeer in New Jersey, Buggsy Siegel, Frank Costello of New York, and "Dandy Phil" Kastel, a partner of Costello's in the slot-machine business who operates out of Louisiana.

The conviction of Dunn, Sheridan, and Gentile came on December 31, 1947. Gentile finally obtained a commutation of his sentence to life imprisonment for having given aid to the prosecution. The execution of Dunn and Sheridan was long delayed. Part of the delay was due to an affidavit by Sheridan, exonerating his two coprisoners and saying he alone had directed the murder. Sheridan said he had been accompanied in it by two gunmen who were either dead or missing. On the basis of this affidavit Dunn and Gentile applied for a new trial.

During the time it took for the original trial judge and the Court of Appeals to find Sheridan's story impossible to believe and for the United States Supreme Court to decline to review the case, Dunn seemed for a while to lose the iron nerve which had marked his long career. He sent word to District Attorney Frank S. Hogan in Manhattan that he wanted to talk. He promised that if his sentence were commuted to life imprisonment he would supply information that would solve some 30 murders along the waterfront. Beyond that, Dunn said, he would name the higher-ups in the field of politics who had protected all the rackets along the docks, including the very top boss of all. One man, Dunn said, was kingpin of all the waterfront rackets, and he was a very powerful man, indeed, with high political connections.

Dunn described the kingpin of New York rackets as a prominent and wealthy businessman, with a reputation for respectability, charitable activity, and prominence in church affairs. Before he could name him, in sworn testimony, he demanded that his sentence be commuted. Commutation first and testimony later. District Attorney Hogan would not consent to the bargain. The commutation, Hogan said, could only come from Governor Dewey, and once signed it would be irrevocable. Dunn might then refuse to carry out his part of the bargain.

The date of the execution of Dunn and Sheridan was set for

the latter part of June, 1949. At Hogan's request it was delayed until July 7. Almost to the moment of execution, Dunn talked frantically to Assistant District Attorney George P. Monaghan, who was Hogan's emissary to Sing Sing. Much of what he told was sensational, Hogan told the press, but it was principally in generalities, unsusceptible of proof. He named one city official, whom he said had been his contact man in getting a fat city contract. He alleged that this official was a participant in some of the waterfront rackets, but he failed to back up his charge with any substantial testimony.

On Monaghan's last visit to Dunn, the killer declined to talk at all. He said very calmly that he was prepared to meet his Maker. At 11 P.M., July 7, 1949, he and Sheridan walked calmly to the chair. In the opinion of Johnson and District Attorney Hogan, a great many people in and around the waterfront must have breathed more easily when Dunn went to the chair, particularly the man Dunn described as kingpin of the rackets, the man who wore the mask of respectability and had been honored by his church.

In Malcolm Johnson's book, entitled *Crime on the Labor Front,* the star reporter had this to say of Dunn's accusation against an alleged big boss of waterfront racketeering:

"What Dunn was saying was no secret on the waterfront. The businessman implicated by Dunn is known to all longshoremen who understand the racket setup."

There was just one aftermath to the execution of Dunn, which close followers of New York City politics have found interesting. Norman Thomas, chairman of the Socialist Party in New York, was the first man to call it to public attention.

Prior to Dunn's execution, when Dunn was threatening to talk, Mayor William F. O'Dwyer had announced that he would not be a candidate for re-election. District Attorney Hogan was the presumptive candidate of the Democratic Party. O'Dwyer had long been under fire for having had a perfect murder case against Albert Anastasia, of Murder, Inc., and having pigeonholed it. Mayor O'Dwyer also had been under fire for his friendship with Frank Costello, the underworld fixer in Tammany Hall.

Two days after Dunn was executed, a committee of labor leaders and so-called Fair Deal Democrats called on Mayor O'Dwyer at City Hall, and asked him if he would change his mind and run for re-election. The mayor said he might. He finally gave his public consent to run on July 14.

During the election campaign Norman Thomas asked publicly whether there was any connection between Dunn's execution, with lips sealed, and the fact Mayor O'Dwyer had changed his mind about running for re-election. The Mayor didn't answer him. Nobody did. But some three years later, long after Mayor O'Dwyer had resigned his office and started an exile in Mexico as ambassador, District Attorney Hogan shed new light on this particular episode in New York politics.

Mr. Hogan gave an exclusive interview to Guy Richards, a reporter for the New York *Journal-American,* in which he told the story of O'Dwyer's change of mind, as he knew it. Armed with the facts given him by Hogan, Richards went to the offices of "Big Bill" McCormack, and talked to him for several hours. The inquiry by the New York State Crime Commission was then in full swing. McCormack had been named often and publicly by this time as the "Mr. Big" of the New York waterfront. Mr. Richards merged the two interviews in a single news story, which was headlined:

HOGAN KNIFED FOR MAYORALTY—HOW PIER CHIEFS GOT BILL O'DWYER TO RUN IN 1949

In this story Mr. Richards went back to the tense days of early July, 1949, when the district attorney's emissary, Mr. Monaghan, was trying to get Dunn to talk on waterfront corruption in the death house at Sing Sing, and Mayor O'Dwyer was declining to make another bid for the mayoralty. His conclusion, after listening both to District Attorney Hogan and "Big Bill" McCormack was as follows:

"The small clique of waterfront leaders known as 'the stable' which has ruled port politics for 30 years was largely responsible for by-passing Frank Hogan and 'persuading' Bill O'Dwyer to run again for mayor."

Mr. Richards named three members of "the stable" as Joe Ryan, head of the I.L.A.; Marty Lacey, president of the Greater New York Trades and Labor Council; and "Joe" Papa, who at that time was boss of the teamsters' union in downtown Manhattan, Local 202. The reporter indicated that all three members of "the stable" were followers of "Big Bill" McCormack, but warned against any oversimplification of the matter. The trio, he said, according to one point of view should be viewed as "wholly independent of Mr. McCormack as well as dependent on him."

With some irony, and a real understanding, Mr. Richards pointed out that in the election to the mayoralty in 1950 these three labor-union leaders each backed a different candidate for mayor. Joe Ryan backed Judge Ferdinand Pecora, Democrat. "Joe" Papa backed the Republican, Edward Corsi. Marty Lacey backed the independent, Impelliteri.

In this way, since all three members of "the stable" were "independent of Mr. McCormack, as well as dependent on him," no matter who won the mayoralty election in 1950, Mr. McCormack would win it, as a power behind the scenes, since one of his followers would have been an influential labor leader in the winner's corner.

"It was almost as if a master strategist had thought of it," Mr. Richards interjected editorially in his news columns, probably with his tongue in his cheek.

"Dunn's death, July 7, brought a perceptible easing of tensions among the mobsters," Mr. Richards wrote in his story. "It was a signal that he hadn't talked enough to suit Hogan. It was also a signal that Hogan had learned enough to make him entirely undesirable to certain groups as a replacement at City Hall. The 'Stop Hogan' campaign was launched almost immediately. The phones started ringing around town and the drive soon gathered a number of respectable businessmen into its growing snowball.

"Starting July 9, McCormack was induced to make two pilgrimages to City Hall to urge O'Dwyer to change his mind. He brought along Marty Lacey and Joe Ryan, both members of 'the stable' and now the biggest wheels in the waterfront union family of the A.F. of L. as bosses respectively of the teamsters and longshoremen.

"Asked who induced him to get into the act, McCormack said: 'I did it as a favor to Eddie Maguire.' [Maguire, by appointment of Mayor Impellitteri, had succeeded in 1951 to the 15,000-dollar-a-year position as Commissioner of the Water Supply Board. The position formerly had been held by Mayor O'Dwyer's friend, James J. Moran, who was sent to prison for extortion and defrauding the city.] 'As for all this talk about Dunn and the tension,' McCormack continued, 'I don't remember any tension. I never met Dunn and Dunn never met me.' "

O'Dwyer's decision to run for re-election, according to Hogan, was made on the afternoon of Monday, July 11. That very morning, Hogan told Richards, O'Dwyer had assured him of his support and said he had persuaded Hugo Rogers, then leader of Tammany Hall, to support him. That gave Hogan the backing of three out of the five borough leaders of the party for the nomination, and he was so informed, he said, by a friend in the National Democratic Club. Hogan told Richards that he telephoned O'Dwyer that very morning to inform him he now had the three leaders back of him, and said he was going up to the National Democratic Club to a meeting to accept their designation as the party's candidate. O'Dwyer asked him to hold off a little until he, O'Dwyer, could persuade Boss Flynn of the Bronx, and Borough President Cashmore of Brooklyn, to be with him. Hogan refused.

"Four or five hours later," Hogan remembered, "O'Dwyer did a complete switch. He denounced all the three leaders who had come out for me. One of those—Rogers—was a man to whom he had devoted more than an hour that very morning persuading to come out for me."

Just why O'Dwyer changed his mind four days after Dunn's execution and again ran for mayor may never be known completely until O'Dwyer himself decides to talk. But to Richards, the *Journal-American* reporter, as to Johnson, the *Sun* reporter, and to Father

Corridan and District Attorney Hogan, the execution of Dunn was a political event of utmost importance at the moment.

Whether Father Corridan's help to Malcolm Johnson as a news source turned him into pamphleteering on the waterfront, on his own account, to help publicize his point of view and that of the men, or whether the longshoremen who were his friends were so impressed by the effect of Johnson's work that they turned to Corridan to help them get out their own publicity is probably an open question. Father Corridan says the men turned to him to help them.

Both he and the dock workers who were his friends were aware at the end of the 1948 strike that one weapon they could use with profit to spread their own point of view on harbor problems among the people most concerned would be a publication of some sort. Consequently a mimeographed, occasional publication, called appropriately enough *The Crusader,* was born one evening from a conversation at the Xavier School early in 1949. As to its founders, Father Corridan even today will say only that Christy Doran, his original follower, was one. There were others, of course. But when *The Crusader* was launched, the atmosphere of physical danger to men rebelling against mob rule on the docks was so real and palpable that it was begun as an underground, conspiratorial affair. The collaborators in it, insofar as the people who read it were concerned, were to remain as anonymous as possible. Some so remain to this day.

"It had to be underground," Father Corridan says. "At the outset I didn't even want people generally to know where it was put out. I didn't want the longshoremen who associated with me to become marked men. There were probably a dozen people along the waterfront with whom I used to discuss the advisability of a longshoremen's paper, representing the interests of the rank and file. Even after the first few issues of *The Crusader* were being read, I used to evade some questions as to who was putting it out, and where the publication office was.

"I got a kick out of it, and so did Christy, particularly as we knew that Joe Ryan and his crowd would immediately brand it as Communist.'

"Right at the outset," Father Corridan says, "Christy and I decided that we would get out a biweekly, mimeographed sheet, usually of one page, legal size, with two columns, and send it by mail to about 500 longshoremen who, we believed, would be receptive to what we had to say. We would talk in longshoremen's language—right down to earth—and we would center the editorial content of our paper on two things we knew everybody would be interested in. One was a running commentary on waterfront events. The other would be about what the union leadership ought to do when it came to negotiate with the New York Shipping Association on the new contract, to replace the one that would expire in August, 1949.

"For secrecy? We went to every precaution. It was real cloak-and-dagger stuff, to keep the enemy guessing. The paper we used was without any watermark, and we never bought it at the same store twice. The typewriter we used for stenciling was never used for any other job, and I kept it under lock and key. The mimeographing machine was a broken-down war-surplus electric A. B. Dick machine, which Father Carey bought for 50 dollars. We had to add some new parts to it to put it into operating condition.

"By January of 1949, I had collected the names and addresses of about 500 longshoremen, mostly on the West Side, but a few in Brooklyn and New Jersey. We ran *The Crusader,* or another paper called *The New Deal,* intermittently from 1949 to 1953. By 1953 our mailing list had grown to more than 3000 persons.

"At first we mailed *The Crusader* out to our subscription list in two-cent open envelopes, because we didn't have much money. As the number of people who knew me increased, more money came in. We turned then to three-cent closed envelopes for more rapid delivery.

"Just to keep the mobsters guessing, *The Crusader* was mailed from all over the metropolitan area. Sometimes it was mailed in bulk. Sometimes it was broken down into four or five bundles and mailed from four or five points. Apart from Christy and myself, as the people who mailed out our propaganda, I sometimes would grab some fellows who were not longshoremen but who would be on their way home from the labor school here. I would ask them to drop a bundle in their neighborhood mailbox. The first few issues we mailed from New Jersey, just to throw up a real smoke screen.

"I'll never forget going out, myself, to mail the first issue. I mailed it from the Erie Railroad station in Jersey City, just off the Hudson and Manhattan tubes. I can even remember the way the night looked, because it was raining cats and dogs and I got soaked for my pains. The weather was perfect for a clandestine operation. The traveling bag of a priest is not usually considered a suspicious object, even if it's loaded with dynamite, of a kind. I believe mine was.

"In the first few copies we enclosed only a single sheet and urged our reader to pass it along to his friends. On getting favorable reactions on some of the docks, it was easy to learn through the grapevine who was helping spread *The Crusader's* message. We stuffed as many as four copies in some of the envelopes, finally. For the first few mailings we put on our list a few of Joe Ryan's pet stooges in some of the locals where we had observers. Then we kept a check of I.L.A. headquarters to see just how many would come running to Ryan with their copy. Once we knew that, we dropped them from our list and picked a few others. There was a little bit of fun in that part of the operation.

"In the beginning Ryan and his friends labeled the paper a Communist production, a Moscow product, and so on, just as we knew they would. It wasn't long, of course, before they knew that I was responsible for it, because once in a while it contained something about me or something I'd said. Then Ryan began calling it the work of a religious fanatic. I didn't mind. What delighted me was the way it was being read.

"The paper's policy? It was devoted to pursuing limited gains for the rank and file, year in and year out, and assailing the I.L.A. leadership for not representing the men more effectively. We harped on the subjects of regularizing the gangs, getting vacation pay, the establishment of welfare funds and pensions, the need for limiting the number of workers by closing the books of the union, and the creation of an effective seniority system.

"These were all subjects the men on the docks could understand. They were things they wanted. They were things they knew they couldn't get without a complete reformation of their union, and the more we could get them thinking about these things, the more, we knew, they would want a reformation of their union.

"Late in 1949 the official *Longshore News* began to be published by Ryan and his stooges. At least we had forced that. Ryan and the mob were beginning to have to use propaganda of their own to keep their own men in line, or to try to. The guns and the blackjacks weren't enough."

Although Father Corridan's archives are rich in material about the problems of the waterfront—social and economic—and in newspaper clippings about almost every event along the harbor's docks since he first took over his assignment at St. Xavier's, they are strangely empty insofar as files of *The Crusader* go. All the copies went into the mails. Father Corridan didn't save any.

Only a few of his longshoremen friends have saved very many, but these few show a vigorous pamphleteer, often working in waterfront lingo, with slang and epithet redolent of the old West Side tenement atmosphere. Derision and invective for Ryan & Co. Sharp cracks at the shipping interests. Sometimes the few remaining issues will be found devoted to the sins of the money-grabbing employers, sometimes to the sins of the union leadership. Both of them—employers and union leaders—throughout all the faded and tattered copies of *The Crusader* which now remain, are portrayed as people who are oppressors of the hard-working and deserving dock worker, who is a good, upright family man and who is being squeezed unmercifully by two allied enemies.

From 1949 onward Father Corridan had the help of another reporter on the New Jersey side of the harbor. He was Robert Greene, of the Jersey *Journal,* in Jersey City. By coincidence, Greene was a graduate of St. Francis Xavier High School in Manhattan, housed in the same gray stone edifice where Father Corridan has made his headquarters.

Greene was a police reporter when he first became interested in the personal relationships existing between the union officials and dock bosses in Jersey City and Hoboken and the officials of government on the municipal, county, and state levels. He found that the I.L.A. on the Jersey waterfront was in the hands of numerous men of criminal records, and that these men were of sufficient political power so that they maintained close relations with the mayors of the two adjoining cities and with the police.

He found that the mayors of the two cities were using the docks as a place to which they could send faithful party workers. The union officials who kept the union books open to anyone naturally became part of the ruling political machine in each city. Just as Joe Ryan, on the West Side of New York, was always a servant of Tammany Hall and a power in its councils through his leadership of the New York City dock workers, so the longshoremen's union leaders in Jersey City and Hoboken were as much politicians as they were labor leaders. Greene found that they were using their power as labor leaders for their own self-enrichment, at the expense of the dock workers whom they purported to lead. He found, also, that they were engaging in criminal activities of various sorts, from which they might expect to get relative immunity from prosecution because of their personal relationship with the mayors and police chiefs of the two waterfront cities, and their participation in the political machine which ruled these cities.

It was entirely on his own initiative, as a reporter with a long nose for the "why" of the news stories he was covering, that Greene began to follow this trail. The trail led him inevitably to Father Corridan on the West Side of Manhattan as a source of information on the personal backgrounds of the men whose activities he was studying, and for tips on daily news stories.

Greene became the outstanding authority on waterfront crime and politics in northern New Jersey—so much of an authority that at one time he was indicted by a political grand jury and then exonerated. He wound up as a special investigator for the New York City Anti-Crime Committee, with which he works today.

"As I see it," Mr. Greene says, "for many years the Jersey piers and the New York West Side piers have been virtually synchronized as parts of a single machine, largely political, in control of large segments of business along the Hudson River waterfront. Take William, or 'Big Bill,' McCormack, who became renowned as the 'Mr. Big' of the whole port, and his late brother, Harry, who was for some years of his life active in labor-union politics with the teamsters. They started their careers in Jersey City, where they were engaged in the highly profitable business of unloading fruit in the New Jersey railroads. Then they went in for their beef-loading operations on the New York West Side.

"It was during their work in Jersey City that they first became acquainted with Mayor Frank Hague, for many years the boss of Hudson County. Later they became very close to him, personally. Peter and Mike Costello also went from control of the Hoboken waterfront to eventual control of the New York Produce Market. To get this control they depended on the political influence of such persons as the late Mayor Bernard McFeeley of Hoboken, Mayor Hague, and the two McCormack brothers, Harry and Bill.

"Now it's been a truism for a generation that Mayor Hague was the absolute political boss of Jersey City. His rule reached out over Hoboken to a large degree. Mayor Hague originally came from the second ward of Jersey City. That's the waterfront ward. He knew from boyhood that more than two thirds of the land area of Jersey City is occupied by the railroads and the docks to which they lead. He knew also that all the major commerce of Jersey City depended on those railroads and those piers. He recognized the fact that to control his city he must control what went on in those railroad yards and along those piers. Once he did that, his rule could be absolute.

"During the 1930's Mayor Hague delegated control of those areas to his most trusted lieutenants. These included his second-ward leader, John V. Kenny, who later became Mayor, 'Shagger' Crimmins, and James 'Happy' Keane. Kenny directed the political aspects of the pier operations. He saw that the people who worked on the piers voted right, and he got jobs for dock workers. 'Shagger' Crimmins was the I.L.A. delegate of Local 1,247. 'Happy' Keane directed loading operations. He was the boss loader.

"This order, as established on the piers of Mayor Hague, was militantly enforced by his Police Department with night sticks. No opposition was tolerated, from the first, and after a while no opposition was ever encountered. The McFeeley machine in Hoboken functioned almost as a subsidiary operation to the Hague machine in Jersey City. Hague was King of the whole county. McFeeley was, maybe, the Duke of Hoboken.

"Hague's empire was solidly entrenched because of his close relations with Big Bill McCormack and Joe Ryan in Manhattan. Big Bill has always done business in New Jersey under most favorable conditions. Because of Hague's friendship, Ryan has always been able to count on a pro-Ryan delegation in the I.L.A. local officials of Hudson County.

"It wasn't until the Hague grip had loosened that Charley 'the Jew' Yanowsky, was able to move in, by sheer muscle, along the Jersey waterfront, as the real power behind the I.L.A. locals, or that Eddie Florio, the former bootlegger, was able to become the real power in the I.L.A. locals of Hoboken. As long as Hague was in power, he had as his police commissioner Daniel Casey, a former member of the teamsters' union on New York's West Side.

"Casey wouldn't have an Alcatraz graduate like Yanowsky around. In fact, an order was quietly given at one time that if ever Yanowsky showed his face on the Jersey City waterfront he was to be thrown into jail. That happened several times. It wasn't until after Hague left the mayoralty to his nephew, Frank Eggers, and Kenny took it away from Eggers, that Yanowsky got his real grip on waterfront labor.

"Yanowsky was in the political camp of Mayor Kenny, who, as second-ward leader, worked with him very closely on waterfront matters when he was out for the mayoralty. When Yanowsky was ice-picked to death in 1948, one of the first moves of the Kenny organization was to set up his brother-in-law, Frank 'Biffo' Di Lorenzo, as I.L.A. delegate from Jersey City's Local 1,247.

"Di Lorenzo, upon his rise to union leadership, as the heir to his criminal brother-in-law, surrounded himself with most of Yanowsky's old lieutenants, Barney 'Cockeye' Brown, George 'the Rape Artist' Donahue, Steve Wilson, and Anthony 'Slim' Lucey.

"Within a month after Kenny's election to the mayoralty in

1949, this gang went down to the piers and demanded the resignation of 'Happy' Keane, Mayor Hague's old lieutenant, as boss loader of Pier D, which served the American Export Line's piers, D and F. The American Export Line refused to oust Keane. The new gang running the I.L.A. on the Jersey docks then called a strike which shut down a large section of the port for about six weeks. A compromise settled the strike. One of Di Lorenzo's friends took over the loading on Pier D, while an old lieutenant of Keane's, Neil McKeon, kept Pier F."

On the night of December 5, 1950, as Greene remembers it, he was sitting in the offices of the Jersey *Journal* when he received a telephone call from a voice which gave the name of George Donahue. The voice named Donahue, purporting to come from George "the Rape Artist" Donahue, told him that an election had been held in Local 1,247 of the I.L.A., in which Di Lorenzo and "Slim" Lucey had been voted out of office and replaced by three men. These were no other than Donahue himself with a man named Barney Brown and one Anthony Marchitto, alias Tony Cheese.

"I didn't buy that," Greene says now. "By that time I had developed quite a few waterfront contacts of my own, so I checked on the facts, and this is what my informants agreed on as the real story of what had happened. There was then a man named Morris Manna, an old-time bootlegger, and a prominent member of the Italian mobs in the New Jersey underworld with a long criminal record. He had determined to move in on the waterfront. This Morris Manna was a close friend of Albert Anastasia, of Murder, Inc., and another Italian mobster named Anthony Strollo, alias Tony Bender.

"Before Donahue phoned me, he, Manna, and Barney Brown had walked into the I.L.A. headquarters on Grand Street. They demanded the resignations of Di Lorenzo and Lucey. Di Lorenzo and Lucey refused to give them. Donahue pulled a gun. At pistol point Di Lorenzo signed his resignation. Lucey refused. Someone knocked Lucey's front teeth out with a gun butt. Then Lucey signed.

"Then they demanded that Lucey open the office safe, but he

refused, despite torture. They finally left. They had control of the union but not of whatever records or money were in the safe. I printed this whole story on the front page of the Jersey *Journal,* on the basis of what my informants had told me. The newspaper demanded a police investigation. No investigation was made.

"I began to check into the background of this union and its political tie-ups more closely. I found that old Charley Yanowsky, the Alcatraz boy, had been a close pal of members of a New York gang called 'The Arsenal Mob.' One of the leaders in that mob was a gangster named Albert Ackalitis, who was prominent on the docks on the West Side of New York. Ackalitis was the real power behind the Di Lorenzo gang in Jersey City, after Yanowsky was slain. When Acky rose to power over the Di Lorenzo mob, he was on parole from Sing Sing, where he had been sent for possession of a machine gun. Although the terms of his parole were such that they forbade him to make a trip to Jersey City, all he had to do to make his power felt over Di Lorenzo was one quick trip once in a while. At other times he would telephone his orders to Di Lorenzo to a tavern on Mercer Street, Jersey City, known as 'Joe the Rebel's.'

"How did he control Di Lorenzo? By terror. Nothing but terror. Di Lorenzo was scared to death of him.

"Just about a month before the Manna mob muscled Di Lorenzo and 'Slim' Lucey out of office, Ackalitis had been sent back to Sing Sing for violation of parole. With Ackalitis out of the way, Manna's project of pushing Di Lorenzo out of office by sheer thuggery was easy.

"If Ackalitis had been around, Manna probably never would have attempted it. Di Lorenzo had been close enough to the Kenny organization so that one might have expected the politicians to back him. But he never was really very smart. He had embarrassed the organization by some pretty loose statements to the press and didn't have any real friends in political circles. He managed to get the I.L.A. to call a special election in Jersey City, however, and the election campaign was fought out on gangster lines. The election was scheduled for March 5, 1951. On January 28, 1951, a bomb went off under the hood of Donahue's automobile when he pressed the starter button. He escaped, miraculously, unhurt. But the blast, which knocked out windows in a fine residential section of Jersey City, served to call public attention to the fact that gangland's election methods were operating as usual. On March 2, three days before election, a bomb was thrown into I.L.A. headquarters, and three men, including Barney Brown, then president of the local, and Armand Faugno, its secretary-treasurer, two of Manna's lieutenants, were sent to Medical Center, badly injured.

"Just before Donahue's car was bombed, I had written stories to the effect that he and Louis Manna were the mob enforcers on the piers and were using guns to keep the men in line. I also wrote four or five stories outlining the criminal records of the men who controlled the union; named Manna as the boss of the piers and Walter Marcinski as the leading loan shark. The Jersey *Journal* kept demanding an investigation. After the bombing of I.L.A. headquarters, one was started. Nothing came of it."

Although the celebrated Kefauver committee hearings on nationwide racketeering brushed but lightly on the subject of the New York waterfront, the committee's interim report of April 17, 1951, was outspoken in its denunciation of the crime-ridden I.L.A. After being rampant in the 1920's and 1930's, "hoodlum penetration of labor unions has decreased steadily over the years," it said. "Today, however, the hoodlum element has been driven to the wall in all but a few important instances. One union which is still infested with hoodlums is the International Longshoremen's Union on the East Coast.

"Here, after twenty years of repeated efforts to correct conditions there still persists one of the ugliest situations in labor-union history."

The first man, actually, to name William McCormack as "Mr. Big" of the New York waterfront in any publication of wide circulation, and to publish some of the accusations which McCormack later denied in testimony before the New York State Crime Commission, was Westbrook Pegler, columnist for the Hearst newspapers. As far back as 1941 he had told the story of an anonymous "Mr. Big" dominating the teamsters' and longshoremen's unions and ruling in business enterprises requiring a great deal of political and union support for successful management. Early in 1951, as the hue and cry about waterfront corruption was making it an issue of national interest, Pegler named McCormack to his readers.

But in 1951 McCormack hired a press agent named Robin Harris, who succeeded in getting a highly eulogistic article placed in the *Daily News* concerning his patron. An effort was being made at that time to get a similar feature article or articles, redounding to Mr. McCormack's credit, in the New York *Times*. One of the *Times'* star writing men, Meyer Berger, was assigned to visit McCormack and to prepare material about his spectacular career, since in any detail it was almost completely unknown to the public at large.

Berger spent several hours interviewing McCormack. He emerged from the interview impressed with the man's personality, his obvious vast abilities, and the fact that he would be able to hold his own, in public controversy, with almost anyone questioning him. Before Berger had completed his researches, however, the *Daily News* had printed its eulogy. The *Times* backed away and printed nothing.

From this time on more and more newspaper, magazine, radio, and television reporters found their way to Father Corridan's offices at the Xavier School.

Budd Schulberg, the author of *What Makes Sammy Run?* and *The Disenchanted,* first arrived in 1949 and kept coming back. Schulberg had read the Malcolm Johnson series in the *Sun,* and the idea of Johnson's "lawless frontier," within a few blocks of Sardi's and Toots Shor's restaurant fascinated him. So did the idea of a "waterfront priest." Schulberg met Johnson and then met Father Corridan. Father Corridan introduced him to "Brownie," the longshoreman. Schulberg never had met anyone like "Brownie" in his life, and before long these two became a mutual-admiration society.

They toured the waterfront. Gradually Schulberg became obsessed with the story of a motion picture which turned out, five years later, to be *On the Waterfront.* Before that motion picture was produced, Schulberg had written eight scripts and submitted the idea to every major motion picture company in Hollywood. Early in his development of the picture he had found a firm ally in Elia Kazan, the director, who wanted to direct it as badly as Schulberg wanted to write it.

For a long time the bigwigs of the studios considered the story too grim, too forbidding, or too hot to handle. There was some question whether unionized cameramen would not sabotage a picture dealing with corruptions of unionism. At one point they had a tentative agreement with Darryl Zanuck to produce the picture, only to have Zanuck change his mind. At this point, as they were discussing their plight in a Los Angeles hotel and wondering whether they shouldn't turn to Broadway and the legitimate theater for a dramatization of their story, they were joined by an independent producer named Sam Spiegel, who lived across the hall. Spiegel listened to their troubles. "I'll produce your picture," he said, and he did. It finally was released by Columbia Pictures, one of the companies that originally had turned it down.

During the making of the picture, on the Hoboken waterfront, Father Corridan was a technical adviser. Through his friend, Austin Tobin, of the New York Port Authority, the producer obtained the use of the Hoboken dock where the picture was shot. Real longshoremen were brought into the production to play themselves.

It was with Father Corridan's advice and help that Dan Bell, labor editor of *Fortune* magazine, wrote trenchantly of waterfront rackets. Murray Kempton, columnist for the New York *Post,* Joe Alvarez of the New York *World-Telegram,* Dick Roth of the Brooklyn *Daily Eagle,* and the late Louis Stark of the New York *Times* editorial board, all consulted him. Father Corridan says that Roth's writings in the Brooklyn *Eagle* were particularly helpful, since Brooklyn harbors the greater part of New York's freighters, and the power of the Anastasia family is mighty along its wharves.

Jules Weinberg for *Look* magazine, Lester Velie for *Collier's,* Dick Carter for *True* magazine, Dennis Howard for *Jubilee,* a Catholic pictorial magazine, Kathleen Donahue for *Time* magazine, and Earl Brown for *Life* magazine, all helped him. Mary Heaton Vorse, an outstanding writer on labor matters for more than a generation, gathered from him much of her material for *The Pirate's Nest of New York,* which *The Reader's Digest* reprinted from *Harper's* magazine.

In the radio and television fields he found willing collaborators in Tex McCrary and Jinx Falkenberg of NBC, Bill Leonard, Irving Gitlin, and Doug Edwards of the Columbia Broadcasting System, and Taylor Grant of ABC News.

In this way, by working through all established mass media of news dissemination, Father Corridan was able to make his influence felt in molding the opinions of many millions of persons who never heard of him personally. For any appraisal of the priest's career through these years of labor, one fact must be set down as highly pertinent. Within the parochial field to which he had been called, he proved himself a master propagandist.

CHAPTER

11

THE STRIKE THAT TURNED THE TIDE

*The wildcat strike of 1951 will always stand out in Father Cor-*ridan's memory as the one crucial struggle in which the tide of battle was turned against the enemy. After that rough-and-tumble conflict Joe Ryan's union was always on the defensive, fighting rear-guard actions to stave off defeat and dissolution.

The defeat of mobster rule in waterfront unionism appeared inevitable to him after the strike, though the rebel unionists who led it fought without victory. Because of this strike the powers of government were brought publicly to examine what had caused it and what had caused all the others which were ruining the harbor.

Only by the active intervention either of the federal government or of the two state governments of New York and New Jersey, Father Corridan maintained, could the dock workers ever gain power enough to overthrow the men who were oppressing them. It was in local politics that the mobsters were firmly entrenched.

Looking back on the struggle today, Father Corridan realizes that the intervention of state and federal administrations could not have been brought about if these higher-up governmental authorities had been parts of the same political machine that dominated the port of New York cities. These municipal machines were all part of the Democratic Party. The landslide for President Eisenhower in 1952 in the nation's voting, coupled with the presence of two Republican governors, Thomas E. Dewey and Alfred E. Driscoll, in Albany and Trenton, made conditions ripe for the final overthrow of Joe Ryan & Co.

Within the framework of Father Corridan's personal career, two events within that strike of 1951 stand out. The first of these was a public prayer he delivered on behalf of the strikers, in their strike committee headquarters, when they were being assailed by influential foes as Communist-led. That public prayer cast a great deal of doubt in many minds as to whether the charges of Communist leadership made against the strikers could possibly be justified, because there in their midst stood a priest of the Church of Rome as their champion and friend. During the 1951 strike, also, when he was ardently and publicly championing the cause of the dock workers, he was called before Cardinal Spellman, at the chancery of the Archdiocese of New York, to answer charges that had been brought against him by a clergyman of his own faith, of higher rank than his within the church, who had been for many years a close personal friend of Joe Ryan. Father Corridan had foreseen this attack from within the very organization to which his life's work and loyalty had been devoted long before it happened. It had even been predicted to him.

The prelude to wage negotiations between the New York Shipping Association and the 125-man wage-scale committee of Joe Ryan's union, which brought on the rebellion of 1951 by the rank and file, was markedly similar to the general pattern of wage negotiations that preceded the rebellions of 1945 and 1948. The union representatives demanded an increase in wages of 25 cents an hour in the straight-time rate, from two dollars to two-twenty-five, with proportionate raises in overtime and specific commodity rates. They demanded one shape a day instead of two, with a guarantee of at least four hours of work at each hiring, 12 paid holidays a year, one week's vacation after 500 hours of work instead of after 800 hours, as was previously the rule, and the establishment of infirmaries at the piers.

The union demands were first presented to J. V. Lyon of the shipping association on Monday, September 10. Although it was announced to the press that progress was being made toward a new agreement, fear was expressed that negotiations would not be completed in time for ratification by the deadline of September 30, when the old contract would expire. Because of this, federal mediators intervened on September 27. They asked both parties to continue negotiations past this formal deadline, "so that the flow of vitally important cargo through the port will not be interrupted." Employers and union leaders agreed.

On Monday, October 8, an agreement was reached providing for an increase of ten cents in the hourly wage rate; a slight reduction in the hours required to be worked before a longshoreman would become eligible for vacation pay; the single shape, with guarantee of four hours' work. On Wednesday, October 10, the I.L.A. distributed 60,000 copies of a special edition of the *Longshore News* to the membership, containing a summary of the new agreement. On Thursday, October 11, a vote on ratification was supposedly taken in every local, although the vote was a fiction in many locals. The result, as announced by Joe Ryan to the press and communicated to the employers' association in a telegram, was a two-to-one vote in favor of ratification. Several locals in New York, including 791 in Chelsea, had voted not to ratify.

On Monday, October 15, dock workers of Local 791 refused to face the daily shape-up at 7:55 A.M., and the costliest wildcat strike in the history of the harbor up to that time was under way.

The strike lasted 25 days. At its close there were 118 piers tied up, with 84 ships lying idle in them. Thirty thousand men went without pay for almost a month. The usual rail embargo delayed freight from the Midwest destined for overseas shipment. Estimates of cost to the port ran as always to many millions of dollars.

Before the strike was ended, Father Corridan was accused by enemies of having started it. "I didn't start it," he says. "Quite the contrary. I argued against it. I advised those men who were closest to me that it would pay the rank and file better to go along with the contract. There didn't seem to me at the time any chance that the rank and file, with the union machinery then in force, could possibly make as their principal demands a decent hiring system and an effective system of seniority rights for men of long service on the waterfront, or a closing of the union's books to get rid of the chronic surplus of labor. The only thing a strike might bring them, I argued, was a slight improvement in the hourly wage rate. I didn't believe a strike would be justified with only that single goal.

"They had a ten-cent rise in the hourly rate. Maybe they might get a few cents more by striking. I told them bluntly I didn't believe that a strike tying up the whole New York waterfront and doing the vast damage to countless people that a walkout in such an essential industry as longshoring would do, could be justified on the single issue of a few cents more hourly pay. I've never believed it. I didn't then, and I don't now.

"I suppose people might ask me why—after telling the men the strike wouldn't be justified—I turned right around and backed them in it, and fought on their side. When the strike broke, as it did, it wasn't a money issue. It wasn't just for a few cents' more pay. It was the spontaneous rebellion of the rank and file, for the most part, against that filthy relationship which existed between a spurious union and a compliant industry.

"The men were certainly right that the contract had not been properly negotiated and ratified. Once they walked out, I believed that their union leaders and the shipping association would either have to capitulate and renegotiate the contract or endure such a strike that the government would be compelled to move toward full intervention. If my judgment on that matter were proved to be true, a long step would be taken toward the destruction of the old racket-ridden I.L.A. and the creation of a decent, honest, democratic trade union to take its place. That was what I was working for.

"I talked to Father Carey and with William J. Keating of the New York City Anti-Crime Committee. They both concurred in my judgment. Besides that, I had growing confidence in some of the men who were on that strike committee, particularly Johnny Dwyer, 'Bibbles' Barrieo, and a few others. Once they were in it, I was with them absolutely, heart and soul, even though I was praying for some break that might cut the strike as short as possible.

"For the first week of the strike, of course, we had to fight hard against the outcry that was always raised by Joe Ryan whenever there was a strike against his leadership. Joe proclaimed loudly that the Communists were back of it. Two newspapers, each influential in different fields, echoed Joe's version of it. One was the New York *Herald Tribune*. In its editorial columns on Thursday, October 18, the fourth day of the strike, it said: 'The Brooklyn walkout quite obviously is inspired by Communist agitators bent on their usual disruptive tactics.' Later on that same day Colonel I. W. Lytell of the Brooklyn Army Base disputed that statement. The strike, he said, was not Communist-inspired. He found that the strikers had nothing against the Army, but were sore at Joe Ryan's leadership. The colonel was absolutely correct. But the mere statement of an army colonel does not gain the public credence of an editorial in the New York *Herald Tribune*.

"How did Ryan spread the word of Communist influence? On the very second day of the strike he issued a statement to the press, saying, 'It looks like Harry Bridges is making his last shot for control of the entire American waterfront.' The *Daily Mirror* editorial a few days later reflected this view. It asked editorially, 'Does Harry Bridges run the United States of America?' The men were so mad that they picketed the *Mirror*. A delegation called on the editor, and the editor retracted his editorial as ill-informed.

"Yet as late as October 30, the sixteenth day of the strike, Captain William Bradley, then head of the tugboat local of the I.L.A. and later to become Joe Ryan's successor as president of the whole I.L.A., was taking out advertisements in all the New York newspapers, denouncing the strike as Communist-inspired.

"From my own vantage point I knew better. As everybody knows, one of the reasons I am in the work I am doing is to fight Communist penetration of labor unions. I have plenty of sources of information about what the Communists are doing any time they are active on the waterfront. From my vantage point I found that this was the pattern of Communist activity during the strike:

"For the first week the Commies were conspicuous by their silence and inactivity. From people I believe to be reliable I learned that it was the Communist Party's original plan to lock up their mimeograph machines during the strike and to infiltrate the rank-and-file strike committees, for purposes of sabotage later on. At the end of the first week, however, they changed their strategy. Batches of Communist Party leaflets began to appear on the waterfront, with an obvious attempt to remove all telltale signs of their origin.

"Then the party tried to louse up the men by organizing phony food drives for strikers outside some of the supermarkets. The non-Communist longshoremen chased them away. In Brooklyn, where an attempted food delivery for strikers was made in a poor neighborhood by C.P. agents, our men dumped the food into the Gowanus Canal, even though some of their families could have used it.

"Attempts at infiltration were at all times blocked by the rank and file, who as everybody knows are 90 per cent Roman Catholic. Gradually news stories about the strike came to discount this Communist Party angle almost completely. Reporters who helped particularly to set the public straight were Murray Kempton of the *Post,* Dick Roth of the Brooklyn *Eagle,* Joe Alvarez of the *World-Telegram,* George Cable Wright of the New York *Times,* and Eddie Markel of the *Mirror.* Bill Keating and Bob Greene of the Anti-Crime Committee worked around the clock, keeping up with every waterfront development and keeping in touch with the press.

"There was one phase of the strike that clouded the picture. It was the participation on the side of the rank and file of a few of the ambitious mobsters, who were then bucking higher-up mobsters in the I.L.A. leadership. They were using the strike to gain their own ends.

"One of these was a hoodlum named Johnny Scanlon, and the other principal one was the iniquitous Albert Ackalitis, then serving a term in Dannemora. 'Acky' was sure some of the higher-up mobsters in the I.L.A. had got him sent back to prison on a parole violator's rap. So he sent word from the prison to Tony 'Cheese' Marchitto, boss of the Jersey City longshore local, to get all his men off the piers and keep them off, even though Ryan, Bradley, & Co. were trying to keep them at work. Tony 'Cheese,' of course, didn't dare stand up to 'Acky,' even though 'Acky' was in Dannemora. He was coming out soon."

In its early stages the strike was much like the big wildcatter of 1948. It was sparked from Chelsea Local 791. It was spearheaded by a local predominantly of Irish stock. Members remembered Ryan and McCormack well.

In the first days of the strike three other locals in Manhattan joined Local 791, of which John J. "Gene" Sampson had for some years been leader. Mr. Sampson, in some newspaper circles had come to be known as "Joe Ryan's loyal opposition." He could normally be counted upon to be a front man for Local 791, at the start of any fight against the Big Fellow, though he would make peace before very long. In the 1951 strike, however, he had young, tough Johnny Dwyer very close to him. Dwyer was beginning to make his own reputation on the waterfront as a man who would face up to the mobsters, whoever they might be.

Johnny Scanlon was also a member of Local 791. It seemed to Father Corridan as if this 31-year-old hoodlum might rise to eminence on the waterfront by the same methods that had brought "Cockeye" Dunn to power.

Born in the Chelsea area, in a slum district, young Scanlon had plenty of brawn and was known in boyhood as a good man with his fists. His mother died when he was 12. At 15 he was haled before the children's court for a minor offense. By 1942, he had been tried twice for assault and robbery and served a term in Elmira. He became the undisputed leader of a gang of street-corner toughies and, in 1947, had established his reputation pretty solidly by beating a charge of homicide. During that year young Scanlon had talked disagreeably to some young Italian kids just as tough as he and been beaten up for his pains. A few nights after the beating someone just about Scanlon's height, weight, and general appearance, dressed the way Scanlon usually was dressed, walked into the Italian neighborhood on West 10th Street. He drew a pistol and fired several times at a group of Italians seated outside a tenement doorway. One old woman, 65 years old, was killed and two teen-agers were wounded.

Back in his own area, Scanlon bragged that he had gained his revenge. He was arrested for murder, tried, and set free by directed acquittal when key witnesses, one a son of the old lady slain, lost their memories.

Thereafter everyone in the neighborhood knew that Scanlon was a man to be reckoned with. Those who knew the waterfront marked him for a potential hiring boss. When the strike opened, Bob Greene, then a Jersey City reporter, commented that "young Scanlon is poised, ready to challenge 'Gene' Sampson for his share of the North River." Actually, for some reason never yet revealed, young Scanlon never made the challenge. On the twentieth day of the strike he changed his mind about its wisdom. He signed a back-to-work petition among the members of Local 791, and thereafter his influence on the Chelsea waterfront was done.

Scanlon never had Johnny Dunn's toughness. To be sure, he and a couple of his cronies beat up two longshoremen shortly after the strike in a West 14th Street saloon—one of them so badly that he lay for two weeks in a hospital with a crushed skull. He pleaded guilty and was sentenced to Sing Sing for five years. But all the waterfront knew by then that Scanlon was not of the caliber with which waterfront rulers had historically been endowed. The day, indeed, when men could rise to eminence on the docks by sheer terror was gradually passing.

It took the strike committee a week to close every pier in the harbor. With 136 piers shut down, 104 ships lying idle, and 3600 railroad cars tied up, Cyrus Ching, as chief federal mediator, sent his ace trouble shooter, Clyde Mills, into the area, to see if he could help bring on a settlement. It took Mills and his aides only two days to report back that they would be helpless in the situation. By this time the strike had reached such proportions that President Truman called a special cabinet meeting to deal with it. After the meeting it was announced that the President had declined to invoke the injunction powers of the Taft-Hartley Law, of which he was a bitter critic. The most he would do was to ask the men to return to their work, "in the national interest."

The men refused. Instead of showing signs of going back to work, they picketed City Hall in downtown Manhattan, 500 strong, protesting the action of the city police in driving their pickets away from the Brooklyn Army Base. This demonstration had only one major result. It drew into the movement of longshore rebels a young lawyer named Peter Johnson, whose father had been a longshoreman. Peter Johnson, himself, had worked on the docks, but he had studied law after returning to the United States from armed combat as a marine in World War II. Johnson, known widely as "Pete" in dockside society, was trying a case in the City Court just back of City Hall, when he heard the demonstrators. He looked out and saw the mackinaws, sweaters, and caps of his West Side boyhood companions. As soon as he was able, he got an adjournment of his case from the judge and went out to join them.

"Hey, Pete, we need a lawyer," one of the strikers told him. Johnson joined up as lawyer for the strike committee, without any pay, and served them with no pay till well after the strike. He served them, indeed, through long sessions of a State Board of Inquiry. The board was appointed by Industrial Commissioner Edward Corsi, and it finally brought the strike to a close. Some time after the strike was ended, a cigar box filled with coins and small bills was brought to Johnson's home one night, as a fee raised by the men he had served. From that day on Johnson was lawyer for the rebel element among the longshoremen, out to buck Joe Ryan's union and organize one that would really meet their needs.

The third week of the strike was crucial both for Ryan's predominant faction in the old I.L.A. and the rebels who had closed the harbor. On Sunday, October 28, Johnny Dwyer and "Gene" Sampson, as cochairmen of the strike committee, wired President Truman an offer to call off the stoppage if he would order an investigation of the strikers' grievances against their own union leadership. Ryan countered with a telegram to the President, saying the strike was practically ended. "We'll have the harbor working tomorrow," he promised the President, and renewed his charges that only the Communists were running the walkout. In an interview with the press Ryan swore that his men would break the rebel picket lines the following day.

"We'll go through them and over them," he said, "but never around them."

Bloodshed seemed imminent. Extra-heavy concentrations of police were thrown around all the docks. At this juncture Father Corridan, hoping for a presidential intervention that never came, determined to dramatize once and for all the fact that the rebellion was not Communist-led. He decided that early on the following morning, Monday, October 29, he would go down to strike headquarters and publicly pray with and for the men who were striking.

During the week end, he had been working with Keating and James Walsh of the New York City Anti-Crime Committee on a telegram for its chairman, former Ambassador Spruille Braden, to send to Governor Dewey, urging the Governor's intervention to end the strike and to bring about a real inquiry into its causes.

"That Sunday I had spent mostly at my mother's home," Father Corridan remembers, "but I got a telephone call from Bill Keating when I returned to Xavier at 11 P.M. Bill asked me if I could come up to Spruille Braden's place and go over the final draft of the wire to the Governor. I took a taxicab and went up there. All through the ride I was deeply depressed. I desperately wanted that strike to be ended, but I wanted the men to get what was rightfully theirs. I was deeply concerned at the prospect of violence. I was afraid that the rebels would doubtless be blamed for it, particularly because of the false stigma of Communist leadership placed upon them by Ryan and the mob for whom Ryan fronted.

"The idea of going down to the waterfront and praying publicly for peace with honor for the men who had fought a good fight in a good cause came to me as I was riding up to Braden's in the cab. I mentioned the idea to Bill Keating, and he thought it was good. I telephoned 'Brownie.' I told him I was coming down to 791's union rooms the following morning at 6 A.M. I asked him to call up some of the men and tell them to be there. Brownie put the calls through.

"When the final draft of the telegram to Governor Dewey was finished I went back to Xavier. It was then about 1 A.M. At 3 A.M. I called up the Associated Press and told them what I was going to do. I knew the AP would notify all the papers. I knew also that the AP would check back by telephone just to make sure they were really being called by Father Corridan from Xavier's and not from somebody in a bar and grill. It so happened that the telephone switchboard was shut down at the school. I had to wake up Father McCarthy and young Father Robert Finley before we got it working. We finally did. The AP call came through.

"Then I went up to my room and sat down in a chair. I smoked a couple of cigarettes and worked out my prayer. I made it very short. These were the words:

" 'God grant that our government may order us back to work in honor. May God protect and preserve us this day. God bless you all.'

"At 4:45 A.M. I shaved and showered and headed for the waterfront. The meeting room was at 164 11th Avenue. Just as I expected, the newspaper reporters and photographers were there. My friends, the longshoremen, wouldn't let the photographers take pictures from the front of the room. There were about 300 men in the room, and a good many of them didn't want their pictures taken. You always have to remember that fear walks that area. The room was pretty noisy when I entered, but quieted down immediately. I told the men what I was going to do, and asked them to repeat the words after me.

"They did—phrase by phrase. 'God grant that our government may order us back to work in honor. May God protect and preserve us this day.' I certainly will always remember those men and will always hear their voices as they repeated the words.

"It didn't take long—just a few minutes, and I walked out of the hall. As I went out, one man grabbed my hand and said, 'Father, I want to thank you from the bottom of my heart.'

"Several people offered to drive me back to the rectory, and I went with one of them. I reported to the acting rector, Father Rowley, what I had done, and then went to see Father Carey, without whose help I never could have done anything.

"All he said was, 'God bless you, Pete.'

"The prayer certainly had the effect I intended. The *World-Telegram* carried the pictures on page one. The *Journal-American* and the *Post* carried the story. I know that it put new heart into a good many of the men on the waterfront. It even led to an editorial in the *Mirror,* rebuking Ryan for his charge of communism against the men.

"That editorial was entitled 'Tyranny's Twilight.' 'Ryan's anguished cry of communism,' the *Mirror* said, 'is answered by a soft-spoken, earnest Catholic priest, who leads the insurgent strikers in prayer. Whatever happens this week, Joe Ryan is through. The terror by which he has maintained his control can never be quite so terrifying again.'

"Of course, Ryan wasn't quite through. But his downfall was coming. Just as I have an absolute faith that someday the rule of the mob will fall—even though it still lingers today. It'll fall down some day."

The very afternoon of the prayer Spruille Braden held a press conference and read his telegram to Governor Dewey asking intervention. The Governor sent in Merlyn S. Pitzele, labor editor of *Business Week* and chairman of the State Mediation Board, to see what he could do to bring about a settlement. Mr. Pitzele met with all parties to the dispute and then told Governor Dewey that settlement was so far away that the whole dispute should be certified under New York's labor law to Industrial Commissioner Edward Corsi as having created "a state of emergency." Under that law Commissioner Corsi was instructed to appoint a Board of Inquiry. The board was appointed. It consisted of M. P. Catherwood, chairman, the Right Reverend John P. Boland, and Dean Alfange. George J. Mintzer was its counsel.

The board began hearings swiftly, but it was badly handicapped. It had dubious powers of subpoena. It was forced to rely on the voluntary cooperation of all the principals in the dispute, the old I.L.A., the shipping association, and the rebel strikers. Young Peter Johnson conducted the case for the rebels before the board and was able to bring about a dozen longshoremen before it to testify as to their grievances against the union leadership. One of the major witnesses was Edward Barry, who later became business agent of the coopers' union, within the I.L.A.

Louis Waldman, veteran labor lawyer, conducted the case for the I.L.A. One of the highlights in the hearing, as Father Corridan remembers, was the testimony of Barry that many locals in the union had never been able to hold elections or even meetings, and that frequent complaints against these conditions had gone unnoticed by the I.L.A. president. Barry attended the hearings in longshoreman's garb, in which his red sweater was the most colorful note. After his testimony about lack of democratic procedures within the union, Waldman cross-examined him. Under instructions from Johnson, Barry had held his fire as to proof of what he had been saying in direct testimony.

"Have you any proof of complaints that were made to Mr. Ryan that remained unanswered?" Waldman asked him.

Barry drew a long file of correspondence from the depths of his sweater and the proof was made.

Father Corridan believes the findings of that Board of Inquiry to be the one great victory won by the rebels in the strike of 1951. For the first time in history a governmental board had listened to testimony concerning the I.L.A. and condemned it officially. The board's report validated on a governmental level all the complaints that the rank-and-file rebels from the Lower West Side had been making against Ryan & Co. The board also was acidly critical of the New York Shipping Association.

In regard to the I.L.A., the board's principal findings were as follows:

1. There was continuous failure over many years by union leaders to maintain democratic standards and procedures in their locals.

2. In many locals there was a failure to hold regular elections, and some locals had been without an election for as long as ten years.

3. Some locals failed to keep bank accounts or to give any accounting to members of dues collected. One local that the board examined had failed to keep any accounts for 16 years, although collecting about 25,000 dollars a year in dues from members.

4. Many locals had failed over many years to hold any meetings.

5. There was a failure in many locals to elect delegates to the wage-scale conference, as required under the union's constitution.

6. Many locals failed to keep records, particularly financial records.

7. There was a failure within I.L.A. locals to bond officers handling funds, even though the constitution of the I.L.A. required it.

8. There were no audits by certified public accountants in many locals.

9. The I.L.A. had failed to correct obviously untenable practices within the longshore and loading industries, whereby officers of the unions were employers of the men they purported to represent.

In summation, the board said of the I.L.A.:

"The board finds that there is an urgent responsibility incumbent on the International Longshoremen's Association to clean its own house. If it fails to fulfill this elementary obligation, it will have failed to do its share in removing the causes that produce costly disturbances on the waterfront."

The board also found, as a matter of fact, that the 1951 strike was not the result of Communist agitation but of long-standing and festering grievances among the rank-and-file workers.

As for the New York Shipping Association, the board had this criticism to make of its members: "Although the time available and the nature of the assignment did not make it possible for the board to explore fully the position of all elements in the shipping industry, the board was disturbed by some of the impressions it received. Substantial sections of the shipping industry seemed to the board to condone practices and abuses which cannot be justified from a moral standpoint. This may be due to apathy, to fear of reprisals, or to financial advantage."

The Board of Inquiry was particularly outspoken on the effect of tolerated crime along the docks. "Many of the conditions on the waterfront," it said, "are a sad commentary not only on the business and labor organizations which have been responsible for, or have tolerated them, but also on the governmental and community forces which have permitted them to exist.

"Criminal activities are economically injurious to the port of New York, and may threaten its pre-eminence as the leading port in the United States. It is clear that if pilferage, extortion, kickbacks, and other rackets that result in excessive charges are allowed to continue and grow, they will force a substantial part of the shipping, both import and export, to be diverted to other ports with injurious consequences to the economy of the city and state of New York."

Before the board reached these conclusions, Father Corridan was called in as a consultant, and the conclusions were a plain statement of his viewpoint. On Friday, November 9, after the strike had lasted 25 days, the members of the Board of Inquiry persuaded the strike committee to end it. It took an all-night session to bring the committee into agreement, and there were compelling circumstances, entirely outside the persuasive powers of the Board of Inquiry, that forced the committeemen to surrender.

On the day before, the Superior Court of New Jersey granted a temporary injunction barring New York pickets from any docks in New Jersey used by members of the N.Y.S.A. The strike in New Jersey immediately collapsed. After 25 days of idleness the strikers themselves were hungry. Their families were clamoring for them to go back to work. Family funds were short or nonexistent. The strike committee had operated from the beginning without any war chest and could give no aid.

The strike committee agreed to lead the men back to work, on assurances of the board that it would see that strikers got fair treatment on their return to the piers. The men were also told that their grievances would be completely publicized in the forthcoming board report. But this was cold comfort. The only finding of the board that the strike committee wanted was one which it was unable to get: They wanted the board to find that the contract against which they complained had been improperly negotiated and ratified, and that therefore their walkout had been justified. They wanted the board to find that a new contract should be negotiated and ratified in accordance with fair, democratic, and constitutional procedure. That was what they wanted. That was what they had struck to obtain. They failed to get it.

When the board's final report was made public, its finding on the issue of proper ratification of the contract was as follows: "On the basis of the evidence adduced at the public hearings and the board's investigation, the board is presented with a close question of fact with regard to the issue of ratification. The evidence of many irregularities creates a strong case against the procedure by which the ratification was obtained.

"However, the board has concluded that these irregularities were insufficient to change the final result. It is well established by the courts of this state that irregularities and fraud are in themselves insufficient to set aside an election unless they establish a pattern of fraud of such magnitude as would have affected the final result."

The strikers, then, went back to work completely beaten except for two victories which they, as hungry men once more prey to mob rule on the piers, were not apt to appreciate. The first one was in the public and official denunciation of their union leadership by a governmental agency. The second victory was that the public hue and cry aroused by this new, disastrous interruption of the port's commerce led Governor Dewey to direct the New York State Crime Commission to investigate the criminal aspects of dockside troubles.

As for the Board of Inquiry's assurances that the men would be protected against reprisals for their share in the rebellion? The men were wise enough in the ways of the waterfront—cynical enough of such assurances—so that they made no complaints against the victors in the fight, the I.L.A. bosses, with their strong-arm henchmen. A good many strikers lost their irregular jobs and drifted away from the docks. The other men took note of their fate. They became even more tight of mouth than ever.

These were dark days for Father Corridan and for the men who had turned to him. Even before the meeting of the board he had cried out publicly, "There is an explosion brewing on this waterfront that will make the strike of today seem like a picnic. The real issue in this strike is the issue of Ryan, and it goes beyond that. There is someone above Ryan who runs the waterfront." This was Father Corridan's first public reference to "Mr. Big."

An attack on Father John, made within his own church, for siding with the rebels against Joe Ryan, "Mr. Big," and all they represented to him, came on Sunday, November 4, the twenty-first day of the strike.

That afternoon he was summoned to appear before Cardinal Spellman, with his immediate superior, the Provincial of the Jesuit Order, to answer charges of misconduct brought against him by another clergyman because of his waterfront activities. The summons came to the priest only a few hours before he was to be heard, and he appreciated the gravity of the summons. To be sure, his Provincial had always backed him in the work he was doing. But he could not know until he appeared before the Cardinal the exact nature of the charges which were to be brought against him. He only knew he must defend himself on anything specific and count on his superior within the Order to speak, in general, on his behalf.

In going to the Cardinal's residence in the rear of St. Patrick's Cathedral, the Provincial took another member of the Order besides Father Corridan who was familiar with the work the waterfront priest had been doing, and the general policy of the Order in relation to it. These three men—priests of no rank—went to face the music together.

His Eminence, when they arrived, was still conducting services in the Cathedral attended by some 12 to 20 bishops and archbishops. The occasion was a solemn benediction in connection with the missionary work of the Church. The three priests waited in the parlor of the Cardinal's home until he returned from these services, by which time several other priests, some of high rank, were present. The Cardinal bowed to these others and conducted the three Jesuits immediately into his study.

Within 48 hours a grapevine of information and conjecture about what happened in that meeting spread through the Catholic priesthood, among police of the waterfront squad, among shipping people, among the dock workers themselves, and those reporters who were covering the strike on a 24-hour basis.

Father Corridan was recognized by most of these people as a very real and potent influence along the docks. The very fact of his appearance at the Cardinal's residence, on a Sunday afternoon in the midst of the strike, raised important questions in many minds. Had anything transpired at that meeting that would interfere with the work which he was doing? Had the priest who was defending the striking longshoremen against powerful adversaries been silenced? Had his enemies in Joe Ryan's union, the shipping association, and New York politics been able to reach into the Chancery of the diocese, by some hook or crook, to destroy him?

There were anxious moments for a good many people as a rumor spread that Corridan had been silenced.

The best account which reporters have been able to piece together from their varied sources as to what transpired in Cardinal Spellman's study is essentially as follows: Father Corridan was told that two charges had been made against him. The first one was that he had been working every other day along the waterfront, frequently as a longshoreman, discarding his clerical garb, and while there had engaged in fisticuffs with various characters. The second charge was that he had started the 1951 strike.

Father Corridan's answer to both of these charges was a simple denial. He told the Cardinal that in the years he had been working on the problems of the longshoremen, he had been on the waterfront very infrequently. He never had worked as a longshoreman and had never engaged in a fist fight on the docks with anyone. Most of the men whom he had been able to help, he said, came to the Xavier School for counsel. He had been in the homes of others.

As to the second charge, Father Corridan said, he had counseled the men against the strike while it was brewing. He told the Cardinal he knew that most of the men around the docks worked under conditions which seemed to him too grievous to be borne without rebellion. Nevertheless, he told the Cardinal, he had not counseled the strike because he felt there was no adequate program drawn up by the men themselves to warrant their striking.

When the strike came, Father Corridan said, he tried to do everything he could to help the strikers, because he believed the walkout was a rebellion against so many tyrannies and injustices that the men were justified in it, even though he had deemed it unwise.

Cardinal Spellman was scheduled to address a convention of the C.I.O. the very next morning. He naturally was anxious to know whether there was anything he might say which would speed the ending of the strike and the re-establishment of peace in the port. Father Corridan said that in his judgment there was not. The ills besetting the port were too grievous and of too long duration. He told him he knew that an investigation by the New York State government was about to begin, and said he felt it ought to be useful in bringing harborwide evils to public attention.

Like many others, the Cardinal is understood to have been curious about the wording of the prayer which Father Corridan had spoken in the union room of local 791. He asked why the priest had used the phrase "in honor" when he prayed that the government would order the men on the waterfront to return to work.

Father Corridan explained that in this particular rebellion the men's condition after two weeks was so desperate that they would have welcomed an injunction against the strike, brought under the provisions of the Taft-Hartley Act, even though they were against the act as a general proposition, and even though the injunction was commonly regarded as an antilabor device.

The only way the men could return to work with their heads up, Father Corridan felt at the time, was to be confronted by a governmental decree. Otherwise they probably would be driven back to the piers by hunger, crawling on their bellies in front of a victory of the mob element within the port. He explained his view to the Cardinal: If he, as a priest, could prevent it, the men would never be driven back to work in that way.

Cardinal Spellman thanked the priest for what he had said, and asked him if he would come to him later, in waterfront matters, and tell him his views. This seemed to the priest a complete exoneration from any charges that had been brought against him. To this day Father Corridan has refused to affirm or deny any of the accounts of his meeting with the Cardinal which were circulated.

"I regretted deeply that I had to reveal almost immediately the true outcome of the meeting with the Cardinal," he says. "A rumor spread like wildfire on and off the waterfront that I had been silenced at the request of the Cardinal for my activity on behalf of the longshoremen. Not only was that rumor utterly false and highly prejudicial to the Cardinal and the Church, but it caused consternation among the striking longshoremen. I had to deny that rumor as forcefully as I knew how—to longshoremen, reporters, and others—for the good of all concerned.

"There began for me a sense of deep peace and real elation. Within a month Governor Dewey ordered the New York State Crime Commission to dig into all the allegations of criminality on the docks. Even in the defeat of the strikers, which was hard to bear, I found some reason for hope in the future. In that sense, and in no other, these men by their sacrifice had won a victory for themselves and for people who would come after them."

CHAPTER 12

OF CRIME AND POLITICS

In Father Corridan's opinion, the ills besetting New York harbor coursed far more deeply within the bloodstream of the city's life than crime itself. But criminal activity and racketeering unionists in every estuary of the harbor afforded the most obvious target for publicized protests. Before any real progress could be made on broader lines for curing deeper ailments of the port of New York, it was absolutely necessary that the magnitude of dockside criminality and the participation in it of labor-union racketeers be proved beyond any dispute. These things not only had to be proved. They had to be proved in all their real enormity so that an angered people would cry out, "We've had enough of it," and act to end it through their governing agents.

The public and irrefutable proof of all the charges that Father Corridan had been making about the harbor for several years was finally spread out beneath the big-type headlines of the entire metropolitan press in 1952 and 1953 by the investigation and hearings of the New York State Crime Commission, ordered into the situation by Governor Dewey as an aftermath of the wildcat strike of 1951.

The cooperation of crooked business and crooked unionism was amply proved. There was some slight reference to political racketeering, closely lined to dockside evils, during those earlier times when William J. O'Dwyer was a district attorney in Brooklyn and Mayor of New York. The alliance of political leaders on the Jersey waterfront, with vote-getting hoodlums, was touched upon. But in the main, the two targets of the New York State Crime Commission's public hearings were:

1. The criminality of union leaders.
2. The cooperation they received, through fear or avarice, from a good many businessmen of fair public repute within the shipping and stevedoring industries.

Right from the outset there was plenty of testimony to the effect that the bribing of labor leaders to betray their followers by giving special favors to employers was a common practice in the shipping industry. Captain Douglas Yates, vice-president of the Jarka Company, testified in an executive session before the commission that he had paid Eddie Florio, ex-bootlegger boss of the I.L.A. in Hoboken, at least 12,000 dollars in the three years between 1949 and 1951, and that he had paid some 5000 dollars to John J. "Gene" Sampson, and James "Jay" O'Connor, business agents of Local 791, on Manhattan's West Side, during the same period. Sampson denied under oath receiving any such payment. Before the public hearings of the commission came along, Captain Yates and Captain Philip G. O'Reilly, another vice-president of the Jarka Corporation, left the jurisdiction of the Crime Commission and remained outside its jurisdiction until the hearings were ended.

Richard J. McGrath, vice-president of the John W. McGrath

Company, stevedores at Pier 88, North River, where the large French liners dock, and at Pier 84, where the American Export liners are berthed, testified that he made secret cash payments to Patrick "Packy" Connolly, executive vice-president of the I.L.A. According to Mr. McGrath he had an understanding with Connolly that half of his payments should go to Harold Bowers, delegate for Local 824, the notorious "Pistol Local." Connolly also denied receiving the payments.

Captain L. C. Howard, president of the Nacirema Operating Company, another large stevedoring company, also testified to payments to Florio. He said he made them payable to Florio's nephew, one Gerald Lamby. Florio also denied receiving this money but was convicted of perjury in the United States court for his false denial, and sentenced to a term of 18½ months.

Daniel J. Keogh, secretary and treasurer of the Pittston Stevedoring Corporation, testified that in 1951 he had paid 1250 dollars to Barney "Cockeye" Brown, business agent for Local 1,478 in Jersey City, and Tony "Cheese" Marchitto, agent for Local 1,247 in the same community. N. J. Palihnich, vice-president of Jarka Corporation, testified that he paid Anthony "Joe the Gent" Giontomasi, the business agent of Local 1,235, Newark, 100 dollars a month regularly. Harold J. Beardell, president of John T. Clark & Sons, Inc., a stevedoring corporation, also testified that he was in the habit of making regular payments to union officials.

The joint testimony of Mr. Palihnich and Mr. Beardell left no doubt in the minds of members of the Crime Commission as to why the officers of stevedoring companies paid off union officials regularly. They paid them, with contempt, to see that the men were always available, always docile, and always ready to do whatever hard work might be asked of them. They paid them to see that the conditions of union contracts were not observed. They paid them as coconspirators—the shipping officials as men with money in their hands for which the union officers were greedy. That the union officers who betrayed the men they purported to lead were as guilty of betrayal as Judas Iscariot made no difference to these shipping men. Nor did they apparently feel any twinges of discomfort over their complicity in the betrayal until the Crime Commission began to subpoena their books to spread them out in the public eye. It was all "business as usual."

Mr. Palihnich even had this to say in defense of "Joe the Gent": "That's one thing I'll say for Joe Gent. He was always available. At one o'clock he came down [to the pier] and settled the matter. The men [who had walked out because of a grievance] returned to their work." Mr. Beardell made very plain the reason for his payment of money regularly to union officials. It was to "prevent quickie strikes."

The stevedoring companies, in some cases subsidiaries to the big and reputable shipping companies, used various devices to disguise the payments they were making to union officers. One device was the placing of "phantoms" on their payrolls. Thus it was testified that the Huron Stevedoring Company, a subsidiary of the Grace Line, placed the names of nonexistent persons on its payroll, in order to pay James "Jay" O'Connor, business agent of Local 791, and Timothy "Timmy" O'Mara, a boss loader on four Hudson River piers, 18,000 dollars in six years and 25,000 dollars in eight years, respectively. The name of the phantom through whom "Timmy" O'Mara drew his 25,000 dollars in eight years was "Edward Joseph Ross." One name was as good as another. This "Timmy" O'Mara, whom the Huron Stevedoring Company was paying off, had been convicted of petty larceny, attempted grand larceny, burglary, and robbery. Although a member of the I.L.A., he was not a union official, yet a Mr. T. Maher, stevedore superintendent for the Huron Company, testified that he certainly was successful in preventing strikes.

Special festive occasions were always a signal for union racketeers to shake down the stevedoring companies that had surrendered to them. Thus, when it came time for the daughter of Mike Clemente, financial secretary and business agent of Local 856 on the Lower East Side docks, to be married in the style to which her father had accustomed her, "Pop" Clemente got a "loan" of 11,000 dollars from Michael Castellana, vice-president of Jules S. Sottneck Company, a stevedoring company with which he did business.

Mr. Clemente, in his testimony before the Crime Commission, said that it was on the stevedoring company's generosity that he took his wife down to Miami Beach, Florida, on a vacation, and the trip was expensive.

Granted the moral atmosphere in which the stevedoring companies were working, there was nothing strange in bribing labor leaders to betray their followers. Some of the chiefs of these companies, especially Frank W. Nolan, president of the Jarka Corporation, which became the biggest of them all, were quite as ready to pay officers of steamship companies, under the table, for giving them their stevedoring contracts, instead of giving them to competitors. On the stand under oath before the Crime Commission, Mr. Nolan admitted that he had paid W. W. Wells, president of the Isthmian Steamship Company, two 10,000-dollar United States Treasury bearer bonds, while there was in existence a contract between Jarka and Isthmian giving Jarka the stevedoring for Isthmian. This contract was signed by Nolan and Wells on behalf of their respective companies. The payments resulted in Nolan's indictment on a charge of commercial bribery and his conviction on a plea of guilty.

This man Nolan also made cash payments of 34,000 dollars to A. Roggeveen, managing director of the Holland-America Line, while it had three contracts with Jarka, the contracts having been signed by Roggeveen and Nolan. Nolan also paid J. C. Bruswitz, managing director of the Colmar Lines, a subsidiary of the Bethlehem Steel Corporation, 47,200 dollars, and E. C. Koenke, operating director of the Ore Steamship Company, another subsidiary of Bethlehem, 56,200 dollars in cash when he was doing business with their two steamship companies, under contracts he had signed with them, as representing their employers. Both men were subsequently indicted and convicted as a result of the Crime Commission's hearings.

The testimony before the Crime Commission brought out the fact that stevedoring company officials, as well as bribing union officers and the officers of companies with which they did business, were accustomed to lavish their money on political leaders in the cities around the harbor, and that when the hot breath of the Crime Commission's investigators was blowing down their necks they altered their books to conceal the payments they had been making. It was brought out that the John W. McGrath Corporation had made substantial payments to Jersey City officials who were in a position to do the company favors, and that the payments were so made as to conceal the identity of the officials who got the money.

The examination of Willam J. McCormack, no other than the alleged "Mr. Big" of the New York waterfront, showed that four companies he owned made "unsubstantiated cash disbursements of 980,000 dollars in the five years between 1947 and 1951." That was almost a million dollars, put out in cash to undisclosed persons, yet when he got on the witness stand, Mr. McCormack said he knew nothing whatever about these great expenditures. Five principal officers of the Jarka Corporation drew about 500,000 dollars out of the petty-cash accounts of the company in the seven years prior to the public hearings. Mr. Nolan, as president of the company, said he knew that 160,000 dollars of this was used to pay off steamship-company officials with whom the Jarka company did business. But the Crime Commission counsel, Theodore W. Kiendl, was unable to elicit any satisfactory response as to where the rest of this "petty cash" had gone.

The books of the Jules S. Sottnek Company, stevedores, showed about 278,000 dollars similarly drawn out and unaccounted for through petty cash and checks made payable to cash in seven years. The accountants of the Crime Commission who went over the company's books were told that all the vouchers for petty cash had been destroyed. The total taken, however, exceeded the net profits of the corporation throughout all those years.

Accountants for the Crime Commission also examined the books of John T. Clark & Sons, stevedores, and found unaccounted cash expenditures of 289,487 dollars in seven years. It was brought out during the public hearings that this company, in an effort to conceal the payments it had been making to officers of the longshoremen's union, altered some of the company's books while the

Crime Commission's accountants were examining others. The alterations were quickly discovered by the crime investigators.

Day after day, in public hearings of witnesses under oath, the Crime Commission spread on the public record the evidence to support its ultimate findings as to the character of the I.L.A. and its leaders. Its major conclusion in regard to the I.L.A. leadership and the leadership of many of its component locals was that for many years they had "flagrantly disregarded the welfare of their members and the public."

"Ryan and many of the I.L.A. organizers are demonstrably unfit for their posts," the commission ruled. "In addition to accepting Christmas and other payments, Ryan also admitted receiving monies from steamship and stevedoring companies which he deposited in the I.L.A. *Journal* account and characterized as "donations to an anti-Communist fund.' From this I.L.A. *Journal* account, Ryan withdrew 31,651 dollars in cash and expended by checks 460 dollars for a cruise to Guatemala, over 1000 dollars for golf-club dues and charges, 10,000 dollars for premiums on his personal insurance, and 817 dollars for such luxury items as expensive shirts and high-priced shoes.

"To summarize, during the period, January 1, 1947, to September 30, 1952, Ryan took out of I.L.A. funds more than 240,000 dollars, of which 115,000 dollars was salary. Among the expenditures for which he used the remainder was 12,494 dollars to buy Cadillac automobiles."

The commission also spread on the records the criminal careers of four major I.L.A. organizers whom Ryan appointed: Eddie McGrath, Harold Bowers, Alex Di Brizzi, and Ed Florio. It called attention particularly to the criminal career of Eddie McGrath, the brother-in-law of the executed murderer, "Cockeye" Dunn.

"Edward J. McGrath, an organizer from 1936 until his resignation in 1951," the commission found, "has a criminal record showing 12 arrests for crimes ranging from petty larceny to murder and including two convictions for burglary. He has never been a working longshoreman, yet Ryan appointed him an organizer less than a year after his release from Sing Sing Prison."

McGrath was called to testify before the Crime Commission in public hearings, and refused to answer 115 questions on the ground of possible self-incrimination. He explained his refusal by reading a statement in which he said he had been branded as a criminal, racketeer, and gangster in the press. He was then asked by Theodore Kiendl, "Now, Mr. McGrath, I would like to ask you one question. Are you in fact a racketeer, criminal, and gangster?"

"I refuse to answer on the grounds that my answer might tend to incriminate me," McGrath replied, and walked out of the hearing.

Aside from his appointment of criminals as organizers for the I.L.A., the commission noted, Ryan named his niece's husband, Joseph J. Schultz, as an organizer in 1948. Schultz had no criminal record. Under oath on the witness stand, Ryan admitted that this nephew of his was no organizer but was his personal assistant. His principal job was the solicitation of lucrative advertisements for the I.L.A. *Journal.* Schultz's 25 per cent commission for all the advertisements in the I.L.A. *Journal,* sold mostly to shipping and stevedoring companies, amounted to more than 26,000 dollars in the four years from 1949 to 1952. "This was sheer graft," the commission commented.

The commission denounced the I.L.A. for failure to exercise any supervision over its locals, particularly the Brooklyn locals, which were under the control first of Emil Camarda as "front man," until Camarda was murdered. The actual control of those six Camarda locals was in the hands of Albert Anastasia, of Murder, Inc., and three of his henchmen, Vincent Mangano, "Dandy Jack" Parisi, and Tony Romeo.

During the commission's hearings new light was shed on the relationship between former Mayor William O'Dwyer, and the longshore mobsters in Brooklyn. "In April, 1940," the commission recounted, "William O'Dwyer, then newly elected district attorney of Kings County, conducted an investigation of these Brooklyn locals in the course of which he obtained evidence of grand larceny and embezzlement of union funds. Soon after receiving the books of the then existing Amen investigation, on May 15, 1940, O'Dwyer closed his investigations of the waterfront rackets, and no prosecutions resulted.

"In June, 1940, O'Dwyer invited Ryan and Emil Camarda, one of the I.L.A. vice-presidents, to a conference in which the facts uncovered by the investigation were disclosed. Ryan announced that a drastic reformation would be carried out and that he would revoke the charters of the Camarda locals." The charters were revoked, but new charters with different numbers were issued to the very same mobsters who controlled the old ones.

The commission's hearings confirmed the fact that 30 per cent of the officials of the I.L.A. locals had police records. "Waterfront criminals," the commission said, "know that control of the local is a prerequisite for conducting racket operations on the piers. Through their power as union officials they place their confederates in key positions on the docks. There they shake down steamship and stevedoring companies by threats of work stoppages, operate the lucrative public loading business, and carry on such activities as pilferage, loan-sharking, and gambling."

These statements by the commission, based on sworn testimony in public hearings, were simply a summary of the stories which had been brought to Father Corridan by longshoremen. They could not be proved, publicly, until told under oath in a governmental proceeding. Before the hearings reporters and others might know, in general, the waterfront setup. But nobody could get it into print, except fractionally and in small pieces, soon to be forgotten, under penalties of the law of libel. The Crime Commission wrapped the whole sorry spectacle of "The Jungle" waterfront up into one big bundle and laid it on the public's lap.

The commission told how importers of a cargo of furs, valued at two million dollars, were not permitted to land it until they paid the Newark business agents, Pasquale "Pat" Ferrone and "Joe the Gent," a fee of 70,000 dollars; how importers of a perishable stock of lemons had been forced to pay a union officer 10,000 dollars to get them off Pier F, in Jersey City, and how another payment of 45,000 dollars had to be made to a union "representative" to get a cargo of tulip bulbs moved in Hoboken. The commission then moved on, in its report, to the mishandling of union funds by union officers.

Thus Constantino "Gus" Scannavino, vice-president of the I.L.A., testified that he had paid a nephew of his, Michael Cosenza, 75 dollars a week and "expenses" for three years, to be a so-called business agent for one of the locals under his control. All that time the nephew stayed in Arizona. Alex Di Brizzi, president of the Staten Island local, allotted himself 937.50 dollars for "expenses" during a convention of the I.L.A., which he attended at the Hotel Commodore in Manhattan. As a matter of fact, Di Brizzi always handled the funds of his locals as his own money and never made any accounting of them.

The so-called financial secretary of his Local 920 told the commission the way union funds were kept. In the first place Di Brizzi would make collections from members without giving any receipts. In the second place he kept no account whatever of disbursements. He just went around picking up the money which the lowly longshoremen had to pay him if they wanted to work. Sometimes there would be a little temporary surplus, which he would hand over to his "financial secretary," one Joseph B. Franklin. Mr. Franklin said that for a long time Di Brizzi might hand him "quite a roll of bills" on a Saturday night, and he would take this money home and place it in a cookie jar until Di Brizzi might want it. Ultimately this practice was discontinued, he said. All the financial records of his local were missing, he testified, prior to 1951. The commission had a hard time finding any financial records of longshoremen's unions that gave a fair picture of the use of members' funds.

"Of the 34 I.L.A. locals whose financial reports were examined by commission accountants," it reported, "those of only 11 were found to be in reasonably good accounting form." Among the more prominent I.L.A. officers whose records were missing, or who admitted that they mingled union funds with their own bank accounts, were John "Ike" Gannon, of the watchmen's union, and Patrick "Packy" Connolly, vice-president of the I.L.A. and generally recognized as second in command only to Ryan. Connolly, president of the Bowers mob's Local 824, said the local never had a bank account before he took office, at first as its treasurer. Therefore he simply kept the union dues in his own bank and his own account.

The "Pistol Local," Mr. Connolly admitted under questioning, had never held an election in the last 20 years.

The commission went into some detail about the failure of the I.L.A. to maintain democratic processes in the locals. Salvatore Camarda, financial secretary of one of the Brooklyn locals, 327, testified that his unit had only held three or four meetings in the three years before the hearings. Tony Di Vincenzo, a member of Hoboken Local 881, testified that his local had not held a meeting of any kind in 30 years, and that another Hoboken local had only held one meeting in ten years, and no election for the past 15.

An example of what might happen to a longshoreman who might happen to object to this lack of elections or union meetings was given to the commission by Mario Frullano, a member of I.L.A. Maintenance Local 1,277. Frullano, it seemed, had noticed the business agent of his local on the pier where he worked one day. He went over to him and asked him what the members were getting for their three-dollar monthly dues. An argument about the way the union was run ensued between Frullano, the business agent, and two men who were accompanying him on the dock. It lasted but briefly. One of the business agent's companions simply kicked Frullano in the groin, and he was carted off to a hospital. One of the things he was objecting to, he told the commission, was that he only had received notice of one union meeting in the four years during which he had been a member of it, and had never received any report whatever concerning the union's finances.

Joe Ryan's absolute control of the union, the commission found, was assured partly by the creation of a good many unnecessary locals, in charge of which he would place close personal friends.

"Some high-ranking officers of the I.L.A. have been given control of several locals," the commission found. "A close personal friend of Ryan, John J. 'Ike' Gannon, is the president of the New

York District Council, I.L.A., vice-president of the Atlantic Coast District, I.L.A., secretary and treasurer of Locals 824-1, and 901-1. He was an organizer and now is salaried adviser of the port watchmen's union. Another close friend of Ryan, Charles P. Spencer, is secretary of the Atlantic Coast District, president of Local 901-1, secretary-treasurer and business agent of Local 866, and a salaried 'adviser' of the port watchmen's union."

The commission found formally that questionable labor leaders within the I.L.A., while neglecting the welfare of the union members, were using their positions to enrich themselves in business ventures aside from the duties they should have been performing as union leaders. Leaders so named included Connie Noonan, president of the platform workers' union, Local 1,730; Thomas W. "Teddy" Gleason, acting president of one local, financial secretary of another, and one of Ryan's picked organizers. Noonan, while a union official, had been an officer of Varick Enterprises, Inc., until it was put out of business by an investigation of the New York district attorney's office. Gleason and Noonan had worked together on deals with "5 per centers" in Washington, D.C., to arrange the sale of armed airplanes to the Dominican Republic and the export of sulfur and nickel to Israel and Brazil.

By all odds the most unsavory story of corruption by labor leaders along the waterfront who engaged in business enterprises as employers of the very men they purported to lead in collective-bargaining negotiations, which the Crime Commission developed, was the story of the A. Costa, Jr., & Son trucking concern. This company for the past eight years had handled about 80 per cent of all the citrus fruit coming into the port of New York from California. It also operated a collection service for truckers doing business along the waterfront.

The union primarily concerned in this story of labor racketeering is the teamsters' union, rather than the longshoremen's union. But revelations about it had a distinct bearing on the close relationship between longshoremen's labor leaders and teamsters' labor leaders, as of the past generation in New York. The revelations also shed light on the unity of both unions in that political power which was called by Guy Richards of the *Journal-American* the "Waterfront Stable." This "stable," as Father Corridan as well as Mr. Richards has seen it, has been operating on both the Republican and Democratic sides of the political fence. Its accent on the Democratic side is only because New York's normal political rule has been Democratic.

The testimony before the commission brought out that the firm of A. Costa, Jr., & Son, insofar as its three partners went, was nothing more nor less than a "front" for "Joe" Papa and his union business agent, Peter Costello. These two men were the real powers in the Costa firm. Nominal partners, Costa and his son, Michael Moretti, and Salvatore Padula were Papa's agents. Moretti was a cousin of "Joe" Papa's wife. He had been a truck driver, earning about 55 dollars a week, and was without business experience or capital, when he was made a partner in the firm, in 1945, the date of organization.

Part of the capital with which the firm was started was a loan of 5000 dollars from Peter Costello. From 1948 to 1952 one of the collectors for the firm, in its activity as a collection agency for truckmen, was James F. Connors. Connors was a brother-in-law of "Cockeye" Dunn, and a half-brother of Eddie McGrath, both I.L.A. officials and gangsters. Connors, for his services to the Costa company, received more than 30,000 dollars after taxes within five years, and many of the checks were cashed by McGrath. Some were cashed by "Cockeye" Dunn's widow. Connors testified before the commission that he actually worked only one morning a week, that his salary was 125 dollars weekly, plus bonuses. There was a fair inference to be drawn from the testimony that the real beneficiary of Connors' job was the widow of "Cockeye" Dunn, the murderer who was tough enough to die in the chair without telling District Attorney Hogan what Hogan wanted to know about the political backers of waterfront racketeering.

Of the operations of A. Costa, Jr., & Son, the commission reported as follows: "Joseph G. Papa, president of Local 202 of the Teamsters' Brotherhood, received at least 46,000 dollars in cash during the 1946-1952 period from Michael Moretti, ostensibly a partner. During this period Moretti, as partner, drew as profits from the partnership over 200,000 dollars, or approximately 25,000 to 30,000 dollars a year.

"Yet he continued to live in extremely simple circumstances at his mother-in-law's house, paying approximately 45 dollars a month rent. Papa, during this period of time, when he was receiving about 8000 dollars a year as president of Local 202, plus loans and gifts from Michael Moretti, managed to build a house costing over 65,000 dollars in Scarsdale, N. Y.

"Moretti, when he first testified before the commission, denied that Papa had anything to do in setting him up as a partner in the trucking company and its affiliated collection service. Later Moretti corrected his testimony to the extent of admitting that Papa had first approached him about the opportunity in the trucking business, and that he had delivered at least 46,000 dollars to Papa.

"Although Padula also received from A. Costa, Jr., & Son over 200,000 dollars, he also continued to live modestly, paying about 45 dollars a month rent. On many of the dates when Padula made substantial cash withdrawals from his bank account, Peter Costello, Sr., visited his safe-deposit box, which was in the bank where Padula had his account. Costello, while denying the receipt of any of this money, refused to fill out a financial questionnaire submitted to him by the commission.

"It is apparent that Moretti and Padula were merely fronts for union president Papa and union delegate Costello in this business enterprise at a time when Papa and Costello were representing the members of Local 202 in negotiating collective-bargaining agreements with A. Costa, Jr. & Son and other trucking companies.

"Local 202 of the International Brotherhood of Teamsters has between 5000 and 6000 dues-paying members, representing employees engaged in the trucking of produce such as fresh fruits and vegetables, butter, eggs, and cheese in the various markets of New York, including the Washington and Gansevoort markets of Manhattan. Papa has been president of the local since May, 1940."

Evidence before the commission also established the fact that

Papa, as president, and Arthur A. Dorf, as treasurer of this union, acted to conceal the defalcation of at least 36,000 dollars of the local's funds. Immediately after the commission's revelations, Papa was removed from his union office by David Beck, president of the Teamsters' Brotherhood, and was removed from his post as a member of the New York State Industrial Council by Governor Dewey.

After spreading plenty of sworn testimony on the record concerning the I.L.A.-sponsored system of hiring called the shape-up, the commission denounced it as an unmitigated evil.

The commission was no less forthright, after its hearings, in denouncing the "public-loading" practices along the waterfront as a racket. Public loading, it said, was a serious drain on business. It placed the responsibility for organizing the racket within the I.L.A. squarely upon the shoulders of Joe Ryan as president.

"On May 6, 1949, Ryan issued an I.L.A. charter for Local 1,757, the so-called 'loaders' local," the commission reported. "The local has no constitution or by-laws of its own and its jurisdiction is not defined. Its members include many officers of corporations and members of partnerships engaged in the loading, and in the hiring of the men who actually do the work. The dues of such members are usually paid as a business expense by the corporation or partnership."

Among the shipping company and stevedoring officials who testified to the unwilling acceptance of so-called public loaders with known criminal records or men known otherwise to be racketeers, were F. M. Rohrer, vice-president of the Grace Line; L. F. O'Meara, terminal manager of the A. H. Bull Steamship Company, Brooklyn; J. F. Devlin of the United States Lines; B. G. Furey of the Moore-McCormack Lines, and P. G. O'Reilly of the Jarka Corporation. It was the consensus of all that acceptance of these loaders, backed by the I.L.A., was necessary if they were to avoid a strike on their piers. Old Captain P. B. Blanchard, president of the Turner & Blanchard stevedoring company, was asked what he thought of the public-loading situation in the port, "I think it stinks," he replied succinctly.

The commission branded the dual employer-union status of public loaders an unmitigated evil. "Although public loaders may operate as individuals, partnerships, or corporations, they are also members of various I.L.A. locals," the commission reported. "They frequently use the labor weapons of picketing and strikes to obtain loading concessions. An example of how some public loaders have developed into big business is George Sellenthin, Inc., which does all the public loading on Staten Island. It employs men at a shape-up and had gross receipts of close to two million dollars for the years 1947 through 1951. Its 31 stockholders are all members of I.L.A. locals.

"Some officers of loading corporations who employ longshore labor at the piers are also shop stewards, whose function it is to represent the longshoremen at those piers. James Doyle and Thomas McGrath of India Wharf Loaders are I.L.A. shop stewards on Pier 33, Brooklyn. Salvatore Trapani, an officer of Kings Loaders, Inc., was at the same time a shop steward on Pier 34. Those shop stewards get paid as longshoremen without performing any work, and also collect additional money as employer-loaders."

The commission named a rogues gallery of public loaders who muscled their way into control of the loading at the Greenpoint Terminal in Brooklyn. One of them, William Sullivan, had served three years in prison for robbery. Another, Edward Taliento, had sentences for unlawful entry and burglary on his record. Vincent Corbett had a couple of convictions for unlawful entry and burglary. Three others, Thomas McGurty, Thomas McGoneghy, and Otto Costello, had prison records for assault, robbery, burglary, and illegal possession of a revolver.

The commission found that in most cases the public loaders kept no financial records adequate even to substantiate their tax statements; but on the basis of available evidence a great deal of their receipts were siphoned off to I.L.A. labor leaders or to known criminals with whom the I.L.A. leaders were working.

The evidence showed that fees paid to loaders on Piers 96 and 97, North River, found their way in large measure to Mickey Bowers, John Ward, and John O'Keefe, the mobster powers in the

"Pistol Local." It found that "Timmy" O'Mara, "a notorious waterfront figure," was exacting a percentage of loading receipts on Piers 61, 62, 73, and 74, North River, and that Eddie Polo, former delegate of I.L.A. Local 1,247, was receiving cash payments of between 5000 and 7000 dollars a year from the loaders on Pier 34, North River, although he admitted to the commission he did nothing whatever to earn the money.

Loaders on Piers 15 and 16, East River, were sharing their receipts on a 50-50 basis, it was testified, with Mike Clemente, I.L.A. delegate with power over that area, while Peter Costello, Sr., the teamsters'-union officer who was hidden partner in A. Costa, Jr., & Son, trucking company, was also enjoying between 10,000 and 15,000 dollars a year for some 20 years, as nominal solicitor for a loaders' collection agency. Costello, under oath before the commission, admitted that he never had solicited any business for the agency whatever. But he and his son, it was revealed, had taken about 20,000 dollars from the agency between 1945 and 1951, for their "good will." Part of their "good will," it was testified, was an agreement to talk personally to any truckman who failed to do business with the loaders' collection agency, and to "persuade" the man to do what was expected of him.

"It is obvious that public loading is a racket seriously affecting the port of New York," the commission concluded, and set the cost of it as probably more than 5,400,000 dollars in 1950.

The Crime Commission's studies of the pier-watchmen system, in connection with widespread pilferage on the docks, revealed the watchmen's union to be under the control of the I.L.A., in fact, although nominally disaffiliated with it after the passage of the Taft-Hartley Act. The commission found there was a complete absence of union democracy in this union setup, and that watchmen, instead of being encouraged to report thievery on the piers, were even reprimanded by their union leaders for reporting thieves.

"Prior to the Taft-Hartley Act of 1947, the port watchmen's union Local 1,456, was an I.L.A. local dominated by Joseph P. Ryan, John J. 'Ike' Gannon, and Charles P. Spencer," the commission reported. "Since the port watchmen were supposed to stop thievery, loan-sharking, gambling, and extortion, and to preserve the peace, they could hardly expect—and did not receive—any support from officials of the I.L.A. or its locals.

"Under the Taft-Hartley Act, the port watchmen's union could not continue its affiliation with the I.L.A. 'Disaffiliation' followed and took the form of the creation of an independent watchmen's association. New charters were issued to the various watchmen's locals, one of which, Port Watchmen's Union Local 1,456, retained jurisdiction over watchmen in the port of New York.

"The disaffiliation was a sham. Gannon and Spencer immediately assumed and have continued in control of the Independent Watchmen's Association, and Port Watchmen's Local 1,456. Gannon continued to represent the I.L.A. hierarchy as the controlling force in the watchmen's union. He also remained as secretary-treasurer of I.L.A. Locals 824-1 and 901-1, as president of the I.L.A. New York District Council, and as vice-president of the I.L.A. Atlantic Coast District, and as business agent for Local 864.

"Spencer, who had been an officer of the I.L.A. watchmen's union, became an officer of the I.W.A., and of Port Watchmen's Local 1,456. He also retained his positions as secretary-treasurer of the I.L.A. Atlantic Coast District Council as president of Local 901-1, and as business agent of Local 866."

The commission found that, in fact, the port watchmen's union had not held a contested election since 1940. When the commission subpoenaed the books of the watchmen's union and of I.L.A. locals under the control of Gannon and Spencer, they were all "missing." Five officers of the watchmen's union, with 1600 dues-paying members, were found to be paying themselves salaries and transportation expenses of 155 dollars a week, plus an automobile apiece.

The commission found pilferage along the docks running at least to four or five million dollars a year, and that Gannon himself had warned one watchman against reporting pilferage on his pier. It found that the I.L.A. had opposed efforts by the steamship companies to improve the watchmen's service at the piers. It found that when a former New York policeman named James Tierney was hired by the Grace Line to make a study of cargo security on its piers, Tierney was threatened with death.

The testimony before the commission of F. M. Rohrer of the Grace Line, and ex-Sergeant Tierney, the retired policeman, told the whole story of the domination of the watchmen's union by the longshoremen's union, and the protection of thievery by the I.L.A. When Mr. Rohrer was testifying concerning the Grace Line's efforts to strengthen its security system, the questioning by counsel for the commission and Mr. Rohrer's answers ran as follows:

Q: Did you tell Mr. Tierney that you had to clear the hiring of Mr. Tierney with "Gene" Sampson, the delegate of Local 791 and "Jay" O'Connor, delegate of 791, and some others?

A: I don't know, as it was mentioned by name, but I probably did tell him it had to be cleared through the union.

Q: That the hiring of head watchmen had to be cleared?

A: With the union delegates.

Q: I.L.A. union delegates?

A: That's right.

Q: Not the watchmen's delegates?

A: No.

Mr. Tierney, when called to the stand, told of violent opposition from within the I.L.A. which he found when he finally was assigned to the task of making a study of pilferage on Grace Line piers. The testimony follows:

Q: Did anything further come out of this study that you made of Pier 45? Did you receive any further communications from anyone as a result of it?

A: Yes, the last day I was at the pier, around seven o'clock in the evening at home, I received a telephone call asking me if I was retired Sergeant Tierney of the New York Police Department, and who formerly worked for the National City Bank. When I replied in the affirmative and asked who was speaking, the man said: "Never mind, but if it wasn't for me you would be floating down the river today. Take my advice. Don't go back to that pier."

Then he immediately hung up, without my being able to learn his identity.

Later on that evening the phone bell rang again. When I answered it, the same voice said: "Tierney?" When I replied "yes," he immediately hung up. This happened at half-hour intervals for four or five hours until it reached the stage where each time the phone rang, I merely picked up the receiver without answering it. That went on until two-thirty in the morning, and then ceased.

The ex-sergeant never went back to the pier.

From the standpoint of Father Corridan, most of the newspapers, and certainly the bulk of the longshoremen around the harbor who had been many years on the waterfront, the high point of the testimony before the commission was the examination of W. J. McCormack, now generally labeled, "Mr. Big." There was some hesitation in the State Crime Commission itself before McCormack was summoned to testify. That he finally was brought to the stand may be due, in part, to the fact that just before the close of the public hearings several New York newspaper reporters and at least one newspaper editor asked counsel for the commission, point-blank, whether McCormack would be called. Before the reporters did this, W. J. Keating of the New York City Anti-Crime Committee, had asked them to.

An attaché of the commission, in talking to Father Corridan in his office at the Xavier School, asked whether he thought McCormack should be put on the stand. Father Corridan replied that old-time longshoremen would never be satisfied until McCormack was placed in a witness chair and required to testify under oath as to any responsibility he might have for the evils of the port against which they were rebelling. As Father Corridan gave that advice, he says, he could look back on only one personal meeting with "Mr. Big." Early in his association with the West Side longshoremen, he had made up his mind he would seek no meeting either with Joe Ryan or McCormack, but would agree to any meeting with either if arranged in such a way it might do some good on the men's behalf.

"The only time I ever met McCormack," Father Corridan says, "was on Good Friday, 1952. About a month before that one of the oldest priests at Xavier, Father Martin Scott, asked me whether McCormack was a man of substantial means and whether I thought it would be proper for him to see McCormack and make a request for funds for one of our Jesuit seminaries. To both questions I answered in the affirmative. Father Scott went to see McCormack, and after their conversation McCormack had Father Scott driven back to Xavier by his chauffeur. There was no commitment about the donation. But Father Scott thought McCormack would think the matter over favorably.

"Personally I couldn't be sure of that, but I thought it was certain that McCormack would recognize that Father Scott came from Xavier, and that I came from Xavier, too. I thought McCormack might be calling me soon thereafter. Sure enough! One afternoon not long afterward, Walter Hamshar, shipping-news reporter for the New York *Herald Tribune,* telephoned and asked me if I would like to meet McCormack. I said, 'I might.' Hamshar said he thought it might be arranged if I would call McCormack's secretary at his office.

"This was only a little while after Lester Velie's articles had been published in *Collier's,* in which McCormack had been named the 'Mr. Big' of the port, and I was described as a priest who was fighting the system that Mr. Big represented. I called McCormack's secretary and in about 15 minutes he called me back.

"It was agreed that since our names had been mentioned in such a way that any meeting in a public place would be news, we should meet at the home of the Provincial of the Jesuit Order, 501 East Fordham Road. I called Father Keogh at the provincial's home and arranged for a time when nobody else would be in the parlor. When McCormack came in at the appointed time, we settled down for a three-hour discussion of the one thing we both were interested in—the port of New York. He seemed to agree with many of my views, and in particular to the great measure of responsibility which the shipping men and the stevedoring companies had for maintaining bad conditions. I had three definite requests to make of him. I wanted his active help, as a man of great power, in straightening out the labor-management conditions throughout the port. I wanted his help in getting at least 100 million dollars invested in the modernization of the harbor to help it compete with other harbors. Last but not least, I wanted him to warn Joe Ryan that if he didn't straighten out the I.L.A. and straighten it out soon, the whole house would come down around his ears, and a good many people would be hurt.

"That was a straight warning that I was delivering. A couple of times I felt that McCormack was pretty angry with what I was saying. But when it was all over he said he would think over what I had said. He said I was welcome to come to see him at any time. I would always be welcome. But when he left, I had a feeling we would not meet again for a long time.

"I doubted personally whether he ever would be of any help in cleaning up the waterfront situation, and so far he hasn't been. Some time later when Father Scott heard the testimony before the State Crime Commission, he came to me highly disturbed. He asked me whether he hadn't compromised the Order in going to ask McCormack for a donation. Father Scott even was a little provoked at me for having advised him to go.

"I said I knew no reason why he shouldn't go. I said I felt that once he went, McCormack would send for me, and I wanted to talk to him about the waterfront. If he could be induced to help the waterfront and the men who worked on the docks, doubtless some contribution to the order might follow. It turned out I was right on both counts, for so far there's been no help to longshoremen from McCormack and no help to the order either."

In view of the commission's revelations in detail of wholesale corruption, tarred by frequent murder, along the waterfront, those who held to the theory that "Mr. Big" had some major responsibility for these conditions were particularly anxious that he be called. They could not forget that as a member of a Committee on the Port Industry, established by Mayor O'Dwyer in 1950, McCormack was signatory of a report that called labor-management relations in the harbor satisfactory to everyone concerned. The report, which he signed and with which he was confronted when on the witness stand, contained the following statements concerning the relations between longshoremen and their employers:

"We have found that the labor situation on the waterfront of the port of New York is generally satisfactory from the standpoint of the worker, the employer, the industry, and the government.

"The longshoremen and management in the port of New York are doing their full share in keeping this nation's postwar economy at a high level. As labor organizations and employers, doing business on the New York City waterfront, they are fully aware of their responsibilities to their members and to industry as a whole. The great progress made so far has been accomplished through collective bargaining inspired by the constructive, progressive, and patriotic outlook of the parties concerned. We recommend that the good will and sense of cooperation which has characterized the relationship of labor and industry in this port be continued and extended."

Having thus placed himself on the record as approving the status of labor-management relations in a harbor that had suffered three harbor-wide wildcat strikes since 1945 and at least 40 quickie strikes in the same time, it seemed to those critics of port-wide rackeetering that an inquiry into McCormack's own relations, if there were any, with known racketeers, criminals of influence, and the political powers of harbor municipalities should be of great public interest. One thing was certain. He had grown to vast wealth by wielding his personal power within the system he defended, and by adjusting his business career to the realities of it. Certainly it was to be presumed that he would know a few facts about almost everyone of any prominence, either in the political world or underworld, during the 50 years he had worked around the port. Critics felt he must have known a great deal about the real, hidden history of the port for that half-century; the way the mobsters and gunmen worked; the links between underworld characters such as "Cockeye" Dunn and Albert Ackalitis, and the leaders of business and government in all the harbor municipalities, since his extensive business interests covered both the Manhattan and New Jersey waterfronts.

On the stand, however, McCormack proved a good witness for McCormack and shed no light whatever on those matters the Crime Commission had been investigating for the past two years. Close-mouthed, defiant, and unshaken, he denied scandalous tales concerning his own career; professed to have little or no knowledge of any of the underworld characters prominent on the docks, and amazingly little knowledge about some phases of his own business operations, as they were called to his attention by counsel Theodore Kiendl.

Since McCormack's testimony consisted principally of denials to questions that might link him closely with matters into which the Crime Commission was delving, or assertions of ignorance, its significance in Father Corridan's campaign for a reformation of the New York waterfront was limited. It was neither greater nor less than the effect which it had upon public opinion.

The headline writers for the New York newspapers, with their training and instinct for supplying newspaper readers with what they wanted to know in capsule form, helped mold the opinion of many people by their handling of McCormack's testimony and the testimony of persons who were close to him. There were three persons, particularly, who went on the witness stand at about the same time as McCormack who shed some light on how his rise to riches fitted into the pattern of New York politics and waterfront business.

One of these was a former New York municipal magistrate, Francis X. McQuade, then 75 years old, who had been treasurer of the National Exhibition Company, operator of the Polo Grounds, and part owner of the New York Giants Baseball Club back in the 1920's. Another was Robert F. Burker, a tall, slender, middle-aged clerical-appearing personality who had been treasurer of McCormack's Penn Stevedoring Company, for many years. A third was Joe Ryan, and the minor characters were members of New York State's Division of Parole.

The first time McCormack's name was brought openly into

the public hearings was when two officials of New York State's Parole Board testified that, as of their knowledge, some 200 criminals, while still in prison, were assured of jobs with McCormack's Penn Stevedoring Company. They linked Mr. Burker and McCormack's late brother, Harry, to efforts to get these convicts paroled, through assurances that they would receive employment with the McCormack enterprises and membership in the longshoremen's union.

Richard J. Malone, supervisor of employment for the Division of Parole, was the first of these witnesses. He said he did not know Mr. McCormack personally but had dealt at times with his brother, Harry. He said he had known Mr. Burker for about 15 years and had also known a few other officials of McCormack enterprises. Because these close associates of McCormack assured him they would provide jobs for the convicts, Mr. Malone said, he had agreed to parole some 200 men from prison. He said that Mr. Burker had made some seven requests for such paroles, and that one of the men he sought to free was no other than the notorious "Acky" Ackalitis. Mr. Malone testified that Mr. Burker told him he wanted to employ Ackalitis as a supervisor with the Jersey Contracting Company. Another parole officer, Ivan H. Laird, told of a talk with Ackalitis, in which Ackalitis told him Mr. Burker had discussed his employment with another union official.

One employment card, released for publication by the two New York parole officers, bore this notation, "Mr. H. F. McCormack will make immediate arrangements for this inmate's union membership upon his release." Ackalitis, the gangster, was brought to the stand by the Crime Commission counsel. He was accompanied by a lawyer. He declined point-blank to answer any questions on the ground he might be testifying against himself. The commission, he protested, was trying to "smear" him. With that he was released.

Then Burker took the stand. After saying he had been in McCormack's employ for 30 years, he said he did not know the name of the president of the Jersey Contracting Company. He said that the piers on which his own company was operating were those of the Pennsylvania Railroad Company and that this company did not permit the employment of ex-convicts. Later he became confused and admitted that when the company discovered ex-convicts working for the Penn Stevedoring Company the railroad protested and the men were discharged.

Burker at first denied he ever interceded with the Parole Board for Ackalitis. Then he said he only knew Malone, the parole officer, slightly. Finally he admitted only to a conversation with one "Chopsy" Plattner, a notorious West Side hoodlum, in which Plattner had asked his help in getting Ackalitis a job. He denied he ever gave it.

The McQuade testimony brought into the open, by testimony under oath, a story of McCormack which was first told as follows by Westbrook Pegler, Hearst columnist, in 1951:

"At one time, McCormack was Al Smith's partner in a trucking business. Long after he ceased to be governor, Mr. Smith told me that they had dissolved their personal friendship. Soon after the Dempsey-Firpo fight at the Polo Grounds, in 1923, Tex Rickard, who promoted the show, claimed that an official of the license committee of the Boxing Commission made him pay 80,000 dollars, more than the appropriate rate. This was reported to Charles F. Murphy, the boss of Tammany, who told Smith.

"Smith said that he ordered the person who had taken the money to give it back. Both Rickard and Smith told me that the person who had received the money never gave it back to him, but claimed to have handed it over to a member of the firm which operated the Giants and the Polo Grounds.

"Smith withdrew his confidence in Bill McCormack because he had appointed him to the license committee and he felt that McCormack had not been duly diligent to protect his administration from scandal. McCormack resigned. When Jim Farley was appointed boxing commissioner, Smith and Murphy both told him to go to Jimmy Walker right away and get straightened out on the facts of an incident that might cause him embarrassment if he did not know them. Farley corroborates the version that I heard from Smith and Rickard, but is careful to insist that Jimmy Walker was not in on the deal and never got any of the money."

The high point to New York newspaper readers of the public hearings of the Crime Commission was the direct questioning of Mr. McCormack by Theodore Kiendl about this story, as whispered or rumored for many years. Mr. Kiendl led into the circumstances surrounding the Dempsey-Firpo fight by asking McCormack whether there was any occurrence in connection with it which he would remember as long as he lived. McCormack answered that there was no such occurrence—outside of a sensational knockout. Questions and answers from that point ran as follows:

Q: Now after the fight was over did there come up some difficulty about the proceeds of the fight?

A: Not that I know of.

Q: Did you make any agreement with Tex Rickard about any division of the proceeds, the gross receipts of the fight?

A: No, sir.

Q: Isn't it a fact that you received in cash from Tex Rickard the sum of 81,000 dollars of the proceeds of that fight?

A: No, sir.

Q: Mr. McCormack, after that fight were you summoned by Judge McQuade to his chambers?

A: No, sir. That makes me laugh. No, sir.

Q: Isn't it a fact that Judge McQuade called you to see him and told you in substance that he knew the facts concerning your attempted shakedown of Tex Rickard?

A: No, sir.

Q: Didn't Judge McQuade make a demand that you bring back this 25 per cent of the gross receipts of the fight, amounting to 81,500 dollars within two hours?

A: No, sir.

Q: Didn't you in fact come back and deliver to Judge McQuade within two hours 81 1000-dollar bills and one 500-dollar bill?

A: No, sir.

The counsel for the commission kept boring in along this line and McCormack kept countering with flat denials. Finally, before turning to a different line of questioning, Mr. Kiendl asked McCormack whether he ever had heard the shakedown story before.

"Oh, I heard about an alcoholic's dream in the paper about a year ago," McCormack answered.

The very next morning former City Magistrate Francis X. McQuade, then 75 years old, who had been an invalid for some time, came limping into the hearing room, leaning on a cane and upon the arm of an attendant. The ex-magistrate's testimony gave McCormack the lie direct. He testified that in 1923 he was not only a magistrate but the treasurer of Horace Stoneham's baseball park and club. It was Stoneham, the retired magistrate said, who first told him Rickard had been forced to pay McCormack 81,500 dollars in order to get a license for the fight.

"Did you tell Stoneham you would try to get the money back?" asked Kiendl.

"I did," said McQuade.

The questioning ran on:

Q: Did Stoneham tell you that unless Tex Rickard agreed to pay before the fight there would be no license?

A: Yes.

Q: Did you get in touch with McCormack?

A: Yes.

After testifying that McCormack visited him in his chambers in the magistrate's court, McQuade said he demanded that McCormack bring him the money he had taken from Rickard within two hours.

"Did he say anything?" Kiendl asked.

"He said nothing but got the 81,500 dollars within two hours and brought it to me." McQuade even testified as to the denominations of the bills and then said that he turned the money over to Stoneham. The commission then introduced into the testimony, in support of McQuade's evidence, a letter written August 24, 1925, to John McGraw, then manager of the Giants, signed by Stoneham. The letter said that the 81,500 dollars was credited to the books of the Polo Grounds Association as of February 1, 1925. Stoneham said that the amount had been carried in cash but had better be in the bank for a true record for tax purposes.

"Ex-Judge Tells Probers of Shakedown," screamed the New York headlines.

Yet the whole story was pertinent to the investigation of New York waterfront evils only as bearing on McCormack's credibility as a witness. The newspapers generally found his testimony of ignorance on specific questions asked him in the hearing room most astounding.

There was the matter of 984,980 dollars carried on the books of his companies the Crime Commission investigators had combed, which had been withdrawn in cash without any explanatory notations. McCormack insisted he knew nothing about it. He acknowledged readily that an item of 19,281 dollars was expended by his big Penn Stevedoring Company on "food for his home," and then charged off as entertainment and dock repairs. He admitted that two of his employees, E. J. Fennelley and Hector McCreary, had been missing since the Crime Commission tried to subpoena them to tell what they knew about the destruction of some of his business records. He admitted that some of the records might have been burned up in a fire in one of his garages.

Mr. Kiendl took up the report of Mayor O'Dwyer's Committee on Port Conditions. McCormack admitted that he and Joe Ryan drew up that part of the report which said the relations between management and labor on the waterfront were satisfactory to all concerned.

As to his political connections, McCormack testified that he never was a close friend of ex-Mayor O'Dwyer, although he was a member of a Draft O'Dwyer Committee in 1949. He said he never knew the gangsters, "Cockeye" Dunn or Albert Ackalitis. He said he never heard of Jimmy McNay, one of Bowers' major mobsters. He said he was a friend of Mayor Hague in Jersey City and a friend of Mayor Impellitteri of New York. Maybe not a close friend of Impellitteri, but friendly enough so he went to prizefights with him. Among his other good friends he listed Harry M. Durning, for many years Collector of the Port of New York, and Albert Goldman, for years the postmaster.

He was quizzed at length about the study he had made prior to the first report he and Joe Ryan made about labor-management relations in the port. He admitted that the report made no mention of the many rackets, such as loan-sharking, wage kickbacks, and extortion, which had plagued the waterfront for years, as previous commission testimony had shown.

"Did you, in your report, make any mention of the fact that many hiring stevedores possessed criminal records," he was asked.

"No, sir," he answered.

"In the investigation of the committee, appointed by the Mayor, you didn't come across the names of hiring bosses with serious criminal records except Danny St. John?" he was asked.

"That's right," he said. "I believe that if the steamship-company officials would have attended the meetings and would have taken an active part in the work of the committee, that was their part, to bring that thing out."

He was asked if he had been informed that the loading concessions on the Lower West Side of Manhattan had been for some years under the control of the mob headed by "Cockeye" Dunn and Eddie McGrath. He said he was not. Similarly he denied knowledge that work stoppages had occurred as the result of shakedowns by union bosses. He denied knowing that employers were unable to discharge workers for stealing at piers. He denied knowing that union dues paid by longshoremen found their way into the pockets of the union officials. He denied knowing of extensive corruption on the waterfront. He said he knew nothing about the waterfront evils as exposed by the commission's hearings, since he had avoided reading the newspapers about them.

The questioning of McCormack on the rates of pay which he paid his own stevedoring labor force drew from him a statement that the reason they received a dollar-fifty-four an hour, instead of the union rate of two dollars and ten cents an hour, was because they worked only on the piers and not in the holds or decks of ships. "Work on the piers is less dangerous," he said. Both Judge Joseph M. Proskauer and Mr. Kiendl tried to show, through questioning him, that the relative freedom from labor troubles which all his enterprises had enjoyed through the years was because of his close relationships with the leaders of labor unions.

McCormack denied this stoutly. "It's because I take a human view of employee problems," he said. "I'm human and they're human." Although the press had branded him Mr. Big, he said he considered himself a very humble man.

When Big Bill McCormack stepped down from the witness stand he stepped down in triumph, as always. Nothing whatever had been revealed in the Crime Commission hearings that could shake the great commercial empire he had built by brawn and brain and fifty years of labor along the waterfront. Nothing whatever had been told that could disturb in any way the great influence he had come to wield over the other practical realists who ruled the harbor in business, politics, and unionism.

Certainly the big man never had posed as a reformer. He never invented that system of rule against which Father Corridan was crying aloud like an Old Testament prophet. McCormack had merely accepted all the hard conditions of that jungle world into which he was born, and fought his way to wealth and power within them. So had all those others in the shipping and stevedoring industries, in politics and unionism around the harbor who had made their mark and acquired their fortunes in the fiercely competitive warfare of commerce allied to politics.

Big Bill was for long years shrewder and tougher and abler than most. If he was pilloried before this Crime Commission, appointed by a Republican Governor to investigate the sins of Democratic New York, it was partly because the very success of his life had made him a symbol of that system of rule against which so many longshoremen along the docks were in rebellion. Father Corridan was their champion.

"It does no good to rail at personalities or to overemphasize their importance," says Father Corridan. "Responsibility for conditions in New York harbor is a social responsibility shared by a great many people, particularly by all those with real power in the community. They have been in some degree the prisoners and captives of that system of corrupt government that has grown up with the years. It is high time to break its chains, if Christ is to walk along the waterfront untroubled—if the essential dignity of man is to be respected in the person of the average worker."

The two-hundred-ninth and final witness in the public hearings of the Crime Commission was no other than old Joe Ryan, lifetime president, then, of the I.L.A., and a great power in politics. After the sensational testimony and headlines concerning his friend and patron, McCormack, Joe Ryan's long day on the stand seemed then an anticlimax, but it resulted directly in his complete downfall, as both union leader and politician, and to his trial in a criminal court on charges of theft of his union's funds.

Ryan left the stand grinning, though shaken. He had been forced to testify concerning the venality and corruption of his close associates and lieutenants. His comment when the day was ended was a laughing question: "When a teller of a bank is guilty of something they don't hold the bank president, do they?"

But under the relentless questioning of Mr. Kiendl, Ryan admitted that he himself had withdrawn 31,650.81 dollars from the funds of the I.L.A. *Journal,* the union's official publication, between 1947 and 1952. A chart introduced by the commission showed that some of his expenditures from union funds were: 816.97 dollars for clothing, 10,775 dollars for insurance premiums, 500 dollars for medical and legal fees, 1,331.60 dollars for golf guest charges, 546.15 dollars for luncheons at the Stork Club, 942.30 dollars for repairs to his Cadillac, and 460 dollars for a cruise to Guatemala.

Ryan insisted that he had replaced all the union funds he took with money from his own personal account. But he was forced to admit that while union accounting showed his personal withdrawals, there was no record kept of his reimbursements.

His examination brought other admissions. He conceded that he had appointed such organizers of criminal record as Eddie

McGrath, Harold Bowers, Alex Di Brizzi, and Edward Florio and that he set up a niece's husband, Joseph J. Schultz, as solicitor for his union magazine, thereby enriching him by 27,343 dollars in five years. This money came principally from shipping companies, who were induced to advertise in the *Journal* under the guise of contributing to the campaign against communism.

Ryan also admitted that in 1948 he had sent a warning to District Attorney Frank S. Hogan that if he continued his investigation of waterfront murders he might precipitate a strike on the piers. He also admitted being told by William J. O'Dwyer, away back when O'Dwyer was district attorney in Brooklyn, that the Camarda locals of the longshoremen's union on the Brooklyn waterfront were really controlled by Albert Anastasia, assassin for Murder, Inc.

It was during this questioning that Kiendl disclosed to Ryan—if he did not know it—that 30 per cent of I.L.A. officials had police records; that more than half of 45 locals could produce no financial records or minutes; and that many of his union officials had increased their own salaries from time to time without consulting their members. Ryan told Kiendl that he had been keeping abreast of the Crime Commission's disclosures by reading the newspapers and that because of them he had called "Ike" Gannon of the watchmen's union on the carpet and told him he would have to give up two of his three I.L.A. jobs.

Asked if he had come in contact, because of his position, with any important officials in New York City, Ryan snapped back that he knew important officials all over the world. Those whom he knew well in the port area, he said, included the late Jimmy Walker, Grover Whalen, Frank Hague, Mayor Frank De Sapio of Hoboken, Hugo Rogers, former borough president of Manhattan, and others. He said one of the city councilmen, James J. Boland, called him "boss," although he never asked him to.

Ryan also admitted knowing Albert Anastasia. He said he met him at "barber shops, golf clubs, dinners, prizefights," and all around the town. He said that when O'Dwyer in Brooklyn asked him to do something about Anastasia's control of the dock workers there, he promised to do what he could but was unable to do anything, actually. To the delight of listeners in the hearing room he branded Anastasia's followers as "a lot of Commies," and said he went among them at the risk of his life.

Asked about union officials who accepted gifts from shipping companies, Ryan said he wouldn't know who did and who didn't. As for himself, he admitted that he had taken 1500 dollars a year for five years from Arthur Kennedy of the Daniels and Kennedy trucking concern. Mr. Keindl produced a chart which showed that Ryan's total salaries and expenses from various positions in the I.L.A., totaled 152,000 dollars in five years. Some of his cash withdrawals were a 1000 dollars for purchase of a bond in a golf club, 222 dollars for shirts at Sulka's, 168 dollars to Nat Lewis, a haberdasher, and a 250-dollar check to a dentist. Old Joe was always what the West Side would call a nifty dresser.

But after headlines like the New York *Herald Tribune's* "Ryan Spent $50,000 on Self from Union Anti-Red Fund," his protestations about fighting Communists would never carry their old-time weight. Even the larger powers behind the old racket-ridden I.L.A., which he had led for a generation, were going to have to drop him as president within the near future, and they knew it.

The American Federation of Labor itself, which has had its share of scandals, was finding Ryan far from an asset. There was a new president now in that great Federation, George Meaney. Meaney was a New Yorker and had known Ryan for years. He had worked with him for years, in labor politics and in the governmental politics of city and state within the state Federation of Labor.

But when Ryan got down off that witness stand at the close of the Crime Commission hearings, with so many of the iniquities of his union lying naked before the public, even Mr. Meaney knew that for the good of the American Federation of Labor as a whole, this rotten racket, which Ryan had led for years, would have to be scrubbed clean or the so-called "union" fired from the Federation of Labor. It stank too badly to be tolerated by anyone pretending any devotion whatever to honest trade unionism.

CHAPTER

13

THE GOVERNMENT STEPS IN

Despite the widespread disclosures of racketeering in the I.L.A. and the shipping industry made by the Crime Commission, the general attitude of the dockside workers when the hearings ended was one of cynicism. "It'll all blow over," was a common comment. "We've seen these investigations before. Nothing ever really comes of them. It's politics, that's all. Nothing will be done." Father Corridan himself was doubtful for many weeks whether the hearings, for all their sensationalism, would bring about any real reform of value.

"We had seen a lot of investigations in the years since Mike Johnson wrote his first waterfront articles," Father Corridan says. "We had seen nine. All of them resulted either in a whitewash of the whole rotten mess or in recommendations that never were followed by governing agencies, by the union, or by the New York Shipping Association.

"First we had the so-called triple investigation, conducted by the city's Commissioner of Investigations John M. Murtagh, by the Department of Marine and Aviation, and by the Police Department. Mr. Murtagh asked the New York Shipping Association members to take over the loading at the piers, and the shipping people declined. Then he asked them to designate the loaders they wanted, and they designated the very men who were browbeating them and extorting money from them. What the Murtagh investigation really led to was to make the loading racket take on a new air of some legitimacy.

"Then we had the reports of the Mayor's Port Industry Committee. Several of these reports were excellent, but the Ryan-McCormack labor report was a whitewash. It was so raw that James A. Farrell, a shipping representative, withdrew from the committee long before it made public its declaration that everything was lovely. Joe Curran, president of the National Maritime Union, refused to sign it. A little later we had hearings of the Kefauver Committee, which was set up on the federal level to delve into organized crime in interstate commerce. The committee denounced the racketeering in the I.L.A., and said it ought to be cleaned up—but nothing happened.

"Then we had the Board of Inquiry after the 1951 strike. That was the first time a real government body pointed out the evils inherent in the shape, in the loading racket, and in the racketeering leadership of the longshoremen's union. What happened after that report? Joe Ryan and his pals in the Central Trades and Labor Council united to defeat the lawyer for the board, George J. Mintzer, when he ran for a judgeship. They got old William Green, the president of the A.F. of L., to create a committee that denounced the board and all its findings.

"After that we had local and federal grand-jury investigations in Brooklyn, New York, and Hudson County, New Jersey. These, of course, brought on a few indictments, and put a few people in jail, but that meant next to nothing in the way of a harbor clean-up. When the State Crime Commission was ending its hearings, who could say there would be any real legislative action. New Jersey, of course, had kept Brigadier General Norman Schwartzkopf in close liaison with the Crime Commission. Governor Driscoll was known to be studying the waterfront ills in New Jersey. But the wise money, generally, was on no real reform."

It wasn't only Father Corridan and the longshoremen who were skeptical. Before the Crime Commission brought in its report, Morris L. Ernst, a lawyer prominent in civil-liberties cases, wrote a letter to the New York *Times*. His letter recalled that these evils, which the Crime Commission had bared in detail, had long been known. He remembered that legislation frequently had been introduced in Albany within the past few years, in a legislature controlled by the Republicans, with Dewey as Governor, to end the shape or otherwise remedy the lot of longshoremen.

"I have checked back and found that as far back as 1948, the District Attorney of New York County (Frank S. Hogan) discussed the basic social ailments and pointed in the direction of the cure," he wrote. "Following Mr. Hogan's bit of social engineering, a bill was introduced into the Assembly on March 1, 1949, amending the penal law in relation to the employment of longshoremen and stevedores in the city of New York. It died in the legislature. On Jan. 18, 1950, a bill was introduced in the Assembly seeking to amend the Labor Law in relation to the employment of longshoremen or stevedores in the city of New York. It died in the Assembly.

"On Jan. 17, 1951, a similar effort was made in the Assembly in terms of assembly bill introductory 806. This also died in the legislature. On Jan. 16, 1952, a further effort was made to amend the labor law by assembly bill 529. It also died.

"All of these bills were introduced by Assemblyman John R. Brooks, Republican of the Ninth Manhattan Assembly District. I should imagine the public is aware of the fact that had the Governor then, as now, been aware of the frightening social aspects of the waterfront, the legislation would have become law without any delays; and maybe even without adequate public hearings, as is so often the case in recent times.

"I hold no brief for any of these bills. But isn't it about time that we stopped playing cops and robbers in this big city and realize that commissions that play for headlines procure a certain number of convictions, but inevitably leave the basic social cancers untouched?"

Then Mr. Ernst urbanely drove the needle into Governor Dewey just a little deeper, in remembrance of the fact that the Governor's rise in politics had been accompanied by many lurid headlines during his prosecution of Jimmy Hines, a notorious Tammany ally of "Dutch" Schultz, the bootlegger in the 1930's, and "Lucky" Luciano, then as now a power in the big-business underworld.

"Does anyone now believe that the conviction of Hines and Luciano," Ernst inquired, "had any effect on the gambling and vice habits of our community? Maybe we should now investigate why the shape-up legislation died so easily."

When Father Corridan read Mr. Ernst's letter to the *Times,* he gave it an appreciative chuckle. To be sure, the lawyer had omitted from his list of legislative efforts against dockside evils the Gracie resolution, which he had helped to draft in 1949, with a Republican legislator. This called for an investigation by the state of the New York waterfront. That little effort of his and Assemblyman Gracie's also got nowhere.

But Father Corridan long since was confident in his own mind why these bills were killed. They were killed because waterfront reform, in itself, was always fought by representatives of the New York Shipping Association, by the I.L.A., and by the Central Trades and Labor Council, where W. J. McCormack's stable of labor leaders wielded power in both the Republican and Democratic parties.

During the Crime Commission hearings Father Corridan was asked whether he would testify, as an expert, before the commission, in private and public hearings. "I told them that my status as a priest was such that I believed it would be most improper for me to testify in an investigation that was primarily an investigation of crime," he said. "I knew that my superiors in the order would not countenance it, and I was quite sure that Cardinal Spellman also would disapprove. I reasoned it this way. Any testimony that I might give would weaken the belief of people around the waterfront in my trustworthiness as a priest to keep confidences. Some of the information I had received had come to me in the confessional. Much of the rest of what I knew had been given me in confidence. Outside of that most of what I knew was of an official nature, from sources the Crime Commission itself could tap.

"The members of the commission conceded the validity of my position and did not call me to testify. They asked me, however, to submit a proposal for waterfront reform.

"Before I drew up the plan, I had a long conversation about it with Ignatius M. Wilkinson, dean of Fordham Law School, who was a member of the Crime Commission, and Leslie H. Arps, assistant chief counsel. Then I waited until there was a lull between the public sessions of the commission. Such a lull came early in January, 1953.

"I was convinced then that the legislation I would be proposing would fail of any lasting result unless it succeeded in giving the longshoremen a chance to organize an honest, democratic labor union. They had never had that chance. In my opinion they never would have it without the intervention of bistate legislation, joined to the approval of the federal government.

"If I could only help bring that intervention about, the longshoremen would have their chance and so would the shipping industry—or the better elements on both sides would have their chance. But ultimately labor and management would have to act together, with a mutual sense of responsibility to the community as a whole, as well as to themselves, of their own volition. Then government controls could be withdrawn.

"I submitted my proposals to the Crime Commission, dated as of Monday, January 12, 1953. Monday has always been a good day in New York for people who want to make news through the daily newspapers. News 'for release' on Monday mornings has been traditionally effective as far back as the days of Theodore Roosevelt. I sent my plan to the newspaper city editors and to the editorial writers three or four days in advance of my release date.

"My proposals embodied eight specific recommendations. Along with these, I sent the newspapers a brief personal statement. I considered the statement almost as important, from the public standpoint, as the recommendations themselves. 'Only major surgery and a radical reconstruction can save the finest port in the world,' I said. 'Halfhearted remedies from halfhearted men are not the answer. It will take men of vision and guts to put this solution into effect. Not only the longshoremen and the harbor workers but also the people of this city and state wonder if we have them. Please God, we do!' "

Father Corridan's eight recommendations follow:

1. Turn over the entire physical assets of the entire port to the Port of New York Authority for rehabilitation and development as one natural unit instead of permitting competition between New York and New Jersey.

2. Outlaw the public-loading concessions and require steamship companies to provide such services when requested by trucking firms.

3. Replace the shape-up with seven longshore hiring centers, three in Manhattan, two in Brooklyn, and two in New Jersey, operated and regulated by the State Employment Services.

4. Register all dock workers, either by state or federal agency, and collect information necessary for a regulated system of hiring.

5. Institute a seniority system for hiring based on job status and length of employment.

6. Provide for dockside arbitration of disputes through the State Labor Department, expenses to be borne equally by the union and management.

7. Encourage the union to adopt democratic procedures, carefully regulated, with election of officers by secret ballot at least every four years. Locals should be reduced to seven, should submit detailed, audited financial reports at least quarterly, and should meet at least once a month.

8. Encourage members of the New York Shipping Association to allow rank-and-file longshoremen to replace the present company union with its gangster dominated leadership by a bonafide union, devoted to the interests of the longshoremen.

The heart of this program, outside of its provision for honest trade unionism, if attainable, was of course the abolition of the daily shape-up, which had for so many years made gangsters and gunmen the absolute masters of the livings of so many thousands of dock workers, and the abolition of the loading rackets whereby the gangsters had allied themselves to the hiring bosses within the I.L.A. for their many criminal activities.

Father Corridan's plan drew strong editorial support from the New York *Daily Mirror* and the New York *Journal-American,* and qualified support from the New York *World-Telegram.*

Then came a three months' wait for the Crime Commission to report its findings, and a six months' wait for Governor Dewey to act. The ponderous machinery of the American Federation of Labor began to move to oust Ryan from his position as I.L.A. president, and either to force the union to clean its own house or to set up another waterfront union to represent the dock workers.

The first move was made at a closed meeting of about 100 I.L.A. leaders in Brooklyn. They agreed that Ryan must be persuaded to become "president emeritus" of their organization. If he declined, the majority said, the A.F. of L. executive committee should suspend the I.L.A. charter until Ryan and his closer lieutenants got out. The proposal of these 100 leaders of the I.L.A. to reform their own union was laughable to Father Corridan. Most of the leaders who wanted to toss Ryan to the wolves were Italian mobsters of dubious repute, including Mike Clemente from Manhattan's East River and the representatives of Anastasia's locals in Brooklyn.

Under the auspices of the Maritime Trades Department of the American Federation of Labor, the I.L.A. officials drew up a paper plan calling for regular monthly meetings of all locals in the I.L.A., the expulsion of all officers or workers found guilty of pilferage or loan-sharking, taking kickbacks on workingmen's wages, or inducing work stoppages for the purpose of maintaining personal rackets. Ryan himself attended this meeting and agreed to most of the program, though he said he was sure the dock workers would vote for continuation of the shape if the question were put to a vote.

He objected, however, to a study by the Maritime Trades Department of the public loaders. As this meeting was being held, officers of Local 791, which had been the sparkplug of numerous wildcat strikes against Ryan leadership and Ryan contracts, announced to the press they had sent a warning to Father Corridan to keep his hands out of waterfront politics and waterfront unionism and confine himself to spiritual advice to the dock workers. As Father Corridan recalls it, he never received any such message of warning and disregarded with a shrug the news in the papers that such a warning had been sent.

On January 16, 1953, United States Senator Charles W. Tobey, Republican, of New Hampshire, a leading figure in the Kefauver Committee's crime investigations, announced that he proposed to have a senatorial investigation of the New York waterfront. Father Corridan wrote the senator a letter, in which he welcomed the inquiry and argued for his own proposals for reform.

The very heart of his proposals, he said, was the registration of longshore workers, conducted by a competent governmental body, federal preferable to the states. He asserted that "nowhere in the world has longshore work been regularized successfully without previous registration." He said his proposals did not imply licensing of the workers. "The vested interests in the harbor," he said, "oppose registration because immediately after it law-enforcement bodies would be in a position to uncover much of the extortion that has not been uncovered."

The inquiry came to nothing because Senator Tobey died.

Within a few days of Father Corridan's letter, Dave Beck, powerful boss of the International Teamsters' Union, announced that he personally would work for a thorough clean-up of the I.L.A. Because of the Crime Commission's revelations he had suspended "Joe" Papa from the presidency of the New York teamsters' local. The A.F. of L. executive committee was meeting early in February in Miami, Florida. Beck said he would present his views there.

On February 3 the A.F. of L. executive committee drafted an executive order in which it ordered the I.L.A. to clean house by April 30 or face expulsion from the federation. The order was adopted unanimously by the committee. It contained a strong implication that the union should throw out virtually all its top officers, since most of them had testified before the Crime Commission that they had taken money from employers or placed known criminals in key position on the wharves. The order demanded an end to the shape-up as a hiring method and the installment of democratic practices in the running of all locals.

This order by the executive committee was a landmark in the history of the A.F. of L. For the first time the principle was laid down that "the exercise of autonomy in government by affiliated unions presupposes the maintenance of minimum standards of trade union decency."

It was a bad day for Ryan. He did not attend the gathering in Miami because he had been ordered by District Attorney Hogan to appear before a New York grand jury investigating the criminal aspects of the waterfront. When he refused to sign a waiver of immunity from prosecution, Hogan refused to let him testify. In interviews with the press Ryan insisted he was trying as best he could to clean up the conditions on the waterfront to which the Crime Commission had called attention. But on the same day he was making his pious protestation, checkers of I.L.A. locals staged wildcat strikes on one pier in Brooklyn and three piers in Staten Island to protest the selection of hiring bosses by the Isthmian Steamship Lines and the Royal Netherlands Steamship Company.

Before the executive committee of the A.F. of L. adjourned in Miami, its members made it clear to newspaper reporters that they had little hope for a real clean-up within the old I.L.A., and so were laying plans for a rival union. They conceded that there would be considerable strife before any rival union could supplant the I.L.A.

On February 11 Father Corridan wrote an open letter to all the longshoremen in New York harbor, urging them to stand by the American Federation of Labor in case of a struggle between its leadership and Ryan. "The A.F.L.," he wrote, "stands for sound trade unionism. Ryan never did."

Between 1951 and the end of 1953 Father Corridan made more than 300 talks to organizations of many kinds, urging action on the waterfront clean-up. He spoke before such organizations of his church as parish sodalities, the Holy Name Societies, and the Knights of Columbus. He talked before schools and colleges. He talked to chambers of commerce, trade associations, businessmen's clubs, and political clubs with particular emphasis on the Young Republican and Young Democratic Clubs. Three speeches a week was his average schedule, and he mixed these in with appearances on television and radio broadcasts. Most of his talks were in New York, New Jersey, and Connecticut, but he made occasional trips to the Middle West, where he found the ills of the New York waterfront and labor-union racketeering subjects of intense popular interest. Particularly in 1953 he kept pressing for action by any political, labor, or business power that was capable of action.

In some of his speeches he bore down on the gradual loss of general cargo shipped from the port of New York, and the gain in such cargo shipped from other ports along the Atlantic seaboard. Speaking at a communion breakfast at St. Joseph's Church, Green Island, he noted that "since 1946, the port of New York has dropped steadily in general civilian cargo from 37 per cent in that year to 31 per cent in 1951. If the port had only held its own it could have handled 2,250,000 more tons in 1951 than it actually did, and this represents cargo valued at more than a billion dollars.

"Beyond that loss in civilian cargo there was a loss last year in military cargo, because of the corruption existing within the I.L.A. leadership, the steamship and stevedoring companies, and the political units of government."

At a luncheon in April before the Labor Management Club of New York he prodded Governor Dewey to swing into action. He reiterated his major theme: That neither the unions concerned, nor the shipping industry, nor the municipalities around the harbor would act to end racketeering. Therefore state and federal governments were obligated to act in the public interest.

Two stormy meetings of the New York District Council of the I.L.A. in March sufficed to show that the union was fighting bitterly within its leadership on the demand by the American Federation of Labor executive committee that it abolish the shape-up. After one of these, on March 8, Ryan told reporters the council had, indeed, voted to end the shape, but would not have any other plan of hiring ready to present to the employers until three months later. Then the wage-negotiation committee would have one prepared. This would be a long while after the April 30 deadline for reform set by the A.F. of L. On March 16 Ryan reversed himself publicly. No decision had been reached to abolish the shape, he said. He personally was still of the opinion that most of the men wanted it, and so a referendum of the rank and file would be held on May 8 to decide the issue.

By this time Ryan had been indicted by the New York County grand jury on a charge of having stolen money from his union, and was under investigation by the FBI, the Federal Bureau of Internal Revenue, and two other grand juries in connection with his tax returns and other matters. There was no visible clean-up within his union on April 30, the deadline for action. On that day he defended himself vigorously in Washington, D.C., at a hearing of Senator Tobey's committee, when Downey Rice, counsel for the committee, asked him about the appointment of gangsters to organizational posts in his union.

"How about Eddie McGrath and Ed Florio and 'Buster' Bell?" he was asked.

"At the time I appointed them I didn't know they had criminal records," he said. The only men he appointed to be organizers already had been elected to some leadership post within different harbor locals, he insisted.

Asked what action had been taken by his union to bar criminals from office in the future, Ryan said there had been a resolution adopted providing for the expulsion of any officer found to have been convicted of any crime.

"Will that apply to you if you are convicted?" Mr. Rice shot at him.

"It certainly will, but I don't expect to be convicted," Ryan retorted.

He admitted on the stand that he had not fulfilled the demands of the A.F. of L. for complete clean-up of his union, but said he would have a progress report ready for the A.F. of L. executive committee meeting, scheduled for Washington, D.C., on May 20.

The referendum of the dock workers on the fate of the shape occurred as scheduled on May 8, following warnings by Father Corridan that, despite the supervision of the Honest Ballot Association, the vote would be a "phony" because of the way the question had been put.

A single question was asked of the dockers: "Are you satisfied with the present method of hiring?" In Father Corridan's opinion this question was so general and vague that an affirmative result in the balloting was the only one possible, since many longshoremen were hired steadily by the gang, and were perfectly satisfied. The machine vote of the I.L.A. leaders could roll up a majority easily, and frauds would swell it. On the day of the voting some of the New York newspaper reporters found it perfectly simple to get I.L.A. cards and cast ballots as longshoremen, thereby proving to public satisfaction that no real machinery for adequate supervision of the polls had been created.

The result was as Father Corridan had predicted. The published count was 7000 in the affirmative, and 3920 in the negative. The result meant little. Less than a week after the vote by the New York locals, the 21 top officers of the I.L.A., meeting in Baltimore, repudiated the result of the voting and ordered the New York locals to follow A.F. of L. policy in their next negotiations of their wage committee with the New York Shipping Association.

On May 20 the A.F. of L. executive committee met in Washington, D.C., and found a so-called "progress report" submitted by Ryan on the reform of his union inadequate. It extended the time for reform, however, to August 10. Since Ryan was still under indictment for theft of union funds, George Meaney sent his new clean-up order to Harry Hasselgren as I.L.A. secretary-treasurer. So far, a clean-up within the union had bogged down completely.

The time had clearly arrived for intervention by the states of New York and New Jersey. On May 20 the Crime Commission made its report.

The Crime Commission's recommendations, naturally, could deal with the problem of the port only from the viewpoint of legislation that might be feasible in one state, but they contained in broad outline most of the provisions of law which were soon to be embodied in a New York-New Jersey compact, ratified by the federal government. The commission asked for the creation of a new State Division of Port Administration, empowered "to abolish the shape-up, and to remove other abuses from the docks."

The commission asked that employment information centers be established under the control of this state authority. It asked that all dock workers be required to register at these centers, and that no one with a criminal record be permitted to work on the docks without specific authorization of the state. The new authority was to receive power to bar from the docks anyone "whose presence on the waterfront will endanger the public peace, safety, and welfare." Employers of dock workers were to be required to employ only registered men, approved by the new authority.

The commission asked that all stevedoring companies be licensed, and that the new state authority receive power to inspect their books. It asked that all pier superintendents and foremen in charge of hiring be licensed, and that the new authority receive the responsibility for denying licenses to persons whose presence on the docks might endanger public security and welfare.

It asked drastic supervision of loading. "No person other than a bona-fide steamship or trucking company, or licensed stevedoring company should be permitted to engage in the business of loading or unloading trucks on the New York waterfronts," its recommendation read. All these loaders should be licensed, it urged. No individual or organization should be licensed, it said, if he or any member of a licensed organization had ever been convicted of a felony or certain misdemeanors, unless a specific exemption should be granted by the new state authority. Licensed loaders should be required to maintain adequate liability insurance and to keep complete books and other business records open at all times to state inspection.

The commission also recommended the licensing of all port watchmen. All applicants for the license should be fingerprinted, have their photographs taken, and fill out a form giving details of previous occupations, and any police record, it said.

The most drastic recommendation of all, from the labor-union standpoint, was one providing statutory requirement of sound financial and democratic practices in all waterfront local unions. A state statute, the commission said, should require that every local union keep adequate books, showing all financial transactions with members and others. A statute should require that these records be audited annually and preserved for six years. A statute, it was said, should also require that all union officers be elected by the membership, at least once every four years, with supervision of the elections by the State Department of Labor.

Evidence that the commission itself recognized some doubt as to whether any legislature would pass so sweeping a control over a labor union's internal affairs was shown in its recommendation that enactment of this legislation be postponed until 1954, to give the labor unions a chance to clean up their own affairs voluntarily.

To Father Corridan, most of the recommendations of the commission were welcome. Bistate administration rather than state administration of any new waterfront regulation, he felt, was reasonably certain. Most of the recommendations of the commission were approved by the members of the Port Authority and were bitterly assailed by officers of the longshoremen's union and their employers in the New York Shipping Association.

By early June, Governor Dewey, acting in close consultation with Governor Driscoll in New Jersey, had the blueprints sufficiently drawn for that ultimate intervention of the two states and of the federal government, which would assure some measure of reform in New York harbor. Since action by the two states in unison would require federal approval, Governor Dewey had preliminary discussions with his old political adviser, Herbert Brownell, Jr., Attorney General of the United States, who by this time was a power in the Eisenhower administration.

Plans had been drawn for special sessions of the legislatures in both states to deal with the diminution of crime in the port, as a minimum objective, and the assignment of some supervision over the stevedoring and longshore industries to a governmental body rather than the municipal governments of the two states. Having laid this foundation for reforms he had in mind, Governor Dewey announced that he would hold public hearings on the recommendations of the Crime Commission in the New York City Bar Association building, just off Fifth Avenue, on West 44th Street—a long way from City Hall and Manhattan's waterfront—on June 8 and 9.

His announcement of public hearings, to which he proposed to bring legislative leaders of both parties, drew immediate outcries of protest or anguish from the longshoremen's union and from the Democratic machine in New York City.

Borough President Robert F. Wagner, Jr., of Manhattan, whose senatorial father had been immortalized during the Roosevelt administration as father of organized labor's charter, the Wagner Act, was one of the first to sneer at Dewey's move as politically inspired. Young Wagner was later to be Mayor. On the eve of the Governor's hearings he complained that during the past "ten years of Dewey rule," public hearings were never held purely as matters of public concern but only when partisan advantage was an issue. As for the I.L.A. longshoremen's leaders, they threatened strike if the Governor went too far, and announced they would picket his hearings. Announcement of the picketing and threat of a wildcat strike in protest were made by William Lynch, secretary of the famous rebel local, 791. Lynch said the rank-and-file longshoremen would be escorted in their picketing by eight posts of the

American Legion and the Veterans of Foreign Wars, composed of dockside workers.

On the day of the hearings the picketing was impressive, but the harbor strike failed to materialize, having been frowned on by the bulk of the rank and file, particularly longshoremen in Hoboken and Jersey City. Heavy police details lined the route of 5000 marching pickets. "This isn't Russia, Mr. Dewey," said the pickets' placards, or, "Hitler had a moustache, too." Massed American flags were carried by the longshoreman paraders. The police turnout was smart. The day was lovely and warm. The crowds in the midtown area watched the show as New Yorkers watch all shows, with sophisticated amusement. There was no disorder.

Twenty-one witnesses were called before the Governor in the two days of public hearings. The recommendation of the commission that drew the strongest fire was that one which urged the creation of a new state agency to supervise the waterfront hiring system. Prior to the hearings Governor Dewey himself had indicated he opposed this recommendation. He even held fruitless conferences with the New York Port Authority, as the one suitable bistate agency, trying to get its commissioners to take over the supervisory job.

Speaking for the I.L.A., Louis Waldman, its counsel, and Ryan—still president though under indictment—charged that the proposed controls would make New York harbor a "slave-labor camp," and were a "blueprint for industrial chaos and the destruction of this great port."

John V. Lyon, representing the New York Shipping Association, said employers generally felt there should be tighter controls in the port, but wanted the commission's recommendations modified drastically, to give the companies greater control over hirings. Warm endorsement for the Crime Commission's proposals came from Austin J. Tobin, executive director, and two other officials of the New York Port Authority.

One of the major witnesses was George Meaney, president of the A.F. of L. Noting that the federation had already gone on record as demanding the abolition of the shape-up, and the clean-up of the racket-ridden I.L.A., Mr. Meaney took the standard labor-union position against the commission's recommendations. The crimes of which the commission complains, he said, have nothing to do with unions or unionism.

"Spelled out in a word," he said, "you've got crime. You've got pilferage and you've got bribery. But the Crime Commission's recommendations that all dock workers be registered smacks strongly of totalitarianism. It smacks strongly of a system of regimentation."

It remained for Father Corridan to counter the Waldman-Ryan claim that laws based on the commission's recommendations would make New York harbor a slave camp.

"The basic problem in this harbor is not crime," he reiterated. "It's how to get a decent labor-management setup, free from the control of racketeers. The problem is not law enforcement. It's how to make law enforcement on the waterfront possible by stripping the racketeers of their false union coloration. The I.L.A. in this harbor is a racket union. We have slave labor today because the men have no voice in their union."

Near the end of the two-day session, Edward F. Cavanagh, Commissioner of Marine and Aviation, spoke as a representative of Mayor Impelliteri. He said that since the harbor was a two-state proposition, no New York State controls would be effective. Some bistate commission should ultimately control. In the meantime, he said, he believed the city and not the state should deal with waterfront problems on the Manhattan side of the port.

The very day following the two public hearings, Governors Dewey and Driscoll announced simultaneously in Trenton and New York that they had reached an agreement for a new bistate agency to control the common waterfront, to wipe out gangsterism on the docks, to police enforcement of union contracts, and to carry out most of the recommendations of the New York State Crime Commission. The cost of supporting this commission was estimated at about 700,000 dollars a year, and this money was to be provided by the shipping and stevedoring industries, through fees and charges for some definite services. Governor Dewey said he would call a special session of the legislature on June 22 or June 29 to enact the necessary legislation, and Governor Driscoll said the New Jersey legislature would adopt similar legislation on June 22.

Governors Dewey and Driscoll were in no mood to await any reformation by industrial or union leaders in the port, and the bulk of newspaper opinion as expressed in editorial columns called for immediate action on the Dewey-Driscoll legislation. Both governors were in complete control of majorities in their own legislatures. Parallel measures setting up a bistate commission to supervise the longshore and stevedoring industries were adopted within a week of each other, in Trenton and Albany, late in June, and by August the United States government had ratified the bistate compact.

After five years, then, of effective agitation, Father Corridan witnessed the complete intervention in port affairs by the state and national governments. With such help by government—one step up from the corrupt municipal machines around the harbor, he was sure the men who worked on the docks would have some chance, at long last, to build an honest labor union to represent them.

All his highest hopes were centered in the men themselves. With the new laws to help them, with the complete public disrepute of their old I.L.A. bosses, with the ruling national committee of the American Federation of Labor itself pledged to a clean-up, surely now the stage was set for the port's longshoremen to set themselves free from old oppressions. With some new, clean union the men could work out decent labor relations with the better elements in the shipping business, Father Corridan believed, and the Bi-State Port Commission would stand by as long as necessary to see that these new arrangements brought a finer moral climate to the deteriorating port.

There would be a stiff fight, of course, before the old mobsters and their corrupt allies surrendered. Father Corridan knew that. But the men had their chance. And the public had its chance. As for himself, foreseeing a battle between some new A.F. of L. union and the old I.L.A., he proposed to roll up his shirt sleeves and get out on the platform, among longshoremen all over the harbor, wherever his friends could get him introduced, to assure the victory for which he was longing.

With ratification by Congress of the bistate compact, Governors Dewey and Driscoll acted swiftly to set up the new Waterfront Commission of New York Harbor, with men of such caliber in directing positions as to inspire public confidence. Governor Driscoll named Major General Edward C. Rose (Retired) as New Jersey's commissioner, and Governor Dewey named Lieutenant General George P. Hays to represent New York. For executive director and chief counsel, Lawrence E. Walsh, a New York lawyer in his early forties, was selected.

Mr. Walsh, who worked in his youth as a seaman, first came to public notice in the late 1930's as an assistant to Dewey in the New York District Attorney's office. Later he became Governor Dewey's personal counsel, and then counsel of the New York State Public Service Commission.

Under the terms of the compact the new commission had five major tasks, all aimed to rid the waterfront of criminal domination. It had:

(1) To license pier superintendents and hiring bosses. Persons who had been convicted of felonies, under terms of the law, were barred from such positions for at least five years, and only persons of demonstrable good character were to be hired.

(2) To license stevedores and port watchmen.

(3) To abolish the public-loading system.

(4) To register longshoremen. The right of registration was to be absolute unless the applicant had been convicted of a crime, was engaged in subversive activity, or was of such a character that his presence on the waterfront was clearly likely to endanger public peace or safety. The commission was also empowered to drop from the register, under some specified conditions, persons not permanently attached to the longshore industry. In this way it was believed that more and steadier work would be supplied to workmen whose primary occupation was longshoring.

(5) To set up 13 regional information centers, in all sections of the port, which would be in effect employment exchanges for registered longshoremen and licensed port watchmen.

In the early autumn a working staff was assembled. The commission began its work of screening undesirable characters off the docks and giving the necessary licenses and working permits so that the work of the port could be carried on without loss of efficiency, after December 1, when all provisions of the law would be made applicable.

As was to be expected, the commission's very existence was fought at the outset by the old I.L.A., first in the courts, where the constitutionality of the compact was challenged by George Brenner, I.L.A. counsel, and then by picketing and work stoppages on the docks.

On October 28 Mr. Brenner argued against the constitutionality of the compact before a three-judge court, composed of Judge Augustus N. Hand of the Federal Circuit Court of Appeals, and Federal District Judges Edward Weinfeld and John F. X. McGohey. Mr. Brenner argued that the act curbed the right of the longshoremen to bargain collectively. He charged that, under the act, the right of a man to work would depend upon the discretion of the commission, and that this would deprive dock workers of "liberty and property on the basis of vague standards."

Mr. Walsh, as counsel for the commission, argued that the only real question before the court was whether the legislature or the commission had acted arbitrarily, or beyond the police power of the states. On November 9 the court upheld the constitutionality of the act as being clearly within the police power of the state.

By this time the commission's work was well under way. It was mailing out notices of registration, with working priority to the regular gangs employed by the stevedoring companies, and setting up supplementary hiring halls. It established two offices for fingerprinting of applicants. There was an effort made by the old I.L.A. to persuade the longshoremen to boycott registration, but the longshoremen balked. They knew they had to register if they were going to work. They did not like the threat of fingerprinting if they failed to register before Sunday midnight, November 18. The act itself was regarded by many as a nuisance or a menace. But the law was in effect, and the men complied with it.

By November 28 the commission was able to announce that it had barred 255 ex-criminals from further work on New York's piers. Out of these, 187 were longshoremen; 24 were hiring bosses. Four were pier superintendents. Forty were port watchmen. Among the more notorious of these hoodlums were Albert Ackalitis, Danny St. John, and John Keefe, the public loader.

It was not until an interim report was made to Governor Dewey by the commission, December 28, 1953, that the public learned how the new leaders of the old I.L.A., Captain William V. Bradley and Teddy Gleason, and some of the employers had tried to thwart the carrying out of the act. On November 30, the day before the act went into effect, Captain Bradley and Gleason warned Lawrence E. Walsh, the commission's executive director, that unless men who had been barred from working were permitted to go back to the piers, they doubted if the longshoremen as a whole would work the next day.

Walsh stood his ground. No barred men, he said, would get either the license or working permit. The next day, as the I.L.A. leaders predicted, there were work stoppages in several parts of the harbor. These work stoppages came, according to the commission, after Bradley and Gleason traveled from pier to pier, shaking hands and talking to a great many people. One of the persons with whom Captain Bradley shook hands was Ackalitis, who was standing in a crowd of workmen outside Pier 32. Pickets were thrown around some of the piers. They carried banners, saying: "We want to work but are locked out by the Bi-State Commission."

That afternoon United States District Attorney J. Edward Lumbard, Jr., issued subpoenas to the pickets to appear before a special grand jury. Subpoenas also were served upon Captain Bradley and Gleason. They were asked to appear for questioning as to whether or not they were violating the Taft-Hartley Act, under which an injunction was prohibiting work stoppages. The next day Captain Bradley capitulated. He sent telegrams to the leaders of locals engaged in picketing. The picketing stopped and work was resumed.

Explaining how opposition from some of the employers was hampering the commission in its efforts, the two commissioners reported:

"The corrupt hiring practices reported by the Crime Commission," they said, "might have been quickly dislodged had there been a willingness on the part of the stevedores to accept the challenge. Although, under the compact, hiring agents can only be licensed on application of the employing stevedores, the stevedores did not seize this opportunity to rid themselves of the persons exposed by the Crime Commission. Of the 23 hiring agents singled out for mention by the Crime Commission, because of their criminal records and corrupt influence on the waterfront, all but six have been renominated by their employers. Those urged for licensure include persons with extensive records for felonies, and one convicted as recently as 1952."

Despite this opposition by I.L.A., and some of the shipping men, the commission was able by the beginning of 1954 to register 28,836 longshoremen and allied dock workers, 643 hiring bosses, 2,546 port watchmen, and 404 pier superintendents—an adequate force to carry on the waterfront, even though the previous longshore working force had run annually to 50,000 persons.

There was one immediate result in cutting down that surplus of labor that had meant so much insecurity for every worker, and given such rich pickings to the loan sharks and kickback racketeers. Municipal employees, who used to work on the docks when they wanted a little extra money, could no longer do so, since the civil-service regulations prohibited their taking outside work. Those who might like to get the extra money by breaking the regulations knew they could not get the necessary working permits under the commission's regulations.

CHAPTER

14

THE MOB FIGHTS BACK

*On September 22, 1953, the top leaders of the American Federa-*tion of Labor, meeting with delegates to the federation's annual convention in St. Louis, Missouri, voted to expel the I.L.A. from its membership. At the same time plans were drawn for a new A.F. of L. longshoremen's union, with the same name but free of all the racketeers who had plagued the port of New York within the old I.L.A., to take the place of Joe Ryan's union.

Not yet formally ousted from the command he had held so long, Ryan was in the lobby of the Hotel Jefferson, in St. Louis, convention headquarters, buttonholing delegates to seek a postponement of federation action, when George Meaney, A.F.L. president, made the historic announcement. It was the first time in the history of the trade-union movement in the United States that the A.F. of L. had expelled a member organization.

"We've given up all hope that the officers or members of that union will reform it," Mr. Meaney said, in making his announcement. "We've given up hope that the I.L.A. will ever live up to the rules, standards, and ethics of a decent trade union."

Informed of Meaney's announcement, Ryan growled, "We'll hold on to what we got." Anyone who knew the mobsters who dominated the I.L.A. in New York would have known they would fight to hang on to all they had, even though Ryan, who was then speaking for the union, was already on his way out of office, and behind the scenes his successor as spokesman, Captain William Bradley, had already been selected by its major powers.

The announcement of expulsion, coupled with the promise that the new clean union would make no deals with any old I.L.A. officer with a criminal record or with a record for having taken employers' money, made inevitable the longest, bitterest strike the New York waterfront had experienced since its docks were first unionized. Even with help from the United States government and the governments of New York and New Jersey, it meant the start of a war of bloodshed and violence, the end of which is not yet in sight. For the leaders of the old harbor criminal gangs, ensconced within the I.L.A., were at last in naked and visible control of the waterfront.

Based on information gathered from the New York City Anti-Crime Committee, the police, and others, James Desmond of the New York *Daily News* wrote the complete roster of the waterfront racketeers, all around the harbor, for the very issue of the *News* that carried word from St. Louis of the I.L.A. expulsion. This was the line-up:

"The big development on the North River piers," Mr. Desmond wrote, "has been the return of Eddie McGrath, boss of the old McGrath-Dunn killer gang and long reputed executioner for gambler Joe Adonis, to active direction of waterfront affairs. McGrath's return, first reported to police after his secret meeting last June with Albert Ackalitis, the old Arsenal Gang robber, who now runs

Pier 32, Desbrosses Street, has been taken by police to mean that the Big Mob—the national crime syndicate exposed by the Senate (Kefauver) crime investigating committee—has decided to go all out to save New York for the racketeers.

"This interpretation has been supported in the last ten days by reports that Vincent 'Jimmy Blue Eyes' Alo, Florida gambler and contact man for Adonis, Frank Costello, and others in the Big Mob, has been seen in New York while McGrath himself was registered at his usual hotel here—although he could not be reached by outsiders.

"A year ago McGrath, although still reported to 'own' Pier 32, was running his dock interests from Florida where he fled when he developed a distaste for New York after his brother-in-law and gang partner, John M. 'Cockeye' Dunn, was executed for murder in 1949.

"Under McGrath there has been a coordination of policy but no change in personnel in the North River mobs. Thus robber Mickey Bowers is still running the luxury piers above 42nd Street, through his extralegal control of 'Pistol Local' 824, I.L.A., and despite federal indictments charging him with income-tax evasion. Mickey was in the same spot a year ago.

"Ackalitis this year as last is at Pier 32. Unlike McGrath, who is under 'strictest investigation' by the U. S. Attorney's office, and Bowers, with his tax troubles, Ackie, one of the most feared men on the waterfront, is not known to be the target of any special prosecution—for the moment at least. Reports to police, however, indicate that his power is growing, particularly on the Jersey shore.

"Running the downtown and East River mobs, now as a year ago, is Mickey Clemente, boss of I.L.A. Local 856. Although indicted and reindicted by federal and state grand juries on income-tax and extortion charges, Mickey is openly representing his local in wage-contract talks. Mickey's lieutenant, Saro Mogavero, also is still on the scene, acting as contact for Rocco Pellegrino, whom U. S. narcotics agents brand as the biggest dope importer—despite the fact that Mogavero's trial on extortion charges is slated for early next month in General Sessions.

"Still around, also, on the Manhattan docks is Philip 'Phil Katz' Albanese, who runs the public loaders on the Pennsylvania Railroad piers. Now, as a year ago, 'Phil Katz,' tabbed by the Federal Bureau of Narcotics as a big dope wholesaler, has income tax worries and is lying low.

"Across the East River on the Brooklyn docks there have been some changes, but the authorities say they are changes of expediency that probably will pass with time. The biggest change is the free hand the underworld has given Anthony 'Tough Tony' Anastasia, brother of murderer Albert Anastasia, in his effort to build up one big union out of 11 I.L.A. locals on the Brooklyn docks. Tony, who was suspended from the I.L.A. by Ryan last July and reinstated secretly last month after the mobs shoved Ryan aside in the District Council, has been allowed to grab the spotlight, police believe, until the bigger bosses see whether the union is going to break up.

"But, authorities say, the big boss in Brooklyn is still Thomas 'Toddo' Marino, 'coordinator' of the mobs and, at least until recently, proprietor of the 20,000-dollar-a-week (net) Italian lottery formerly owned by Vito Genovese. 'Toddo' is now fighting a deportation order and is lying low along with his lieutenant, Constantino 'Gus' Scannevino, a brother-in-law of Vincent Mangano, who is a partner of 'Lucky' Luciano, the white-slaver, in the Florida-Cuba dope racket. Mangano is a member of the Big Mob in his own right and still gives a Brooklyn address every time the Florida cops pick him up as a murder suspect—which is just about every time there is a murder.

"Whatever the validity of the official belief that 'Tough Tony' is conducting only a 'holding' operation in Brooklyn, the fact remains that he is getting impressive support in his new role. . . . for example, Murderer Al has been seen, gabardine-clad and debonair as usual, strolling the Brooklyn waterfront with his brother. This is a substantial indication of Tony's present prestige, because Albert has been rarely seen on the docks since he moved into his 65,000-dollar mansion in Jersey several years ago.

"There has been one major change on the Jersey shore. Ed

Florio, the I.L.A. organizer, extortionist, and alien importer who was actively bossing the Hoboken and Weehawken docks a year ago and had a hand in running Claremont Terminal, through his boss, Anthony 'Tony Bender' Strollo, is gone from the scene temporarily. Florio is doing 18 months in the penitentiary for lying to a federal grand jury about a dock's shakedown. His place has been taken, Hoboken detectives say, by Angelo 'Gyp' De Carlo, convicted counterfeiter (FBI No. 29837; Newark Police Department No. 8670). De Carlo, a Florida and Newark gangster, with ties to Abner 'Longy' Zwillman, doesn't show on the docks often but has put in his cousin, Pete De Carlo, who was never a longshoreman, as a hiring boss in Weehawken.

"In Jersey City the situation is what the military men call 'fluid' as, in fact, it has been ever since Charley Yanowsky was ice-picked to death five years ago. Anthony 'Tony Cheese' Marchitto has been booted out of I.L.A. Bomb Local 1247 (without a bombing this time) and a new faction has taken over. The new faction is made up of the followers of the late Biffo Di Lorenzo, who was in turn an ally of Albert Ackalitis now of Manhattan's Pier 32. Ackie, who was a friend and ally of the late Yanowsky, has always had ambitions to take over Jersey; but if he has at last achieved his ambition, no direct evidence of it has come to the attention of authorities.

"Staten Island, now as a year ago, is a satrapy run by Alex 'The Ox' Di Brizzi and his notorious nephews, the Dee boys. All are under tax investigation or prosecution at the present moment, but no new figures have appeared to challenge their power or cut into their perquisites."

Such was the line-up of the real powers in the old I.L.A., as linked to the national crime syndicate, when the union was expelled from the A.F. of L., and these powers had been forewarned for months that expulsion was coming.

There was one enormous advantage the strong-arm rulers of the old I.L.A. had in fighting back against the powers of government, and against interference by any new A.F. of L. union. The working contract that their union had with the New York Shipping Association was to expire on October 1. The union's wage committee was the only one with which the N.Y.S.A. could deal, as the new A.F. of L. union, slated by George Meaney, Dave Beck, and others, to take over the harbor had not yet been created.

The old I.L.A. leaders had been "negotiating" with the shipping men, as usual, since August 1. These shipping men continued to meet them, just as if they were still the unchallenged representatives of all the longshoremen in the port, after their expulsion by the A.F. of L., as they had before it. It was a very easy position for the shipowners and stevedores. They always had found the I.L.A. easy to get along with. If there was to be any trouble in the harbor as a result of the reform movement, they could always cry out—as they later did—"we were caught in the middle."

As contract negotiations started, in the Governor Clinton Hotel, the old I.L.A. asked a half-dollar raise in the basic hourly wage rate. There was no counteroffer from the employers until word came that the union had been expelled by its parent organization. Then the employers offered a raise of seven cents, to include any advance in welfare fund.

There was the usual shadowboxing, following exactly the classic pattern set by a union that never in all its history up to that moment had conducted a strike against its opponents in collective bargaining. "Packy" Connolly, said the men wanted a jobless relief plan based on a tax on payrolls. They wanted lighter sling loads. They wanted a bigger welfare fund payment. They wanted a guaranteed eight hours of work at a single hiring, instead of four. On these points the employers were adamant.

"Tough Tony" Anastasia spoke up, quite out of turn. He wanted the employers, he said, to add 13 cents instead of seven to the basic hourly rate. Tony was shushed by his own nominal leader, "Packy" Connolly. Connolly told Tony that if he had any proposals to make to the shipping association, he could make them first to his union committee. Tony shrugged and sat down.

The stage was all set. The orphaned I.L.A. at that time was practically pleading with the shipping men for any old contract it could get. If only given that contract, for another one year, or maybe two, all attempts by the A.F. of L. to break the contract would immediately become a "wildcat" strike—or even maybe one inspired by Communists—or at most a "jurisdictional" strike. Public opinion, with its educated regard for the sanctity of contracts, would be bound to be on the side of the joint effort by industry and union to uphold that contract and let the business of the port go on.

J. V. Lyon, chairman of the employers' wage-bargaining committee, gave the position of the shipping association perfectly when he emerged from an early meeting with the union, and was reminded that it had just been expelled from the American Federation of Labor as dominated by criminals and racketeers.

"We don't much care what goes on in St. Louis," he said. "We're bargaining here today."

Then came an interruption. It was a telegram to the shipping association, sent also to the press, by John Dwyer, leader of the 1951 so-called "wildcat" strike, and Peter Johnson, youthful counsel for the rebels within the union who had fought twice in harbor-wide strikes in the past five years to throw off the weight of the mob-union's alliance with employers. Both of these young men had been in consultation with Father Corridan before they sent their telegram and gave it to the newspapers.

The telegram sent to J. V. Lyon by Dwyer and Johnson follows: "Grave implications in signing an agreement with the I.L.A. hierarchy, who no longer speak for the rank and file, should be screamingly evident to your group. We urgently advise you to remember that the rank and file of the I.L.A. will resist any mob-signed contract."

That telegram gave pause to both the shipping men and the old-time union leaders. They knew from the experience of 1951 that Dwyer had a big following around the harbor. They knew that a cheap, quick contract, with little obtained by the men, would help make the bid of the new A.F. of L. union for support by the rank and file a great deal stronger when the showdown came.

Prior to that telegram the negotiations between the N.Y.S.A.

and the I.L.A. had moved at a leisurely pace. Now they took on speed. The very next day the employers came up to an offer of eight and a half cents, and the New York *Times* reported: "Employers and I.L.A. officials both want an agreement within the next six days—the shipping association to avert a port tie-up and the I.L.A. to strengthen its position as bargaining agent against the new waterfront union that the American Federation of Labor plans to set up."

Federal, state, and New Jersey mediators were in the lobby of the Governor Clinton Hotel, by now, at J. V. Lyon's request, but were not taking any part in trying to bring about any agreement until asked by both sides. On the same day there was an indication from Brooklyn that the old I.L.A. leaders were going to have a rough fight to maintain their power before the coming port-wide struggle was ended. One of the biggest Brooklyn locals, headed by Vincent and John Erato and Johnny Passante, wired George Meaney that they proposed to join the new A.F. of L. union when it was formed.

"Tough Tony" Anastasia, though criticizing Lyon loudly for having given him only a picayune raise to take back to his men, announced that the locals he controlled in Brooklyn would continue to work the following week, no matter what was the outcome of the conference. As Tony was warning there might be violence along the docks, Police Commissioner George Monaghan called a conference with the district attorneys of the five boroughs of New York, and with U. S. Coast Guard officers and New Jersey law-enforcement officials, to see how the threat of violence was to be met.

Already the challenging new A.F. of L. union was opening its campaign to become bargaining agent for all the longshoremen of the port. As the shipping association raised its ante to the old I.L.A. to eight and a half cents an hour, caravans of A.F. of L. organizers began motor parades along the Brooklyn piers. They were loaded with about 300 members of the A.F. of L. Seafarers' and Teamsters' Unions. They received a few catcalls in Tony

Anastasia's territory, but otherwise distributed their A.F. of L. literature in relative peace.

The outline of the A.F. of L. effort, both in strength and weakness, began to appear. No A.F. of L. longshoremen's union, manned by longshoremen, officered by longshoremen, and financed by longshoremen, was yet in existence. What President Meaney of the parent body had done was to set up a five-man committee to organize the new union, with himself as nominal chief.

The four other top-ranking members of this committee were Dave Beck, boss of a million of the nation's teamsters; Paul Hall, secretary-treasurer of the Atlantic District of the Seafarers, with headquarters in Brooklyn; William C. Doherty, president of the National Association of Letter Carriers; and A. J. Hayes, president of the International Association of Machinists. The major assignment in carrying out the purposes of this committee was naturally given to Paul Hall, of the Seafarers, since his headquarters was in New York harbor. The major assistance, at least in strong-arm conflict, with the goons of the old I.L.A., would of course have to come from the teamsters and seafarers, familiar with the New York waterfront.

Within a day after the first caravan of A.F. of L. organizers appeared on the Brooklyn docks, police halted a truck driven by a member of the seafarer's union. They arrested the driver, Albert D. Thompson, and seized some 20 sawed-off baseball bats and 40-odd other wooden bludgeons—pieces of wood about one and a half feet long and two inches thick, with fashioned hand grips and round edges. Just who was going to receive these weapons was never made known. A few flying squads of seamen and teamsters, however, were beginning to unload from similar trucks around the harbor—even on the piers dominated by Mickey Bowers and his "Pistol Local"—and were passing out literature urging longshoremen to join up with a new clean union, dedicated to their welfare as the old one never had been.

At this point Joe Ryan's union, which had hovered on the brink of accepting a ten-cent raise in the hourly rate from the employers, suddenly raised its demands to 13 cents, with a few extra fringe benefits the employers had formerly turned down. "Impossible to grant," the employers' representatives snarled back (for publication) at the old I.L.A. leaders. On the afternoon of September 30, the old I.L.A. issued its first official strike call throughout the harbor, after some 60 years of history. The 1948 wildcat strike became "official" three days after the men went out. The 1953 strike was to start at 12:01 A.M., October 1, since no work contract would then be in existence.

No sooner had "Packy" Connolly walked out of the meeting room in the Governor Clinton Hotel, September 30, announcing that his Independent I.L.A. would strike the port at midnight, than J. V. Lyon, for the N.Y.S.A., appealed directly by telegram to President Eisenhower at the White House for help. He informed the President that the strike, in the opinion of the shipping industry, would seriously imperil the national health and safety. The New York State Chamber of Commerce made a similar plea to the White House. Employers' organizations also appealed to the two Republican governors of New York and New Jersey to use their influence with the President on their behalf.

Within a day the President acted, although members of the Federal Mediation and Conciliation Service, who had been in New York keeping track of waterfront maneuveurs, had already notified the Defense Department and other interested agencies that a jurisdictional struggle, tying up the whole port in the conflict between A.F. of L. and old I.L.A., would be inevitable. There was doubt for a moment only whether Eisenhower would act.

During his campaign for the presidency, he had maintained that one of the principal reasons why labor-management relations got snarled up was that the federal government stuck in its oar too often. His prescription for handling labor disputes, during the election campaign had been to "keep the White House out of them." Prior to this New York emergency he had ridden through three serious labor controversies, in atomic-energy production, the production of jet aircraft, and in the maritime trades, without taking any action.

But within a day he had taken the first step, under that Taft-

Hartley Act so reviled by labor, for full federal intervention in New York's waterfront conflict. He set up a fact-finding board consisting of David L. Cole, a New Jersey lawyer; Dr. Harry Carman, dean emeritus of Columbia College, and the Reverend Dennis J. Comey, a priest of the Jesuit Order and director of the St. Joseph's College Institute of Industrial Relations in Philadelphia, Pennsylvania. These men sped a report to the President within five days. The report merely detailed the complicated issues involved, and called any settlement through normal collective-bargaining procedures extremely unlikely.

President Eisenhower immediately asked Attorney General Brownell to go into the Federal Court for a temporary injunction to halt the strike then in progress. Federal Judge Edward Weinfeld issued a ten-day restraining order that night. Strikers returned to work without incident, quite as expected, October 6, and the injunction process, thus begun, was continued twice by Judge Weinfeld, once for ten days, and then for the full 80-day cooling-off period, envisaged by the promoters of the Taft-Hartley Act. This automatically deferred the inevitable conflict at least until Christmas Eve, when the injunction would expire. It lent a little time for the two major antagonists, A.F. of L.-I.L.A. and Independent I.L.A., to get ready for battle. It was just a breathing space before the full collision; an interim, marred both by dockside brawling and at least one unsolved drowning of a Pier 32 hiring boss—believed by many to be another case of murder.

The mysterious death of Michael Brogan, assistant hiring boss on Pier 32, North River, who disappeared on the very morning of September 30, when "Packy" Connolly announced the old Independent I.L.A. would strike the next day, has a deep and very real significance in the story of mob rule along the New York waterfront. Pier 32 for a considerable time up to then, insofar as union labor went, was considered by the New York Anti-Crime Committee and police, to be under the control principally of Albert Ackalitis. Eddie McGrath also had a share in the I.L.A. public-loading racket, of still undisclosed extent, at piers in the immediate neighborhood. The shipping line operating from the pier is the Moore-McCormack Line.

For eight years before the day he disappeared, Brogan, a member of Local 895, I.L.A., had been an assistant hiring boss on the pier, the principal boss being "U-Boat" Kelley, a pal of McGrath's. Brogan, a quiet type but tough enough for his job, was a cousin of Billy McMahon, an ex-prizefighter who for several years had been shop steward on the pier for the old I.L.A., and who later became briefly a shop steward in the new A.F. of L. union. Brogan was also a friend of Johnny Dwyer, who became chief Manhattan organizer for the new A.F. of L. union, early in the 1953 battle, and then the chairman of its port committee. Several days before his disappearance Brogan told McMahon he was having some trouble with Ackalitis. "The big fellow told me to move off the dock," he said. McMahon told him to stand his ground but to watch his step.

On September 28, Local 895, to which Brogan and McMahon belonged, voted 5-to-1 to quit the old I.L.A. and join the A.F. of L. The Moore-McCormack Line was then rushing the loading of its freighter, the *Mormacreed,* for a trip to Buenos Aires. In the absence of the regular hiring boss, Brogan as his assistant blew the whistle for work the morning after the vote of his local. Then he began to inspect the loading of the ship. As he and his gangs were working, several "organizers" for the old I.L.A. on the pier handed the men loyalty cards for their signatures. Unless they signed these cards, they were told, they never would get any more work on the pier. After an argument, some of the men signed. Whether Brogan signed is not known, but it is known that friends of Brogan gave the "organizers" an argument.

Loading of the cargo was finished well before 6 A.M., and most of the men left the pier. Mail was to be brought before the ship sailed. According to one account, Brogan stayed on. A longshoreman told the police that Brogan was seen on the pier, "pretty drunk," at 5:45 A.M. Another longshoreman later told the police he saw Brogan leave the pier about 6 A.M., and this longshoreman also said Brogan was pretty drunk. This testimony, as narrated in the newspapers, was startling to Brogan's friends, who agreed that although Brogan took a drink now and then, he never drank while on the job. If these two longshoremen actually saw him on the pier drunk at 6 A.M., or thereabouts, they are the last persons known to the police who saw him alive.

Brogan was then living apart from his wife, in a furnished rooming house uptown. He never returned to that rooming house. The day after he disappeared was his birthday. The following day was payday. He never collected his pay. He had a rendezvous with his teen-age daughter, Marie, the day after payday, when he was to bring her that part of his wages which he gave to her mother, and at which she was to give her father a birthday present. Brogan never appeared. His landlady told the police of his disappearance, October 7.

This report, in police routine, was merely an ordinary matter for investigation by the Missing Persons Bureau, and the case might never have come to the attention of the public had not a sister of Brogan come to see Father Corridan. To the priest, whose attention was fixed on the longshore struggle, Brogan's disappearance immediately seemed sinister. A few inquiries among his dockside friends, and it seemed even more so. He telephoned W. J. Keating at the New York Anti-Crime Committee. To Keating also it seemed as if Brogan's body someday might be found under some cargo, somewhere, or perhaps in the river. Maybe it never would be found. But both to Father Corridan and Keating, when they heard the story, Brogan was as good as dead.

On Saturday or Sunday of the October 20 week end, someone notified Brogan's sister that her brother had shipped overseas, being tired of New York and anxious to get off the docks. The very afternoon after her brother's body was found floating in the river just south of Pier 32, Brogan's sister dropped into the Xavier Labor School to see Father Corridan. She told him with relief what she had heard about her brother's having gone overseas. Father Corridan then had the sad task of breaking the news to her that her brother was dead.

One of the strange things about the discovery of Brogan's

body was that it should be afloat, more than three weeks after the hiring boss' disappearance, next to the pier where he was last seen. A strong current runs there. If the man was drowned at any time near that early morning when witnesses last placed him on the pier, his body presumably should have been found either well downstream or somewhere up the Hudson.

To West Side longshoremen, about to vote in an election as between the old I.L.A., and the new A.F. of L. union, the story of the disappearance of Brogan on the eve of the five-day strike could have only one meaning. Brogan was breaking away from the old crowd who still ruled the docks, and he talked openly of his decision. His death—not so unusual in dockside struggles for power—was a warning to longshoremen generally not to espouse the cause of the rebel group in this particular area too openly. It might be all right to vote for a new union in a secret ballot, but to get out and work for it openly was another matter.

What if the old crowd should win, after all? Any dock worker would know there would be reprisals against anybody active in an ill-fated rebellion. Economic reprisals, such as the loss of a job, at the least possible reckoning. A fate such as Brogan's, if the mobsters willed. As an election maneuver by the McGrath-Ackalitis coterie—if that is what Brogan's death really was—it was a very effective job. The case, of course, has never been solved by law authorities, although Brogan's friends in the new A.F. of L. faction offered a reward of 10,000 dollars soon after the body was found to anyone who would help identify his murderer.

Thanks to the combined efforts of about 1500 New York policemen constantly guarding the waterfront, United States District Attorney, Mr. Lumbard in Manhattan, three grand juries, and the officers of local courts, the expected violence during the period of rival organization prior to Christmas Eve, 1953, was kept to a minimum. There were several minor work stoppages, when A.F. of L. locals collided with the old I.L.A. leaders led by Tony Anastasia on the Brooklyn piers. One bomb was found in Brooklyn, close to the Todd shipyards, and was taken away by the police. There was only one pitched battle of any major proportion.

This occurred on November 12 outside the Breakwater Pier in the Erie Basin, Brooklyn, where a local in Tony Anastasia's territory that had switched to the A.F. of L. decided to run a gauntlet of Anastasia's faithfuls and unload a cargo of canned Hawaiian pineapple from the Isthmian Line steamship *Steel Vendor.* This steamer had been idled for five days, after the new union members had induced the Jarka Stevedoring Company, as agent for the Isthmian Line, to drop one of Tony's lieutenants, Anthony "Tony Spanish" Calvo, as hiring boss, and to pick an A.F. of L. man.

When the new A.F. of L. man blew his whistle that Wednesday morning, a big crowd of Anastasia's henchmen stood by and jeered. Nobody answered. Shortly after 1 P.M. the word spread along Columbia Street, at the head of the piers, that the A.F. of L. union was bringing in workers from another pier, nearby, to unload the ship. The street near the pier contained ten mounted patrolmen, five motorcycle men, three emergency trucks with a plentiful supply of tear gas, 40 detectives, about 100 patrolmen on foot, and 25 patrolmen from the New York Port Authority who were there to guard an adjacent grain elevator.

There were only about 200 of Tony Anastasia's faithfuls on guard, and the police pushed them back from the entrance to the pier. Suddenly, with a great screaming of sirens, a motorcade loaded with about 60 A.F. of L. men came along the street at 40 miles an hour. Two motorcycle men led them to the dock and two police patrol cars brought up their rear. Since a strike had been outlawed on the port, by federal injunction, the new A.F. of L. union was now in the position of crossing Tony Anastasia's picket lines, with police protection.

As the A.F. of L. longshoremen neared the pier, the old I.L.A. boys rushed forward throwing rocks, beer bottles, bricks, and chunks of wood at the trucks. The A.F. of L. men simply threw out leaflets, urging Anastasia's men to desert their leader and join the new union. Instead of that, Anastasia's 200 rushed the police who guarded the pier gate. In the following melee the police used clubs only. Three of the I.L.A. men were taken to a hospital with minor injuries. Following this, and another minor battle that evening, 13 I.L.A. men were under arrest, including Gerardo "Bang Bang" Anastasia, Tony's younger brother.

Not until the fighting was ended did "Tough Tony" appear on the scene. He railed for a while at the police for their interference, then said he would bring out 10,000 longshoremen on the morrow to teach these A.F. of L. interlopers a lesson. His threat failed to materialize. The next day it was announced that a federal grand jury was investigating work stoppages on the Brooklyn piers, and that Anastasia was facing a possible citation for contempt of court.

The long-overdue resignation of Joe Ryan from the presidency of the Independent I.L.A. was staged in mid-November at a special convention of that organization at Philadelphia. It took several days before the front men for the mobs could iron out all the fine details that must accompany Ryan's departure in the style to which he was accustomed, and bring about the succession of Captain William V. Bradley, chief of the I.L.A. tugboat division, to the presidency.

The start of the convention was delayed for two hours, on November 16, because of an effort the leaders made to have it opened by the prayer of a Catholic clergyman, as usual in I.L.A. conventions. An effort was made to get the Reverend Dennis J. Comey, Philadelphia's waterfront arbiter, who had but recently been one of President Eisenhower's board of inquiry on the New York waterfront troubles, to deliver the proper invocation. Father Comey explained that because of his official position he could not appear.

After the two-hour wait for some other clergyman, Mr. Ryan called his old followers to order for the last time, with a bang of the gavel. He turned to one of the I.L.A. vice-presidents, William "Preacher" Jones of New Orleans, Louisiana, to deliver the invocation. Preacher Jones delivered. In his prayer for God's blessing upon the gathering, "Preacher" Jones spoke of his old friend and leader, the retiring president, as a man who was being sacrificed to make the union great. He then recited the words of a hymn entitled, "The Mercy Seat."

The first thing that had to be done, of course, was to take such action as would help old Joe in a trial he was facing for theft of the union's funds. Ryan had been indicted by a New York County grand jury, on 51 counts, for having used about 45,000 dollars of union monies for his own personal needs. He had pleaded not guilty and was free under 3500-dollar bail. Having been in and out of a hospital for some months, the 69-year-old president had not actually been running the Independent I.L.A. for a long time. Now in his closing hours, his old associates were supercharged with emotion. They took pains in a formal resolution to answer every part of the grand jury's indictment, with the countercharge that as far as they were concerned Ryan was guilty of no wrongdoing whatever.

One of the charges Ryan was to face was that he had stolen about 23,000 dollars of the funds of the I.L.A. *Journal,* an annual publication. The resolution recalled that the I.L.A. in 1943 had voted to give Ryan power to use the funds as he saw fit. The resolution said it was the purpose of the I.L.A. that Ryan should use whatever money he needed for himself and family, and that the union certainly had no complaint to make about anything Ryan had ever done with union money.

This resolution was adopted midst cheers and applause. As the applause died down a lone delegate leaped to his feet and yelled, "Let's do it again. He's a good old fellow." This set off another demonstration for Ryan, who sat with head bowed in thought on the platform. When the chairman *pro tem* asked if anybody was opposed to the resolution, there were cries of "Let Meaney oppose it," and "Let Dewey oppose it." That finished, the convention voted Ryan a 10,000 dollar-a-year pension for life and gave him the position of "President Emeritus." The delegates also initiated a constitutional change that would limit the term of any future president to four years.

The boys in the back room had only temporary difficulty in putting over Captain Bradley as Ryan's successor. As far back as December 12, 1952, before the final public hearings of the New York State Crime Commission had ended, James Desmond of the New York *Daily News* was able to report that Ryan ultimately would be shelved and that Bradley would be his successor. Bradley was known to be a good friend of Bill McCormack, and had been helpful to the waterfront industrialist in settling a tugboat wage controversy without a strike. He had no criminal record of any kind. Throughout the port he was looked on as representing "the better elements" in the I.L.A. Although "Packy" Connolly as I.L.A. vice-president had been fronting for the union during recent wage negotiations with the shipping men, the brief strike, and maneuverings with governmental agencies, it was well known that Bradley was on the inner board of strategy. The only momentary hitch in the proceedings was caused by the efforts of a couple of outport aspirants to get the job, and these were soon squelched. The presidency of the I.L.A. certainly had to go to a man from the world's greatest seaport, where the biggest longshore force of potential dues-payers was gathered.

When Captain Bradley took the rostrum to accept the election result, he denied that he was being backed by any "Mr. Big" in New York City. He said he would welcome the support of everyone. Then he singled out Thomas "Teddy" Gleason, business agent of the Checkers Local 1,346, of Staten Island, as the man who was most responsible for his election. Gleason took a bow but later disclaimed the assertion.

During the Crime Commission hearings Gleason had been described as a labor official who consorted with gangsters and who had received gratuities from steamship and stevedoring companies. Gleason admitted at the hearings that he had recommended Ackalitis for the job of hiring boss on Pier 18, North River. Statistics offered by the Crime Commission's accountants at the hearings showed Gleason's hands relatively clean of taking money from employers. He only had received 1725 dollars in such gratuities, between 1947 and 1951. Gleason apparently was one of those Ryan lieutenants who expected old Joe to throw them to the wolves in the final showdown, and so had turned early to Captain Bradley as a more acceptable president.

With violence held to a minimum, all parties in the waterfront controversy turned to the normal, legal procedures under the

Taft-Hartley Act. By these, the National Labor Relations Board, after hearings, may hold an election and certify which of two unions in a jurisdictional dispute is entitled to represent enrolled union workers. The new A.F. of L. union tried to get the old I.L.A. ruled off the ballot of any election as a company union, and failed. Then there was jockeying before the board as to just who should vote in the election everyone knew was coming. In this matter the old I.L.A. pressed for a vote by all 40,000 members of the longshoremen's union up and down the East coast. The new A.F. of L. union wanted only the 19,000 longshoremen in New York harbor. The New York Shipping Association asked that the vote include some 25,000 workers in New York harbor, not only the longshoremen but affiliated crafts usually represented by the I.L.A. in collective bargaining. The board's final eligibility ruling covered about 23,000 workers.

During this period of organization and jockeying before the federal agency, three events occurred that influenced the final result. The first was the intervention of John L. Lewis, president of the United Mine Workers, as financier of the old I.L.A. The second was a claim by Dave Beck, national president of the teamsters, that his union proposed to take over jurisdiction of loading on the piers, when public loading would be outlawed under the terms of the bistate compact. The third was the pressure exerted upon the Republican administrations in Albany, Trenton, and Washington by the New York Shipping Association for a vote at the earliest possible moment, so that some bargaining agent for the men involved would be certified before the end of the injunction period on Christmas Eve.

At the outset of the organizing campaign the A.F. of L. had appropriated 200,000 dollars for the port-wide campaign. While Paul Hall of the Seafarers' Union, with Local 807 as his only ally among the teamsters, furnished the first shock troops for actual waterfront campaigning, a port-wide committee of local longshoremen was formed with reasonable speed. John Dwyer was chairman. Peter Johnson and Howard Shulman were local counsels. Then Mr. Meaney, as chairman of the trustees' committee, sent in a personal representative, Ace M. Keeney, former organizer of the machinists' union to head up the New York effort.

By mid-November the new union had 40 paid, full-time organizers at work around the harbor, and had opened six offices, one in Hoboken, one in Jersey City, two in Manhattan, one in Brooklyn, and one on Staten Island. Mr. Keeney, upon his arrival, claimed that already his new union had about 12,000 men pledged to it. At this time the old I.L.A., which never in all its history had gathered a war chest, was painfully short of cash. It was not until mid-December that negotiations between Captain Bradley and Mr. Lewis brought 50,000 dollars into the I.L.A. coffers.

Neither Mr. Lewis nor Captain Bradley would announce publicly a fact that became speedily known. Fifteen paid organizers were newly enrolled in the staff of the Independent I.L.A., and the word went out from Washington and New York that Lewis was preparing to back the old union with even greater funds, if it would meet some clean-up requirements he would lay down, and then join his heterogeneous District 50, United Mine Workers. The funds obtained, Captain Bradley exclaimed jubilantly that he believed his union would win the coming election by a margin of 5-to-1. The earlier the election could be held, he said, the better for everyone concerned.

Already the New York Shipping Association was pressing for a quick election, and the new A.F. of L. union was seeking to delay it, so it could have more time to organize the harbor. The shipping men had been urging action ever since November 8, protesting that the N.L.R.B., under Charles T. Douds, its regional director, was dilatory in hearing all parties to the controversy. On November 8, J. V. Lyon, for the association, telegraphed President Eisenhower, with copies for Governors Driscoll and Dewey, and for Guy Farmer, chairman of the N.L.R.B. in Washington, turning the heat upon Mr. Douds, as local administrator.

"We believe you will agree," Mr. Lyon's telegram to Eisenhower read, "that unless the governmental agencies operating under the Taft-Hartley Law keep pace with your emergency order, the injunctive relief will become a futile gesture, and on December 24, the disastrous situation which caused you to act so expeditiously will be renewed."

President Eisenhower let the plea go by, and let his new labor relations board take its time for more than a month. Within that month Mr. Beck, chief of the nation's teamsters, saw fit to issue a charter for a waterfront teamsters' union in New York harbor, to be known as Teamsters Local 507, Waterfront Motor Truck Loaders of Metropolitan New York and New Jersey. He let it be known that he looked upon the job of loading and unloading trucks at the pier heads as properly within the jurisdiction of the teamsters' union, even though historically in New York it had been done by men carrying longshoremen's union cards. He said he would try to enroll some 2500 loading laborers in his own union, since public loading was to be outlawed under the New York-New Jersey compact on December 1. This enrollment, he said, would be supervised by Thomas L. Hickey, New York regional vice-president of his union.

No action calculated to estrange the average New York longshoreman from the new A.F. of L. union and to keep him faithful to his old I.L.A., corrupt though it was, could ever have been taken more effectively than this effort of Dave Beck's to shoulder his way into control of jobs traditionally held by longshoremen rather than teamsters. A great many of the older longshoremen were suspicious enough of the part played in organizing the new union by Paul Hall of the seafarers. Historically there always has been a little distrust of the seamen among many of the longshoremen, since today's seaman may be tomorrow's rival for a job on the docks. Beyond that, Hall had long been known as an associate of Ryan, and had helped him in fighting the rank-and-file rebellion of dock workers in 1951. Early in 1953, many longshoremen remembered, Hall had been prominent in the Maritime Council, formed within the harbor in an effort to stage such an effective clean-up, within the old I.L.A., as might keep the old gang in power, despite the Crime Commission's revelations. Then when Dave Beck came along, organizing a new local of teamsters to take over longshoremen's jobs in the loading at the piers, the old-timers knew that they were caught up in union politics, no matter whether the new A.F. of L. union won, or the old I.L.A.

Six months before he made that attempted excursion, Father Corridan had been discussing waterfront problems with Mr. Beck in Washington and had begged him to keep his hands off the pier loaders. The priest did not want the new A.F. of L. union to feed the I.L.A. propagandists with factual material that the A.F. of L. craft system might chop up the longshoremen.

On December 17, pressed by the shipping association and other business groups in New York for a quick election, the National Labor Relations Board in Washington suddenly ordered one for the following Tuesday and Wednesday, December 22 and 23. They did that in spite of the fact that normally an N.L.R.B. order for an election provides for at least a month of campaigning time for union jurisdictional rivals. They ordered it despite warnings to go slowly by James P. Mitchell, Secretary of Labor, Governor Dewey, Judge Proskauer of the State Crime Commission, and Mr. Walsh for the Waterfront Commission.

Apparently the board was impressed by the argument that the issue must be settled before Christmas Eve to head off a strike in the harbor, in absence of union contract. Spruille Braden, chairman of New York's Anti-Crime Committee, joined in the bitter protests, made when the board announced its decision for a quick vote. The newspapers, cognizant of the divided command in the A.F. of L. and the fact that the new A.F. of L. union had received far less time to campaign for converts than it had expected, rightly interpreted this to be a great victory for the old I.L.A., whose leaders were openly jubilant. They predicted victory by a landslide, maybe even 10-to-1. Mr. Meaney, for the A.F. of L., predicted soberly that he would win, but nobody took his prediction seriously.

During two days of voting, under N.L.R.B. supervision, some 20,000 dock workers walked grimly to the polling places, casting their ballots and saying little. Violence was centered principally at Prospect Hall, the Brooklyn polling place. It was visited by Ackalitis, Harold and Mickey Bowers, Danny St. John, "Machine

Gun" Campbell, and Johnny Keefe. The day before the voting, the Waterfront Commission had barred Ackalitis from any further work on the waterfront, but that did not stop his union activities.

Three seamen were stabbed and four other men badly beaten as the mob's leading plug-uglies toured Brooklyn.

The count of the votes proved startling to everyone. Instead of a walk-away for the old I.L.A., as had ben predicted, the I.L.A. was out in front by the slender margin of 9060 votes to 7568. Ninety-five votes were voided. A total of 4405 votes were challenged. The challenged votes might possibly change the result. These ballots were locked up carefully by the N.L.R.B. As the New Year of 1954 was dawning, prior to the greatest strike in the history of the harbor, the rule of the mob-ridden longshoremen's union had not yet been broken, but apparently tottered.

CHAPTER

15

A STATE OF SIEGE

To Father Corridan the startling result of the quickie election of December 22-23, 1953, was a defeat for everyone concerned. It was a defeat for both unions, for the state and federal agencies working for a clean-up of the harbor, for the shipping industry, and for the long-suffering public. By showing an almost even division between longshoremen favoring the old and new unions, it merely tightened the battle lines.

The priest had held himself aloof from electioneering. He was in touch continually with Johnny Dwyer, chief of the A.F. of L. union's port committee, with "Pete" Johnson, one of the counsel for the rebels' union, and with a few other key A.F. of L. insurgents around the docks. He gave what advice he could concerning strategy. But in his opinion the job of tossing off the mobsters' rule was now up to the dock workers. As the election neared, he hoped for an A.F. of L. victory but was doubtful of it. As far as he could see there were just two net gains for all his campaigning.

The rebellion of the rank and file had grown, even though it might not be strong enough for victory. His major victory had been the advent of government, on a level higher than the harbor municipalities, taking a hand in solving port problems. When the deadlocked election result was announced, Father Corridan simply sat by patiently, awaiting events. The next move was up to government. The move came swiftly.

No sooner had the Christmas holidays passed than Governor Dewey acted to stave off any triumph for the old I.L.A. If time were granted, the quickie election could be found invalid. Perhaps in a new one the A.F. of L. union might win.

By preventing the certification of the old I.L.A. for the time being as collective-bargaining agent for the dock workers, Governor Dewey could give more time, too, for the new Bi-State Waterfront Commission to complete its task of banning the most notorious criminals from the waterfront. He could gain time for the federal and local grand juries to do their share in bringing such indictments against the old unionist racketeers as might land a few more behind the bars.

The Governor called on Mr. Pitzele, chairman of the State Mediation Board, Police Commissioner George P. Monaghan, and Mr. Walsh, of the Waterfront Commission, to submit reports to him on the conduct of the election. These reports were rushed to him within three days. They showed what everyone knew they would show: plenty of violence around the polling places—enough so that many a longshoreman who might have liked to cast a vote could have decided to stay out of the way. They also showed that supervisory employees for the shipping companies and public loaders had helped to herd voting employees into busses, with admonitions to vote for the old I.L.A. if they wanted work in the future. Goon squads from the Manhattan West Side, had gone over to Brooklyn, assaulted distributors of A.F. of L. literature, and left a trail of beaten-up or stabbed antagonists in their wake.

The Governor's intervention drew bitter comment from Captain Bradley. He charged Dewey with "trying to steal a bona-fide election, in a deal with George Meaney, A.F. of L. president, for support in the next state election."

At the same time counsel for the new A.F. of L. union succeeded in delaying the count of disputed votes by the simple expedient of refusing to sit down with counsel for the rival I.L.A. and help supervise the count. Counsel for the A.F. of L. planned another legal move to invalidate the result. The old union, they pointed out, had been "adopted" by John L. Lewis. Since Mr. Lewis and his fellow officers in the United Mine Workers had refused to sign the non-Communist affidavits required under the Taft-Hartley Act, no unit of the mine union could appear on any ballot. This might have been pettifoggery, but it was at least a point.

Captain Bradley's countermoves were two. He hired detectives to trace the alleged criminal records of some of his opponents in the Meaney-sponsored dock workers' union, and thereby show that the so-called reformers in the harbor were no better than some of the people in his own camp. The other move was to ask President Eisenhower to name a "coordinator" of federal agencies, dealing with the jurisdictional dispute, and thereby speed up a settlement. The President ignored the request.

On New Year's Day Governor Dewey made a move without parallel in the history of the National Labor Relations Board. He informed the board that the State of New York would send a representative to its hearings, to tell of "coercion and intimidation" surrounding the recent election. His action put the full weight of the state government behind the A.F. of L. campaign, even though he did not specifically demand that the board invalidate the result of the poll.

By this time the old I.L.A., which had given a ten-day guarantee of peace in the harbor, was beginning to mutter of the influence of wildcat strikes if the N.L.R.B. did not get a move on and certify the election winner. Foreseeing trouble, Mayor Wagner increased the dockside police force. Judge Samuel Leibowitz in Brooklyn summoned his rackets grand jury to investigate the disorders attending the election in his county.

Traditionally the courts move slowly. By this time "Tough Tony" Anastasia was on trial, charged with violating the antistrike injunction of the previous October. He beat the rap. "Jay" O'Connor, business agent for Local 791, was under indictment for income-tax evasion. Another federal indictment had been brought by a grand jury of which Laurence S. Rockefeller was chairman, charging old Joe Ryan and five of his union officers with extortion.

One of the weaknesses of the A.F. of L. effort to clean up the harbor was highlighted to the public by a quarrel in January in the Central Trades and Labor Council. Paul Hall of the seafarers charged openly that Marty Lacey, president of the council for the last 20 years, was backing the old I.L.A., against federation policy. He charged that Tony Anastasia was bragging publicly of support in the council. Hall ran against Lacey for the council presidency and was supported in his fight by David Dubinsky, leader of the International Ladies' Garment Workers' Union. Lacey won reelection by 374 votes to 216.

Some close followers of labor politics pointed out that George Meaney had lost in terms of influence within the A.F. of L., since Hall and Meaney were working to break up the old I.L.A., and Lacey, to say the least, was dragging his feet. Lacey was one of Beck's recalcitrant lieutenants. Apart from action by Local 807 of the teamsters, Beck's only discernible movement in the New York situation had been to try to grab the dockside loaders into his union.

The quarrel served only to point up the fact that interunion rivalry, within the A.F. of L. itself, and the intrigues of its principal leaders for greater power, was a weakness in the campaign of the federation to organize the dock workers. The new A.F. of L. union got no public support whatever in its fight from most of the New York City federation stalwarts. In Father Corridan's opinion the only local unions that gave the new union any help at all were Local 807 of the teamsters, and Paul Hall's seafarers.

Far from the New York waterfront, the new A.F. of L. union won some slight victory in obtaining the allegiance of about 5000 dock workers in Puerto Rico. But this was a diversion from the main New York struggle.

In February Marty Lacey and other friends of the old I.L.A. made a futile effort to get the discredited union back into the fold of the parent national organization. Meaney slammed the door on any "negotiated peace." The new I.L.A. leadership also approached Walter Reuther of the Congress of Industrial Organizations, to seek affiliation. Reuther turned the union down.

But the old I.L.A. scored a very real victory when it succeeded in getting new contracts ratified with employer associations in seven Eastern ports outside of New York, thereby giving it stability in Portland, Maine; Boston, Massachusetts; Providence, Rhode Island; Chester and Philadelphia, Pennsylvania; Baltimore, Maryland; and Hampton Roads, Virginia. It was further strengthened, even in New York, by the announcement that these outside ports, as I.L.A. organized, would be affiliated with Lewis' mine workers, thereby assuring themselves of support against A.F. of L. raids in the future. Old I.L.A. leaders were to make a great point of this in the coming fight within New York. As between leadership by either Meaney or Beck and leadership by John L. Lewis, a good many dock workers preferred Lewis. Of course the mine workers' union never was conspicuous for democratic practices. But the dock workers never had known any democratic practices. They knew Lewis as a leader who brought his followers concrete, material benefits.

It was not until February 17 that the N.L.R.B. got around to ordering public hearings in New York on the election of the preceding December. They set the first hearing for March 1. As February waned, there was an increasing tempo of violence along the docks. On February 19 four men entered the offices of Local 1,199 of the old I.L.A., in the Red Hook section of Brooklyn, one of the toughest neighborhoods in the city. Two of the men, armed with a baseball bat and a piece of iron pipe, beat up Thomas Rubino, 46, the local's financial secretary. He was taken to Long

Island College Hospital with a broken skull, broken nose, jaw, and arms, and for a time lay near death, but he recovered.

In the hospital, Rubino named as his assailants Frank Russo, a delegate of Local 327, and Salvatore Trapani, a shop steward of Local 327-1. They were arrested and charged with felonious assault. According to the police, the beating was a sequel to a quarrel that had occurred between Rubino and "Tough Tony" Anastasia in Tony's Longshoremen and Clerks' Social Club, during a meeting there in which Tony had outlined a plan to merge 11 Brooklyn locals of the old I.L.A. into a single one, with himself as boss.

Rubino was a brother-in-law of Anthony Camarda, treasurer of one of the six Brooklyn locals. Rubino objected violently during the meeting to "Tough Tony's" plan and was joined in his objections by representatives of four other locals. He stalked out of the club, leading his followers with him. Both the Brooklyn police and federal agents were at that moment looking for Tony, but he had left the city suddenly for a brief stay in Florida.

Before the National Labor Relations Board could begin its hearings, the wildcat strike started and spread through all the harbor, lasting 29 days. At the end of that time it was conceded by leaders of the old I.L.A. to be an official strike, conducted with union leadership, despite the fact of a federal court's restraining order.

The incident that sparked the strike might have occurred on any one of many piers in the harbor, where the two rival unions were battling, but by chance occurred on Pier 32, North River—once the territory of the Dunn-McGrath mob, and later of Ackalitis. It was set by the insistence of the new A.F. of L. union that Billy McMahon, Brogan's cousin, be made shop steward for A.F. of L. men on that particular dock. The Moore-McCormack Line, which operated the pier, acceded to the A.F. of L. demand. Immediately partisans of the old I.L.A. began picketing the place. McMahon was fired. Then A.F. of L. pickets showed up to take the place of the I.L.A. pickets. McMahon got his job back when A.F. of L. teamsters from Local 807 stopped deliveries until McMahon did. Thereat the old I.L.A. began a boycott of all the Local 807 trucks. This was on February 26. On March 4 Federal Judge Edward J.

Dimock, at the request of the N.L.R.B., issued a restraining writ, ordering the I.L.A. to do nothing whatever to interfere with the trucks operated by Local 807.

The original boycott of Local 807 trucks was announced by Teddy Gleason, I.L.A. general organizer. He said it would only affect some 30 per cent of the cargo around the port, and promised that the union would continue to work all piers and all cargo except that handled by the one teamsters' local. On the very day after Judge Dimock's restraining order was handed down, Captain Bradley intimated that one probable result of it would be harborwide stoppage. As the stoppage began to spread, the N.L.R.B. went before Federal Judge David N. Edelstein and asked for an order requiring three I.L.A. officials, eight locals, and the international union itself to show cause why they should not be held in civil and criminal contempt for violating the Dimock writ. Possible penalties for the officers and the union were jail terms of a year, a fine of 100,000 dollars, and additional fines of 5000 dollars a day for every day the strike was continued.

The three union officials against whom the contempt order was sought were Harold Bowers, as business agent of the "Pistol Local," William P. Lynch, secretary of Chelsea's Local 791, and William Ackalitis, business agent of Local 874, a brother of the more notorious "Acky." "Acky" was then being sought by the police to answer for his possible part in three stabbings outside the Brooklyn polling place, the December before.

Judge Edelstein issued the order that the N.L.R.B. requested on March 9. Then the courtroom process of curbing the mobsters came to a complete halt. Federal Judge William Bondy postponed the contempt case three times, at request of defense counsel, and then sent the case along to Senior Judge John C. Knox of the Southern New York Judicial District, who said he had no judge at liberty, for the moment, to sit in the case. He would act as soon as some judge was available, he said, but nobody knew when that would be.

By this time the old I.L.A. leaders were so emboldened that they had made the strike official. Their followers had staged a so-called "spontaneous" picketing demonstration outside the federal courthouse in Foley Square to protest against court action against their leaders. Now the leaders said the strike would continue, regardless of the pendency of another N.L.R.B. election, until the New York Shipping Association or its individual members negotiated final contracts with the I.L.A., as bargaining agent for the harbor.

On the level of municipal government, Mayor Wagner at first appealed to the old I.L.A. leaders to quit the strike and start a back-to-work movement. At first they said they were trying to get their men back, but were failing. Then the Mayor got tougher. He increased police patrols. He guaranteed protection for anyone who wanted to work, but he never was able to deliver it completely.

Leaders of the new A.F. of L. union, who from the start had denounced the strike as a "phony," set out in earnest toward the middle of March to get their own followers back on the piers, bringing them to their work in trucks under heavy police escort. It was not until March 19, when Mayor Wagner had stepped up police protection for their trucks, that the A.F. of L. began to break the mob-run strike.

From March 19 to March 25, according to a report by the Waterfront Commission, they had raised the number of longshoremen running the I.L.A. picket lines from 1330 to 3646, and the number of piers worked from 23 to 34. The back-to-work movement was impeded, the commission reported, by lack of cooperation, or even opposition, on the part of hiring bosses in the employ of some of the steamship lines, and in some cases by the insistence of the lines themselves that they would hire only members of the old I.L.A. It was impeded also by continued intimidation and assaults upon members of the new union by members of the old.

In an interim report to Governor Dewey the commission was able to list daily brawls between the rival factions from March 13 to March 24, in which tires were slashed, the families and relatives of A.F. of L. organizers threatened or beaten, and attempts of the would-be workers to get to the docks halted by mass picketing. One A.F. of L. worker was stabbed. Trucks under police escort bringing workers to the docks were stoned. Nails were strewn on the streets near the docks to stop the trucks or get in the feet of horses carrying the mounted police. It was a war of muscle in which the police only gradually acquired an upper hand.

At one point in the strike Governor Dewey waspishly reminded Mayor Wagner and Police Commissioner Francis W. H. Adams that under the laws of the state he had the power to remove them both, if they failed to keep order. At another time Joseph M. Adelizzi, managing director of the Empire State Highway Transportation Association, appealed to Attorney General Brownell, in Washington, D.C., for the use of the United States Army to restore order, at bayonet point if necessary.

In the final analysis, it required the combined and coordinated powers of the national government and two state governments, acting through the courts, the National Labor Relations Board, and the Waterfront Commission to end the I.L.A. walkout. Before it was ended there had been a great diversion of the harbor's shipping to Baltimore and Philadelphia, and several shipping lines were threatening to quit New York harbor for good and all. A personal appeal to President Eisenhower for his intervention was made by Mayor Wagner on March 24.

The President said nothing. On March 26 Arthur Leff, examiner of the N.L.R.B., made a formal recommendation to the board that the December election be set aside because of the violence and intimidation accompanying it. No count of the challenged votes was made, and this drew bitter comment from "Packy" Connolly as I.L.A. vice-president. "They're afraid to count it," he said. "They got orders from Governor Dewey. If any honest jury heard the evidence about that election they'd decide in our favor."

On the same day President Eisenhower sent new Secretary of Labor James P. Mitchell to New York to confer with Governor Dewey. Mayor Wagner, who had been suffering from a bad cold for a week, thereupon praised the N.L.R.B. examiner for paving the way to a solution of the problem. He then took off to Bermuda for a week's vacation with his family. As he departed he said he believed that President Eisenhower might have taken a more active part than he did in ending the port's paralysis.

Then followed a conference between Governor Dewey, Secretary Mitchell, and U. S. Attorney Lumbard of the Southern District of New York, at the Hotel Roosevelt, in which the final strategy was drafted for breaking the strike by governmental action. At the end of the conference a joint communiqué was issued in which the strike was branded "a criminal conspiracy" rather than a jurisdictional labor dispute.

The old I.L.A. answered this by sending about 600 men in busses and automobiles to Washington to picket the White House. The pickets were orderly. "We served you in 1941. Now serve us in '54," read one of the banners. "Heroes in '44 and Hoodlums in '54," said another. There was no comment from the White House, but strength was being added to a movement in Congress to ban picketing of the White House by any organization whatever, as detrimental to the dignity of the federal government.

In the closing hours of the battle Captain Bradley's old tugboat local walked out briefly to aid him. But with labor divided there was no power to stem the combined drive of Governor Dewey and his allies in the federal administration. The strike was to be cracked as an illegal racket, by all the arrests, indictments, and injunctions necessary to break it. Not only the union leaders of it but any shipping and stevedoring companies that had connived with the union leaders were to be the targets of this governmental campaign.

The N.L.R.B. drew up a petition to the courts to stop the tugboat strike. U. S. Attorney Lumbard summoned "dozens" of witnesses to a federal grand jury to investigate charges of collusion between the shipping companies and the old I.L.A. His aides drew up a list of 18 shipping companies and 23 stevedoring concerns alleged to have helped the old I.L.A. leaders by letting their ships remain unloaded rather than hire any A.F. of L. workers. Local and federal judges began to issue injunctions limiting the number of pickets at any pier. An I.L.A. picket, charged with throwing a block of cement at a policeman, was indicted by a New York County Grand Jury on the very day of his arrest—a record for speed in the city's courts.

Leaders of the old I.L.A. made only two more moves before throwing in the sponge. They tried to make a deal in federal court whereby their three officers, Harold Bowers, William Lynch, and William Ackalitis, might make pleas to some lesser offense than contempt of court, for which they were about to stand trial. And they tried to get the Waterfront Commission to return working cards to 65 longshoremen barred from the docks because of their activities in violence during the strike. The agencies of government rebuffed them.

The move that finally broke the strike was an announcement by Charles T. Douds, regional director of the N.L.R.B., that if the leaders of the old I.L.A. did not end the walkout "forthwith," the union would be barred from the ballot in a new election, which would give the victory automatically to the new A.F. of L. organization. That ultimatum was the final knockout.

On the night of April 2, after a stormy meeting of about 180 of the old I.L.A. leaders, Captain Bradley announced that all the men in the I.L.A. would be ordered back to work the following morning at 8 A.M. The 29-day battle was ended. Strong and determined government ended it, using powers within the N.L.R.B. and the Taft-Hartley Act as they had never been used before. The A.F. of L., though normally a bitter critic of this act, made no criticism of the government's action, of which it hoped at the time to be a beneficiary. Captain Bradley, for the defeated I.L.A., said merely that in any future election his union would be found a victor, by vote of the rank and file, as it had been victor in December.

The long-idled port returned to life. Longshoremen of both camps went gladly to work. The men had lost wages totaling more than three million dollars. Their families were in many cases hungry. The usual newspaper estimate gave the loss to the shippers and the shipping industry as probably more than 30 million dollars, and estimated that cargoes valued at more than 300 million dollars had been tied up for that long, frustrating month of strike. Only the outports benefited, and no issue affecting the future of labor-management relations, New York's greatest weakness in competition with other seaports, had as yet been settled.

Left in the wake of the disastrous strike were a score of uncompleted court actions and problems of getting members of the two rival unions to work together in peace. At some undetermined time in the future there was to be another election, to see what organization would be the bargaining agent for the men. As members of the old I.L.A. went back to the piers on which A.F. of L. men had tried to break the strike, they found the A.F. of L. men in possession of jobs that formerly were theirs. That added to the bitterness.

The I.L.A. continued to press its legal fight against the exercise of Bi-State Waterfront Commission powers, but on April 8 the board's hands were strengthened by a Supreme Court decision upholding its right to bar ex-convicts from the docks. The commission finally got around to barring Danny St. John, the "Pistol Local" plug-ugly. The I.L.A. also protested to the N.L.R.B. that the new commission was guilty of unfair labor practices, in a conspiracy to deprive its members of jobs and hand them over to the A.F. of L. Chairman Douds tossed this contention out the window.

One court decision in this relatively peaceful time pointed straight to a major waterfront evil that Father Corridan had been fighting. That was the conviction of the Jarka Corporation, one of the largest stevedoring companies in the world, of having resorted to commercial bribery to increase its business. A three-judge bench in the Court of Special Sessions slapped the corporation's wrist gently with a fine of 2000 dollars, and gave its president, Frank W. Nolan, a six months' suspended sentence, on the plea of Sol Gelb, his attorney, that Nolan had been ignorant that what he was doing was against the law.

Toward the last of April Mr. Douds set the date for another dockers' election as May 26. He drew up a set of rules to govern its procedure. He rejected an effort by the New York Shipping Association to make some of the supervisory employees eligible to ballot with the men they supervised.

In the midst of the campaign of rival unions for the votes of the workers, Federal Judge Harold P. Burke, of Rochester, New York, fined the old I.L.A. 50,000 dollars and imposed smaller fines on eight of its locals for having violated the court order of Judge Dimock on March 4 and conducted an illegal strike. The fine affected the mob not at all. John L. Lewis was now financing the old I.L.A. in its fight for survival. Jail sentences of six months, pronounced gravely against Harold Bowers, William P. Lynch, and William Ackalitis, could hardly have had much of an effect upon I.L.A. conduct. Many of its major chieftains were graduates of terms in Dannemora or Sing Sing, and could shrug off a six months' jail term as a brief retreat or vacation from more strenuous labors.

In the final campaigning of the second election plenty of money was spent on both sides. Pamphlets, mass meetings, caravan parades, and oratory all played their part. One minor sensation of the campaign was the fact that Tony Anastasia, driving hard to become the boss of one unified union along the Brooklyn waterfront, sent two of his aides, Anthony Impliazzo, president of Local 327-1, and Tom Di Bella, an organizer, out to the West Coast to get money from Harry Bridges, chief of the left-wing longshoremen's union and long-time target for federal prosecutions as a disguised Communist.

The two emissaries spoke up and down the San Francisco, Portland, and Seattle waterfronts in praise of Bridges, and came home with 3675 dollars from the three locals of the Bridges union. The A.F. of L. organizers of course capitalized on this amazing liaison, in their electioneering, charging "Tough Tony" with bringing Communist influence back into the port.

As the day for the new election approached, the police of New York mustered 2500 men to see that no violence such as had characterized the December polling should invalidate the vote. By election morning the new A.F. of L. union was generally conceded in the public mind to be a sure winner. It had the open support of the national government, of the two state governments of New York and New Jersey, and of the entire metropolitan press of Greater New York. Editorials urging the men to vote A.F. of

L. were printed by the New York *Times* and the New York *Daily News,* supposedly the two newspapers of greatest public influence in the city.

The A.F. of L. union organizers were certainly confident of victory. No other than George Meaney himself had come to New York in the final stages and campaigned before the television camera. The votes, when counted, told a different story. Crime-ridden though everyone in New York knew the old union to be, discredited as eveyone knew it was, expelled from the A.F. of L., faced with new charges of Communist infiltration, short of funds, and with many of its old leaders barred from the docks, indicted, or actually imprisoned, the old union squeezed out a bare, temporarily official majority of 319 votes over its reformist rival, and 268 over both its rival and those men voting for no union at all. The official count was 9110 votes for the I.L.A., to 8791 for the A.F. of L., with 1797 ballots in dispute, 49 void, and 51 for neither union.

As for the challenged votes, 961 were impounded because the men who cast them had faulty identification as eligible voters. Another 762 votes were under challenge because they were allegedly cast by supervisors. In order to win certification, the old I.L.A. would have to pick up another 770 votes, if all the challenged votes were counted. The vote was temporarily a stalemate.

Although the result came as a shocking surprise to most of the New York community, it was a vote that no one could laugh off. As the *Daily Mirror* said, editorially, "You can't pretend it didn't happen." During the last few weeks of the electoral campaign Father Corridan was actively on the stump, at longshoremen's meetings, campaigning for an A.F. of L. triumph. He circulated an open letter to longshoremen all around the harbor, asking their votes for the new union. He believed that he and his rebel friends would win. The result was a deep disappointment to him.

CHAPTER 16

INDICTMENT AND CHALLENGE

On a street suitably called "Liberty" in downtown Manhattan stands an ornate old building, filled with fine portraits of affluent leaders of the city's financial and commercial community, dating back for many years. This is the headquarters of the New York State Chamber of Commerce. The principal speaker at the annual meeting of this influential organization, May 6, 1954, was Austin J. Tobin, executive director of the Port of New York Authority. Mr. Tobin for some years has been a friend of Father Corridan, and their views on the ills that have plagued the harbor for the last generation have been in general agreement.

Mr. Tobin's speech in the Chamber was delivered very shortly after the close of the harbor's most devastating strike. His topic was the future of the port. He spoke out bluntly.

"In any frank appraisal of the future of the port of New York," he said, "a review of the position and policies of the New York Shipping Association by the real leaders of our great shipping services is one of the first orders of business. It is a tragic thing to see the house flags of fine old companies soiled by association, placed in the unhappy and unfair position of being privy to the policies of an association which deprecated the work of the New York State Crime Commission; deplored and covertly opposed the creation of the Waterfront Commission; and played the I.L.A. game in the recent strike.

"This shabby, servile record does not represent the policies or the principles of the majority of our shipping companies. And in their own interests, and in the interests of the port, I trust that the decent and honorable majority will review the association's position and policies."

Ever since his earliest studies of the waterfront Father Corridan had been hammering away at the theme of employer responsibility for the rackets that were ruining the port. The report of the State Board of Inquiry, which helped end the 1951 strike, supported his viewpoint to some degree. The revelations of the Crime Commission helped. In the spring of 1954 two more governmental reports upheld his original thesis. One was by the Bi-State Waterfront Commission. The other was the final presentment of the special grand jury in Brooklyn, which had been investigating rackets in that borough for four years.

The report of the Waterfront Commission involved only happenings during the 1954 strike. The commission charged, in its report to Governor Dewey, that some of the shipping companies and stevedoring companies, instead of helping to revive the stricken port, were helping the mobsters to maintain their control over it.

"A factor seriously retarding the efforts to resume work in the port is the resistance of steamship lines and stevedores to accepting on their piers longshoremen other than their former employees," the commission said. "Although the shipping association has made a studied effort to give the impression that their members were willing to work their piers, in fact, most of them have not been willing to work them except with their old employees. Resistance to the employment of A.F. of L. longshoremen has been manifest in different ways.

"First, the outright insistence upon old I.L.A. longshoremen. In the daily survey conducted by the managers of the Waterfront Commission's information centers, certain lines have specified and still specify that they will only employ old I.L.A. men. Second, the refusal to ask for men. Certain companies have shut down their piers, stating that they did not need men, although they had ships in port.

"Third, unrealistic rigidity in standards for accepting new men. It is, of course, difficult to persuade men to pass through picket lines faced with jeering and actual physical injury. To require on the first day a pier is opened that gangs be perfectly balanced between winchmen, holdmen, deckmen, and machine-drivers is to require the impossible. The way men are encouraged to come back to work is by seeing other men working on the piers in safety. Companies which have accepted the men supplied by the A.F. of L. in irregular gangs have found that within a day or two they have been supplied with better-balanced gangs. Certain other companies have been unrealistically setting standards for accepting new men."

In an appendix to its report the commission submitted to Governor Dewey a list of the shipping and stevedoring companies which, it maintained, had ships in port during the strike but failed to cooperate in getting the harbor back to work. These shipping companies included the Furness, Cunard, Panama, Despatch Terminal, Isbrandtsen, Flomarcy, National Sugar, Sealand Dock, Costa, Grancolombiana, Brigantine Terminal, Cosmopolitan, Barber, Black Diamond, International Freighting, Lloyd Brasileiro, Farrell, and Seaboard Constructing Corporation lines. The stevedoring companies named by the commission included the Bay Ridge Operating, John T. Clark, Pellegrino, Universal, Jarka, Federal, American, Sottnek, Commercial, Atlantic, Marra, J. K.

Hanson, Anchor Stevedoring, Pittston Stevedoring, and McGrath companies.

In all fairness to the companies cited by the commission, it must be said they were under no legal compulsion to work their ships throughout the struggle, and could justify their failure to cooperate with governmental efforts at reform of the harbor by several sound business principles. Badly-made-up gangs can be dangerous. Loyalty to old employees, even though they may belong to a racketeers' union, may be said to be a commendable principle. The most the commission was able to charge against these shipping and stevedoring concerns was a failure to cooperate.

The final presentment of the Brooklyn Grand Jury to Judge Samuel S. Leibowitz, April 28, 1954, was similarly critical of employers in the shipping industry.

"Waterfront employers," the grand jury found, "have shown a distinct tendency to resort to bribery as a way out of the harassments of the racketeers, instead of manfully invoking the protection of the law. They have not been known to lift a finger over many years against operators of the infamous loading rackets. They have 'bleated' much about quickie strikes, but they bear much of the direct responsibility for these themselves because they have permitted racketeers and corrupt union leaders to violate contracts with impunity. They have turned a blind eye to the large-scale pilfering of merchandise, sometimes in carload lots, from piers and warehouses. They have unprotestingly permitted thieves with long criminal records to occupy positions of trust in their employ."

The grand jury considered untenable the contention of shipping and stevedoring companies that they had to capitulate to the mobsters or suffer larger financial loss through strikes. "There can be no justification for subordinating law enforcement and decent dealing between labor and management to a desire for profit," it said.

In all Father Corridan's considerations of the role of the shipping and stevedoring companies in complicity with gangsters to make their individual profits regardless of the welfare of the port, he has always recognized that the shipping industry is highly competitive. Within it there are elements of very diverse interests—

often conflicting interests. He had recognized also that many officials of the companies involved, who might have liked to alter waterfront labor-management practices, have inherited those practices and have not been completely the master of their own decisions.

Some of the shipping lines have operated within the fold of conference, and others outside it. Some of them are independent and others are subsidiaries. Some are subsidized. Others are not. As for the shipping association that represents the great majority of them, its decisions have of necessity been group decisions, and not the decisions of individual men. For any individual or small group of individuals to attempt to abolish historic harbor evils, deeply rooted in the historic development of the port, would require an effort no less than Herculean. It would be an effort accompanied by risk, sometimes by loss. At any time prior to the revelations of the State Crime Commission and the establishment of the Waterfront Commission, it would have required courage of the highest order.

Today, however, Father Corridan believes such an effort by the shipping industry's employers would not be fraught with yesterday's difficulties or perils. Father Corridan, like Mr. Tobin, ranks this change in the policies of the New York Shipping Association as today's urgent business, if the port of New York is to thrive once more, and if the steady deterioration of its commercial prestige is to be stopped.

"In one of his reports to Mayor Impelliteri, Bill McCormack made a wonderful suggestion," Father Corridan says. "He told the Mayor that plans for bettering the port should come from men of the stature of General John M. Franklin of the United States Lines, Harold Borer of the Cunard Line, R. R. Adams [deceased] of the Grace Line, A. V. Moore [deceased] of the Moore-McCormack Lines, and J. E. Slater of the American Export Lines.

"He certainly pointed to people of power. If people like that would only join in cleaning up the New York Shipping Association, so that its labor policies would be modern and decent, it would help a great deal."

Father Corridan, discussing port problems as a religionist, stresses social responsibility of men in business as something demanded by Christian teachings. "Everyone has social as well as personal responsibilities in the community," he says. "But all people do not have them to the same degree. How great one's responsibility may be is determined in large part by one's position in life. The heads of the great shipping industry have far greater responsibility for what happens in the port than the rank-and-file longshoreman. They have the power to remedy many of the harbor's evils, if only they will. Leaders of the automobile and steel industries have long since risen to the challenge of accepting modern trade unionism, and real collective bargaining, as required under present-day industrial conditions. How long will the shipping industry cling to the older concept of company unionism, or captive unionism, in which helpless men are coerced by thugs?"

As Father Corridan analyzes the situation in New York harbor in the autumn of 1954, the old I.L.A., mob-dominated, unreformed, and unrepentant, stands clearly the winner of the great battle fought for the past few years. To be sure, old Joe Ryan, completely discredited, was tossed to the wolves by the union bosses for whom he had long been a mouthpiece. A jury in downtown Manhattan disagreed as to whether he actually had stolen funds of the union that voted him his 10,000-dollar annual pension for life. The jury stood 10-to-2 for conviction. He still faces trial in a federal court on a charge of extortion.

But late in August the old I.L.A. was certified by the National Labor Relations Board as collective-bargaining agent for New York dock workers. At this writing it is now engaged in "bargaining" with the New York Shipping Association for a new contract. One of its demands is a complete union shop, which would, of course, end all chances of employment by members of the newly created International Brotherhood of Longshoremen, A.F. of L. It would give the old I.L.A. absolute control of all new workers by requiring them to join the union within a month of their being hired on the docks.

As far as the great American Federation of Labor goes, it has to all intents and purposes abandoned support of the fledgling "reform" union which came within 319 votes of overthrowing the old one.

"Tough Tony" Anastasia has consolidated his rule over all the Brooklyn waterfront. His power is greater within the old I.L.A. than ever before. He is now to rule the dock workers at the United States Army Base, who temporarily were on civil service before many of them joined the new A.F. of L. brotherhood. The Bowers mob still reigns along the piers where the luxury liners dock on New York's Upper West Side.

Eddie Florio is back in power in New Jersey. Mike Clemente, to be sure, is away in prison for a little while, but according to the dock wallopers themselves, conditions haven't changed much. There is no security of employment for anyone who incurs the displeasure of a hiring boss. The loan sharks still prey on men long out of work. There is still an oversupply of workers on the piers, and no system of seniority to protect men long on a job.

At the end of its first year of operation the new Bi-State Waterfront Commission has issued a hopeful report, saying "great progress" has been made in eliminating some of the worst of the abuses pointed up by the State Crime Commission's hearings. It has banned 120 persons of criminal record from working as longshoremen and is suspending from ten to 60 days the work permits of dockers convicted of thievery. It is promising more drastic penalties if necessary. It has barred ten persons from supervisory positions on the docks, and expressed a belief, since other applicants withdrew, that racketeers' grip on the piers has been weakened."

But the commission concedes it has no power over the internal management of a labor union. There was one interesting item in the report of the commission as it relates to Father Corridan. A picture of the priest was shown talking to three dock workers on a pier. The faces of all three were blacked out to prevent their identification by enemies of the waterfront priest.

Captain William V. Bradley, new head of the I.L.A., has entered the presidency with some prestige, and is representing the "cleaner elements within the union." Whether he can control the real powers within his union is doubtful.

By a change in the policy of the shipping association, no stevedoring concerns are now represented on its executive board. How far the change will go remains to be seen. New York's latest mayor has created the latest grandiose committee of eminent citizens to do all within their power to promote the welfare of the port as a whole. The name of "Mr. Big" does not appear on it, as he has retired from public life.

"On the whole, the outlook on the waterfront is dark," says Father Corridan. There are strong rumors that a new blood purge is in the offing, just as soon as the old I.L.A. consolidates its position through the new contract. There may be no more to this than rumor. But the word is being passed around quietly, quite in the old evil tradition.

"Several veteran detectives of the Police Department's waterfront squad believe it, and are planning to retire rather than go through it. One of them recently predicted that the 'new Korea' would come within the year."

In his offices at the Xavier School, Father Corridan recently reviewed his eight years of effort on the waterfront. A thickset, burly, bald-headed man in the prime of life, he brims with energy. His moods can run within very few minutes all the way from uproarious laughter to a quiet scorn and burning wrath. He gives the impression of a man too busy to be occupied long with contemplation. Yet once in a while the priest turns back in his mind and conversation to the basic faith of his church, and his own mission within it. These carry him far beyond the immediate fortunes of the New York waterfront, or the men and women of this generation who work around it.

"Remember when Father Carey asked me to try my hand at the waterfront?" says Father Corridan. "I certainly didn't come to this place as a knight in shining armor. I came as a priest, and a lot of people have asked me what business a priest has doing the kind of thing I've been doing. A lot of priests have gone before me and a great many more will follow, long after I'm gone.

"But if you'll go to the Gospel of St. Luke, in Chapter Five, you'll find these words: 'Launch out into the deep and let down your nets.' Those words, 'launch out into the deep,' have always had a great appeal to me. Remember the scene? Christ had been standing in the fishing boat of Simon Peter, speaking to a crowd on the shore of Lake Gennesaret. When He had finished speaking, He took note of the fact that the fishermen's nets were empty. So He bade His friends leave shore again and make another try. They did as they were told, and their nets brought up so many fish that they broke.

"That was the time that Peter fell on his knees, and Jesus told him that henceforth he would be a fisher of men. That's part of the job of any priest. He is looking for men—and women, too—who will truly serve God.

"That's been one of my great rewards in working with longshoremen around the docks. I've found some. I've found men who will stand up and resist evil. I've found men who will risk their lives to fight against tyranny. I've found men who can really go home each night and sleep with a clean conscience. I'm looking for more.

"Of course I've been pretty discouraged sometimes. There are some things I take pretty hard. I hate to see the casualties in the war that's going on. I know that men who have fought for the right as they've seen it have often lost their jobs. I know that some are killed. But when I think about these people there's always one thing I can say. A great many people in times to come are going to be better off because these men lived and made their fight. I can read you chapter and verse on that. Just go to St. John. Chapter Four. Christ was talking to the Apostles. 'It is one man that soweth and another that reapeth.' That's always true. A good many people have to sow seeds in their lives and be content if they never see the harvest."

There is usually a chuckle pretty near the surface with Father Corridan. You seldom see a man any happier. He can veer back and forth between slang and formal diction, chain-smoking cigarettes sometimes, and pausing in his talk to ask the score of some ball game. In his daily life, of course, he puts in his time reading the offices required of him by his priesthood. In West Side parlance he calls this "pushing the Book."

He takes an almost childish delight in the fact that his work among longshoremen is coming increasingly to the attention of young men beginning their studies for the priesthood. "You know I was a child of the Depression," he says. "Some of the priests that are coming along now are ex-GIs. They know now there's plenty of room in the church for priests who do other things than swing a smoke pot."

Father Corridan believes that a great deal of the work of serving God has to be done outside church buildings. "It's nothing new," he says, "to realize you can serve God by helping people. The Catholic Church lays great stress on the sanctity of marriage, and the home. Men who are insecure in their jobs or home are men in trouble. I've been trying to make longshoremen more secure both in jobs and homes."

The priest's eyes light up when he tells the names of longshoremen, dead and living, who have become his friends and helped him. He really loves them and loves his work.

As for the fight he has made to help clean up New York's waterfront, Father Corridan says that fight has been lost. "You can't close this story with any happy ending," says the priest. "If you're going to tell the truth, you will have to ram one fact home. The rank-and-file dockworkers have lost this fight, and they won't make another for a long time to come. I've lost. I believe the city and people of New York have lost.

"The mobsters won. They're still on the docks. The more unscrupulous elements within the shipping industry won. They still try to maintain that surplus working force, insecure and dependent for daily bread on the daily favor of the man who blows the morning whistle. They're trying to push the old degrading shape-up into the new job information centers."

To corroborate his charge the priest turns to a speech made by General George P. Hays, New York State representative in the new Bi-State Waterfront Commission, November 4, 1954, asserting that the principal trouble at the employment centers now is the "enlarged requests for manpower" by employers. "They call for about 500 men," said General Hays, and then they just pick and choose the men they need and send the rest away. This defeats the purpose of the centers and virtually returns the shape-up. Under this call system the union officials still get their chance at control, and often force the hiring of certain men, an abuse the commission seeks to end."

"Sometimes I mourn for my city," says Father Corridan. "The time is running out. Its prosperous traffic is being diverted to other ports. The St. Lawrence seaway will soon be in competition. But this, of course, is only the economic aspect of the matter. Far more grave is the city's defeat in the relationships between man and man and between man and God.

"Remember? It was Pope Pius XI who told us the 'issue of our time is FOR God or AGAINST God.' Not until we can bring the spirit of Almighty God into our daily economic, political, and social lives can our city prosper. We have a longer and harder fight here than the fight against communism. Communism is just the Russian version of materialism. On the waterfront we've got the American version."

INDEX